POOLSCAPING

POOL
SCAPING

Gardening and Landscaping Around
Your Swimming Pool and Spa

Catriona Tudor Erler

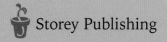

To my sons, Ashton and Nicholas Erler

The mission of Storey Publishing is to serve our customers
by publishing practical information that encourages personal
independence in harmony with the environment.

Edited by Gwen Steege and Karen Levy
Art direction by Wendy Palitz and Cynthia McFarland
Design by Susi Oberhelman
Photographs by Catriona Tudor Erler, except for those
     noted on page 198
Illustrations © Elayne Sears, except for those on pages 14, 127, and
     159 by Alison Kolesar; page 128 by Steven Hughes; and page
     160 by David Stiles
Cover photographs by © Joseph De Sciose (front flap); © Catriona
     Tudor Erler (back cover left and back flap); © Roger Foley
     (front cover and spine); © Harry Haralambou (back cover right)
Text production by Jennifer Jepson Smith
Indexed by Ann W. Truesdale

Printed in Hong Kong by Elegance

10 9 8 7 6 5 4

Library of Congress Cataloging-in-Publication Data
Erler, Catriona T.
     Poolscaping : gardening and landscaping around your swimming
     pool and spa / Catriona Tudor Erler.
     p. cm.
     ISBN 1-58017-386-1 (hardcover : alk. paper) —
          ISBN 1-58017-385-3
(pbk. : alk. paper)
1. Swimming pools. 2. Landscape design. I. Title.
TH4763 .E75 2003
712—dc21   2002151300

CONTENTS

CHAPTER ONE

IN, OUT, AND ABOUT
YOUR POOL

Swimming pools have come a long way from the turquoise water holes surrounded by stark paving. Increasingly, pools are being integrated into the design of the house and garden so that they blend seamlessly with the setting, rather than standing out as a jarring addition. Instead of just being a vessel for swimming in and lounging around, the pool is treated as a waterscape. Indeed, the swimming pool has become an important garden feature, the centerpiece for entertaining, dining, relaxing, and playing. To add to the comfort, convenience, and fun, many remodeled or new pool plans include such amenities as an outdoor kitchen, built-in barbecue and fireplace, "floating" fire, waterfall, fountain, grotto, water slide, spa, underwater shelves to display sculpture, and wide shallow shelves just a few inches deep where preschoolers can wade and adults can lounge. In addition, new technologies have opened the door to myriad features.

▲ Vanishing-edge pools give the illusion of merging with the surrounding landscape. In fact, the water spills over the edge into a hidden catchment basin.

▶ Palm trees and other lush tropical plantings around the pool make this family feel as though they are on an exotic vacation when they are enjoying their own home.

Among the many possibilities are underwater speakers for piped-in music; fiber-optic lights, with all the magical effects they can produce; safety features, such as sensor alarms that go off if anyone goes near the pool; and remote-controlled fountains, waterfalls, and water slides that turn on at the press of a button.

With sophisticated engineering, people are able to fit pools into spaces that were previously thought impossible, even the edge of a cliff. Designers are creating "vanishing-edge" pools that appear to merge with a distant view, as well as pools with "zero depth access." Instead of the standard stairs for pool entry, zero depth access pools have a natural "shore" that gradually gets deeper. Besides being an interesting architectural element, the shallow water is an ideal play area for supervised little ones who don't yet know how to swim.

A lot of homeowners want a poolscape that reminds them of tropical holiday destinations. To evoke a sense of Bali, the Caribbean, Tahiti, Brazil, Mexico, or Hawaii, they select bright turquoise or a lagoon blue for their pool color, then fill the garden with tropical plantings. Even in cold climates, people can achieve an exotic look by landscaping with tender tropical plants used as annuals intermixed with hardy plant material that conveys a tropical feel.

Skip Phillips, owner of Questar Pools and Spas in Escondido, California, and a founding member of the national swimming pool design group called Genesis, suggests that whatever you do for your pool, make it artistic. "If you want your pool to increase your property value," he says, "opt for high design."

Phillips recommends using rich, eye-catching materials, including aggregate stone finishes, limestone, and stamped-concrete decking, to add visual appeal. Also, pay attention to such details as decorative tile trim, dramatic lighting (with fiber-optic lights, you can achieve all sorts of special effects), and underwater statues. Fountains and waterfalls will broaden a pool's appeal to potential buyers, as well as add to your own enjoyment of the setting. Most important, the pool should complement your home both in its style and in the materials you use.

Making Your Pool Landscape Plan

Whether you are starting from scratch or looking to dress up an old swimming pool, think carefully about your goals for the overall landscape before you begin. What look do you want to achieve? Possibilities include modern, classic, tropical, and any number of other styles. How will you fit the style you choose with other existing features on your property, particularly your house? Have a brainstorming session with your family to generate a wish list of all the wonderful features you'd like your pool to have. Don't worry about budget or what's "realistic" at this point; a creative designer may be able to incorporate more features than you think, and you don't want to stifle creativity by squelching any potentially good ideas. The following checklist will help you get started:

How will I use the pool?

EXERCISE

☐ Swimming laps
☐ Water aerobics
☐ Low-impact exercise

THERAPY

☐ Easy entry
☐ Stairs
☐ "Beach" entry
☐ Shallow shelf entry
☐ Hot tub
☐ Spa (bubbles, jets, both)

WATER SPORTS

☐ Volleyball
☐ Basketball
☐ Water polo

GENERAL PLAY AND RECREATION

☐ Water slide
☐ Diving board
☐ "Beach" entry area or shallow shelf for nonswimmers
☐ Centerpiece for outdoor entertaining

What visual/architectural impression do I want from the pool?

CENTRAL FEATURE

☐ Major element in design
☐ Pool integrated with garden and house
☐ Enhance view from house and garden

SECONDARY ELEMENT, HIDDEN FROM VIEW

☐ Isolated from garden immediately around house
☐ In its own "room"

SEASONAL CONSIDERATIONS

☐ Summer sun
☐ Autumn leaves
☐ Winter view
☐ Spa location and usage (easy to get to in winter?)
☐ Entertaining in spring and autumn — the "between" seasons

NIGHTTIME CONSIDERATIONS

- ☐ Pool lighting
- ☐ Deck and garden lighting
- ☐ Color filters, plain white
- ☐ Fiber-optic lights
- ☐ Low-voltage systems
- ☐ Nighttime view from the house

STYLE OPTIONS

- ☐ Naturalistic (pond, tropical lagoon)
- ☐ Classic (geometric, symmetrical)
- ☐ Contemporary
- ☐ Evoking style typical of a foreign country
- ☐ Pool color

How much paving do I want around the pool?

PARTIAL DECKING

- ☐ Garden or lawn edge
- ☐ Waterfall, stone edge
- ☐ Deck only at entry point
- ☐ Extensive decking

DECK USES

- ☐ Sunbathing
- ☐ Entertaining
- ☐ Traffic-flow considerations
- ☐ Integrate deck with house

SEATING

- ☐ Lounge chairs for sunning — how many? _____
- ☐ Hammock
- ☐ Benches
- ☐ Other chairs

DINING

- ☐ Dining table that seats _____
- ☐ Barbecue area
- ☐ Extra table(s) for serving trays, etc.

ENTERTAINING

- ☐ Sit-down dinners
  Small: How many people? _____
  How often? _____
  Large: How many people? _____
  How often? _____
- ☐ Stand-up cocktail parties
  Small: How many people? _____
  How often? _____
  Large: How many people? _____
  How often? _____

DECK MATERIALS

- ☐ Consistent with architecture
- ☐ Comfortable for bare feet
- ☐ Not too slippery when wet
- ☐ No electrostatic properties (plastics can be a problem)
  - ☐ Stone
  - ☐ Brick
  - ☐ Tile
  - ☐ Wood
  - ☐ Wood composite and vinyl
  - ☐ Poured concrete
  - ☐ Interlocking pavers

How do I want the pool enclosed?

- ☐ Area to be enclosed
- ☐ Visual impact of fence or wall
- ☐ Practical/convenience considerations
- ☐ Fence
- ☐ Gates
  - ☐ Around property or just around pool
  - ☐ Height (check local codes)
- ☐ Wall
  - ☐ Gates
  - ☐ Around property or just around pool
  - ☐ Height (check local codes)

What other features would I like?

- ☐ Waterfall
- ☐ Fountain
  - ☐ Inside pool
  - ☐ Outside pool
- ☐ Water slide
- ☐ Pond
- ☐ Pool house
- ☐ Cabana
- ☐ Arbor
- ☐ Pergola
- ☐ Bridge
- ☐ Spa or hot tub
- ☐ Sound system
  - ☐ Underwater speakers
  - ☐ Speakers in the garden
- ☐ Garden train
- ☐ Sculpture
  - ☐ Under water
  - ☐ Around pool
  - ☐ In garden

- ☐ Grotto
- ☐ Firepit
  - ☐ Inside pool
  - ☐ Outside pool
- ☐ Underwater seating

How much storage do I need?

- ☐ Pool games and toys
- ☐ Cushions for furniture
- ☐ Pool chemicals and maintenance supplies
- ☐ Barbecue, charcoal, cooking utensils
- ☐ Pool equipment

What design and construction issues do I face?

PUMP/HEATER LOCATION

- ☐ Visual issues
- ☐ Practical limitations
- ☐ Noise

UTILITIES

- ☐ Underground
- ☐ Electric
- ☐ Gas
- ☐ Water
- ☐ Sewer/septic
- ☐ Cable
- ☐ Aboveground
- ☐ Overhead electric wires

LEGAL AND MUNICIPAL REGULATIONS

- ☐ Setbacks
- ☐ Fencing requirements
- ☐ Building permits
- ☐ Building codes

SOIL AND SITE CONSIDERATIONS

- ☐ Small space
- ☐ Steep slope
- ☐ Waterlogged soil
- ☐ Bedrock, rocky soil
- ☐ Tree roots/trees to be protected during construction
- ☐ Access to site for large equipment

PERFORMING A SITE ANALYSIS

When you decorate a room in your house, you normally measure the room's dimensions, noting the location of windows and doors as well as any other built-in features, such as a fireplace, a wall niche, and bookcases. You also assess what furniture and accessories you already have and want to keep, then decide what you want to replace. The same process applies to a garden space. Whether you are installing a new pool or giving an existing one a new look, before you rush off and purchase plants for the landscaping around it, it's a good idea to do a

▼ **Having a blueprint of your pool and the surrounding area drawn up by a pool builder is a useful start for creating a site analysis of your property.**

site analysis that includes a scale drawing of the area and an inventory of what already exists.

You can start from scratch, drawing the property to scale and noting where the house, pool, and other structures are on the lot, but you'll save a lot of trouble if you have a copy of your plat or property survey (plats are available, usually at no cost, from your tax assessor's office) or a blueprint of the pool area already drawn up by the contractor or designer. Those documents will include a footprint of the house and other structures on your property and should also have clearly marked easements, setback lines, and the location of overhead and underground utility lines owned by the county or city. Have the plat enlarged so you have room to write comfortably, and make several copies so you have them on hand.

When you have your scale drawing of the property, add existing landscape features, such as beds, borders, and planters; patio paving; trees and shrubs (draw circles to scale that approximate the overall diameter to the drip line); arbors; fences, walkways, and steps; and a pond or stream on the property. Be sure to mark where doors and windows open onto the pool area, as well as other significant house features, such as chimneys, and indicate the location of air conditioners, water spigots, and electrical outlets.

Next, note items that affect the character of the site — views (both nice ones that you want to preserve and unpleasant ones that you may want to screen), prevailing wind and microclimates, changing patterns of sun and shade throughout the day, type of soil, slopes, rock outcrops, and drainage, for example. You will find it helpful to make a note of traffic patterns around the area. People generally prefer to take the most direct route and will even walk through flower beds to cut corners. You'll want to keep that fact in mind as you lay out paths and work out the traffic flow around the pool. Once you have all this information in one place, you're well equipped to make decisions about how and where you can incorporate the various landscape features you'd like to have around your swimming pool.

SWIMMING POOL MAKEOVERS

Although new swimming pools are being created with extraordinary designs and state-of-the-art accessories, there is still hope for the old pool that needs a facelift. Many pool designers, including the current "stars" whose projects are featured in shelter magazines, are willing to take on makeover projects, applying their creativity and engineering knowledge to bring an old pool into the twenty-first century. These designers will discuss possibilities with you, from obvious, basic ideas, such as resurfacing an old deck — or even the pool itself — to adding features such as waterfalls and slides to update and enhance the appearance and pleasure of the pool experience. With the information in this book, you will be well prepared to ask about incorporating ideas and features you see and like into your home and pool landscape.

In addition, the landscape around the pool may be grossly overgrown, or minimal, because nobody bothered much with planting. If an old garden has grown beyond what's attractive, a good landscape designer can help you determine which plants are worth keeping (perhaps with some judicious — or even draconian — pruning) and which should be replaced. Don't forget that most plants, even very large trees and shrubs, can be transplanted. If you have the right plant in the wrong place, try to transplant it rather than just chopping it down. Refer to a landscape design book that has information on restoring an established landscape.

Renewing Old Tile

Sometimes the tile on an older spa or pool begins to look dated. Taste in colors and patterns change, and what is considered the height of fashion in one decade appears tired and quaint — or downright ugly — in another. Where tile is more exposed, such as on a wall dividing a spa from a swimming pool, pieces may begin to fall off. Finding replacements for the missing tiles that will coordinate with what's left may be difficult.

Laurie Connable of Poway, California, had just that problem. After a year of searching for something that would go with the outdated brown '70s tile used in her pool and spa, she decided to approach the problem from another angle. She remembered the motifs of Hawaiian fish, squid, and crabs that her mother had painted on the tiles rimming their swimming pool in Hawaii. "My little friends and I often played pirates in the pool. We'd find immense treasure aided by the sea creatures my mother had painted on the tiles around the pool," said Connable.

Inspired by the happy memory, Connable, who started out as an art major in college, set about painting her own spa tiles. The supplies and information for doing the job correctly were all available from a local ceramic store. (Check the Yellow Pages under "Ceramics" and "Craft Instruction" for a shop near you.) She chose colors that went well with the existing tile — avocado green, orange, brown, and yellow, with a turquoise background to pull all the colors together and tie the tile to the color of the pool water — and used a layering watercolor technique to paint the dragonflies, frogs, and turtles she had seen around her garden pond.

If you don't feel confident about your artistic skills, consider using stencils to create a pattern on tiles. Most craft supply stores stock a wide selection of stencils ranging in style from Colonial and other historic periods to modern. Have fun creating a whole new look for your pool or spa while spending very little money.

Siting and Designing Your Pool

Because you can't easily change your mind and put the pool in a different place later, it's very important that you get it right when you decide where you want the pool to be. Think about how you plan to use your pool and whether you want to see it from the house or have it hidden away in a corner of the garden. If the pool is visible from the house, how will it look in winter? In many parts of the United States, the winter season represents a big percentage of the year, so it's important that the prospect from the house during those months be a pleasing one. You'll probably want the pool in a sunny situation out of the way of prevailing winds, as you won't want the spot to be too cold for sun-

bathing or swimmers to be chilled by cool breezes. Involve the entire family in the discussion of where the pool will go and what it will be like.

In addition to aesthetic considerations, there are many practical issues to take into account. Most communities and cities have zoning regulations regarding setbacks from the property line, and there will be other codes to keep in mind (some communities prohibit electric lines passing over or within 10 feet of a pool, for example) as well as building permits required. Your pool builder may discover that certain engineering issues must be addressed, such as ground stability and underground water levels. Buried electric, gas, water, telephone, and TV cable lines may run through the area where you want to build the pool, or you may find that the sewer lines or septic fields are in the way. All these potential problems can be solved (underground cables can be moved, earth can be stabilized, shallow underground water can be pumped away), but they cost money. As a result, it may be much more expensive to put the pool in one area of your property than another. In those cases, you'll have to weigh the potential benefits of a specific, more expensive site against the lower costs of another spot.

Drainage is another important consideration when you site the pool. Whether the pool is placed at the bottom of a slope or on the highest point of the property, the drains must be built to funnel the runoff away from the pool. The surrounding decking also must be gently sloped so excess water runs away from the pool.

The ideal location for a swimming pool isn't always obvious, and you may want to discuss the

▼ If you live in a region where swimming pools are kept running all year, you may want it to be a stunning centerpiece and focal point in your garden design.

matter with a good landscape designer or architect before you make your final decision. For example, when the Heekins family of western Massachusetts first began thinking about putting in a swimming pool, they planned to put it in the middle of an expanse of lawn in full view of the house. Because the winter in their region is long, it meant they'd be looking at a covered hole in the ground for much of the year. Fortunately their daughter,

Elizabeth Bartels, is a landscape architect with a good eye. She convinced them to move the pool a few feet to a spot that's screened from the house by a stand of old hemlocks. The pool is in full sun, but the trees provide welcome shade for those who want a sheltered place to sit.

Those who have the luxury of a large property may prefer to situate the pool some distance from the house in an out-of-the-way spot. When the

▲ The Heekins in western Massachusetts are grateful that their swimming pool cannot be seen from the house during the winter months, when the pool is covered.

famous Edwardian architect and garden designer Sir Edwin Lutyens laid out the gardens for the British Embassy in Washington, D.C., he placed the swimming pool and tennis court in a corner of the property discreetly out of sight. Cole Porter, who had a swimming pool built in the early 1940s at his Williamstown, Massachusetts, home, also opted to put the pool far away from the house. In these cases, the pool becomes a destination, and the area around the pool has a character of its own distinct from the more formal parts of the garden closer to the house.

CHANGES IN LEVEL

A pool landscape doesn't have to be all on one level. In fact, changes in level make a space more interesting. On a sloping lot, you'll gain more living space near the pool — and a more interesting design — by creating different spaces on different levels. For example, consider installing a series of terraced patios leading to a swimming pool at the bottom of the property. It is very appealing to look down on a swimming pool from a deck or patio on a higher level. You get the sense of an aerial view from that vantage point, with the shape of the pool and the

> "One of the greatest pleasures of the garden is the walk through the meadow to the pool. There is a sense of a journey to a special destination."
>
> **Jane G. Briggs, Williamstown, Massachusetts**

layout of landscape features readily apparent. It also is pleasant for adults to have a place to relax that is slightly removed from the hubbub of children playing in the pool but in clear view of their activities.

Changes in level can serve pleasing practical functions as well. When landscape architect Ned Bosworth of Fullerton, California, designed a pool house for a steep lot, he used the lower level, which was built into the slope, as storage space for pool supplies and the solar heating equipment. The main floor of the pool house is surrounded by a large wooden deck that overlooks the pool. A spa is built into the edge of the deck. Here is a spot where adults can relax while they supervise children in the pool. Several designers who are in the vanguard of modern pool design have used sloped lots to create multilevel swimming pools connected with water slides or waterfalls. (See chapter 7, pages 132 and 136 for details about specific projects.)

If your soil is poor, consider building a retaining wall that extends out of the far side of the swimming pool to create a raised bed, then fill the bed with high-quality loam. Make the wall wide enough to provide a buffer between the bed and the pool so there isn't a problem with soil or plant debris falling into the water. The raised bed behind will make the swimming pool appear sunken (very chic), and on a small property, the change in level will increase the perception of size.

POOL SIZE AND DEPTH

Size and scale are important aspects of a satisfying garden design. When you begin thinking about a swimming pool in your own garden, you need to evaluate what space is available and what percent of the yard you want to take up with the pool. Ideally, a pool should be in scale with the size of the house and lot, but there are exceptions to every rule. Many successful swimming pools are squeezed

into tiny lots and take up most of the available space, but they nevertheless bring huge amounts of pleasure to their owners.

Think about how you want to use the pool. Ask yourself whether it will be mainly a play space for children or a lap pool for exercise. Do you have a budding competitive diver or a racer in training in the house? Involve the entire family in this discussion, as your personal goals may not be the same as those of a teenager or 10-year-old. Although you may have to compromise because of space or budget constraints, a good designer can often accommodate a lot more than you might expect.

There are minimum depths and widths recommended for specific activities. Lap swimmers need a minimum length of 40 feet. Longer is even better. If two people want to swim laps side by side, the pool should be 12 to 14 feet wide. For racing, where swimmers make the speedy flip turnarounds, the pool needs to be at least 4 feet deep at both ends. Diving requires much deeper water and more volume. Serious divers generally need a pool that is at least 36 feet long, 18 feet wide, and 9 feet deep. Recreational divers don't need as much space, but the water must be deep enough and the pool wide enough for safety. If playing water games, such as water basketball and volleyball, will be the primary activity, then you want a pool that's only 3 feet deep at both ends and about 5 feet deep in the middle.

The latest trend in swimming pool design is a shallow shelf that is just a few inches deep. Known by multiple names, including Baja step, tanning bench, kiddie play platform, grandparents' step, and thermal ledge, this new twist on pool design and water depth is praised by owners who say they spent about 1 percent of their pool-building budget on this one corner of the pool that they use almost 100 percent of the time.

POOLS IN SMALL SPACES

Almost no garden space is too small for a swimming pool, though it may take some engineering and design creativity to make it work. Mary Walsh had always admired the swimming pool that designer Charlie Bowers, of Garden Gate Landscaping in Bethesda, Maryland, had created for her parents. "It was built just as I finished high school," she remembers. "They used a crane to lift four-ton rocks over the house to the backyard. We had to move out of the house while they did it because it was so dangerous." The boulders were required to create the illusion that the swimming pool was actually a natural mountain pond. A waterfall and a large stone slab that protruded over the pool as a diving platform completed the impression.

When her parents died, Walsh wanted some way to have a part of their wonderful garden on her own property. Thinking her diminutive backyard might be too small, she called Bowers and asked whether he thought he could fit a pool like the one he designed for her parents onto the property. He agreed to try, and the result is an award-winning success.

To allow as much room as possible for the pool, Bowers positioned it very close to the back fence and left only enough paving for a pathway at the foot of the pool and along the side opposite the boundary fence. The sitting area is a preexisting wooden deck off the family room and is several feet above the level of the pool. The spa, which also is raised above pool level, is accessed from the deck. Both the deck and the spa are wonderful vantage points from which to look down on the beautiful stone-rimmed swimming pool.

In Southern California, coastal land is costly, so lots tend to be small, and all sorts of unlikely plots on a steep slope or perched on the edge of a canyon are made to work as building sites. To fit as much swimming pool as possible into a small lot, landscape designer Gary Stone recommends placing the pool right up against the edge of the property. Another solution is to dig into the slope and build a retaining wall to acquire more room, then tuck the pool against the retaining wall and along the property line.

Landscape designer Phillippe Lizarraga, of Unlimited Landscape in Escondido, California, specializes in small properties as well as large estate projects. For a small backyard in Carlsbad, California, he managed to fit in a 10- by 31-foot pool, a raised spa, a patio space, and an outdoor kitchen. He put the outdoor kitchen at a 45-degree angle to the house, thus contributing to the illusion that there is more space and providing a niche for the triangle-shaped spa. An arbor attached to the house links the building with the outdoor kitchen.

◄ **You can squeeze a long, narrow lap pool into a very small space. Ideally, lap swimmers require a minimum length of 40 feet. Longer is even better.**

▼ **By squeezing the swimming pool right up against the back fence and leaving just a narrow walkway on the opposite side, designer Charlie Bowers fit a comfortable-size pool into a tiny lot.**

trees and shrubs that create privacy but do not take up a lot of space. Choices include specimens with narrow, vertical growth habits and plants that take well to severe pruning to keep them in bounds. Another way to create an illusion with plants is to grow large, bold-leafed plants in the foreground of your setting, then put smaller, finer-textured plants farther away. Because we are trained to know that things are smaller when they are far away, our eyes are tricked into believing that the smaller plants are indeed far off. Dark-colored foliage and flowers, such as those with deep reds and blues, will visually recede into the distance; bright colors, such as yellow, tend to jump forward.

In the case of a plot that really is too tiny for even a scaled-down pool, a swim spa may fit. This mini lap pool contains a major water jet that produces a current strong enough to swim against. Because it is smaller than a traditional-size pool and can double as a spa if you turn up the heat and turn on more water jets, some people find it is the perfect solution (see page 165).

CONSTRUCTION MATERIALS

In-ground swimming pools are made of concrete, vinyl, or fiberglass. Each material has specific benefits; the best choice for your situation will be determined by your budget and region of the country. For example, in northern climates where winter is harsh, many people opt for a vinyl pool because it tends to flex more with ground movement during freezes and thaws. Once the pool is filled with water, it can be difficult to tell which material was used.

Concrete. Most pools in warmer climates are built of gunite or shotcrete, which is concrete pneumatically applied to a reinforced structure with a system of pumps and hoses. The concrete is then surfaced with a choice of a plaster and marble

▲ **An attractive stone planter at the back of the lot gives this pool a chic sunken effect. The change of level and layered plantings also visually enlarge the small space.**

Other illusionary devices to "create a perception of bigness," as Lizarraga puts it, are to use multiple levels in the design and a variety of textures and materials for paving various surfaces. The change in levels defines spaces and creates a sense of depth, both of which make the area feel larger. Using a combination of paving materials has the same effect. For example, a brick border around a small concrete patio sets that apart and clearly defines the space. The same brick might line a narrow path that passes beside the pool to the patio area. The pathway is defined, and the strips of bricks make it appear longer than it actually is.

Lizarraga also uses plants as tools to give a sense of increased size. For example, he opts for mixture, plaster, pebbles, exposed aggregate, or tile. The advantage of a concrete pool is that it can be any shape or size. In cold climates, or in regions where earthquakes are an issue, a concrete pool must be reinforced with steel and additional concrete.

Vinyl. Vinyl pools cost about half of what you'll expect to pay for a concrete pool. However, they are not nearly as long-lived. There are concrete pools still in good working order that were built 50 or 60 years ago. In contrast, a vinyl liner will probably need to be replaced in 10 to 20 years, depending on the quality of material used. Manufacturers are developing ever more durable vinyl materials, so it's worth springing for a more expensive option with a long guarantee. Even so, vinyl is subject to tearing and ripping. Although it can be repaired with an underwater patch kit, you can avoid the problem if you ban any sharp objects in a vinyl pool. Sunlight, excessive chlorine, and other imbalances in the water's chemistry are all damaging to vinyl pools. Some vinyl liners are impregnated with sunlight and fungus inhibitors, which help extend their life.

Vinyl liners are supported by a metal, wood, or plastic framework that is built inside the pool excavation (which must be sized precisely for the liner to fit properly). Like vinyl flooring, vinyl liners can be made to look like tile, marble, or other more expensive materials. The coping for vinyl pools is generally made of aluminum or PVC.

Fiberglass. In terms of cost, fiberglass pools are in the middle. They are more durable than vinyl pools (one manufacturer offers a 50-year limited warranty against structural failure), but they do not come with the choice of shapes and sizes that are available with custom-made gunite pools. Most fiberglass pools are molded at the factory, then lowered into the prepared hole in the ground with a crane. There is a trend now for pool builders

to construct the fiberglass on site, however, greatly increasing the design choices available.

Fiberglass pools are simple to maintain because of the smooth, colorfast surface that makes them easy to wipe clean. To protect the finish from scratches, avoid using abrasive sponges and cleaning powders.

Fitting a Swimming Pool into a Tight Space

In addition to physical room on the ground for a swimming pool, builders need to be able to get large equipment, such as diggers, to the area where the pool will be built. In situations where there isn't access to the backyard, cranes may be required to bring material and equipment over the house. Needless to say, such a measure adds significantly to the expense of building a pool. Here are some ideas to maximize space and minimize cost:

- Build the pool parallel to the back boundary of your property so the side yard spaces add to the potential length.
- Set the pool on the diagonal to gain greater length.
- Set the pool as close to the property line as allowed by local codes to maximize space on the opposite side.
- Build an L-shaped pool that runs across the back of the property with a leg down the side.
- Minimize the amount of decking around the pool.
- On a downward-sloping hillside lot, increase the area for the pool by terracing the slope and holding the soil in place with retaining walls. Of course, these walls need to be professionally engineered to support the weight of the soil and water.
- In cases where the hillside slopes up from the house, dig into the slope — using retaining walls to hold the soil in place — to create more level ground near the house.
- Squeeze a narrow lap pool along the side of your property, rather than in the back.

▲ To make the pool blend harmoniously with its surroundings, Allen Mushinsky had it painted a deep charcoal gray. The result is a natural-looking pond one might find in a woodland clearing.

POOL COLOR

Just as early cars were all painted a standard black, the first swimming pools all had a white bottom. This preference for a white plaster finish on swimming pools continued for nearly half a century so that even today, when you fly over any major city in the United States, you can see the suburban neighborhoods dotted with turquoise rectangle and kidney-shaped pools, as the white bottom reflects the color of the water. The traditional turquoise pool is still extremely popular. It makes its owners feel they have escaped to a favorite holiday place without leaving their own property. As one family in western Massachusetts put it, "We refer to our pool as the 'L.A. pool' because its turquoise color makes us feel like we're in California."

Nevertheless, many designers are choosing to soften the stark white finish with varying amounts of gray or beige. The result is pools with deeper colors that reflect water's natural chromatic variations. For the "starry night" pool (see pages 120–121), Ron Gibbons custom-blended marble-dust aggregate and three hues of colored crystal aggregate into the finish coating to give the pool its deep navy blue shade.

Allen Mushinsky, of Potomac, Maryland, set out to make his swimming pool blend with its woodland setting. He opted for a charcoal gray that contributes to the impression of the pool being a pond happened upon in a woodland glade. For some people, a black or marine blue pool is a safety concern because the dark color makes it difficult to see changes in water depth. Other people are not bothered by that issue. Certainly, a dark-colored pool will absorb more heat from the sun, so the water will tend to be warmer.

When the worker arrived to paint the newly finished bottom of Mary Walsh's pool in Bethesda, Maryland, she told him she wanted the water to look tropical, with the feel that her family was in Bali. He custom-mixed the color while she watched, then painted the pool when they got just the right shade.

Pebble tech is another way to surface swimming pools that is rapidly gaining in popularity. In this technique, concrete is embedded with tiny pebbles to resemble the bottom of a sandy pond. You can also achieve a certain pool color with lights. With appropriate-colored filters, a nighttime pool can be any color you desire, from cotton-candy pink to emerald green to passionate purple.

A very expensive but dramatic approach to swimming pool color is an all-tile finish. On average, mosaic tiles are five times more expensive than a plaster finish. If you have the budget for it, however, you can achieve striking results, and the tiles are extremely durable and versatile. Linda Bateman, of Rancho Santa Fe, California, chose a combination of five blue shades of Italian mosaic tile for her pool. The result is a rich blend of color and texture that stands out in bold contrast to the terra-cotta paving around the pool (see page 168). To achieve the design benefit of tile without quite the high cost, many people combine tile — around the water line of the pool, say, or in a central pattern or motif on the bottom of the pool, or to outline steps or define swim lanes — with a less expensive plaster finish.

Skip Phillips, owner of Questar Pools in Escondido, California, advises homeowners to be careful to choose materials for cosmetic finishes that do not "date" the pool. "If you make the right selections," he says, "your pool will still look up-to-date years from now."

▼ Mary Walsh of Bethesda, Maryland, had the paint for her swimming pool, left, hand mixed to achieve this "lagoon" shade of blue. The tile edging on the steps, below, is an attractive highlight as well as a safety feature, clearly outlining the steps' presence.

Aboveground Pools

Nearly half the swimming pools in the United States are above ground. It's not surprising, as a typical aboveground pool costs less than $4,000, making it affordable for a large number of people. You can even save money by doing the installation yourself, which is meant to be an easy job. Some manufacturers claim their pools can be installed by the homeowner in just 1 hour without any specialty tools. In contrast, the price tag for an in-ground pool typically starts at $15,000 to $20,000 and can ratchet up quickly if you opt for customized features.

There are three types of aboveground pools: those constructed with a rigid steel or aluminum frame with a vinyl liner; new soft-wall pools made of durable, ultraviolet-light-treated material for long life; and inflatable pools. In the past, aboveground pools came in limited shapes and sizes. Today, the choices are much greater. Pools range from 9 to 30 feet in diameter and may be round, oval, or rectangular. For serious lap swimmers, 40-foot-long aboveground lap pools are available. Buyers can select a pool depth between 48 and 52 inches.

▼ Soft, feathery grasses layered with brightly colored flowering annuals and perennials successfully hide the unattractive sides of this aboveground pool.

On the negative side, an aboveground pool will not add to your home's value, and unless it is dressed up, it is an unattractive feature in the yard. In an effort to improve the appearance of aboveground pools, manufacturers have introduced liner designs that imitate stone and tile, and the outside walls come in a variety of colors and patterns. One, called the Coliseum, has regularly spaced faux fluted columns around the outside walls. The material between the columns looks like the walls of an ancient building, and the pool rim is capped with a circle of faux bricks. There are no bare metal parts showing; the overall effect is clean, finished, and attractive.

Perhaps the nicest way to disguise an aboveground pool is to incorporate it into a deck so that none of the sides is exposed. Dolphin Pools, of Dallas, Texas, rose to the challenge of making a standard aboveground pool resemble its more expensive cousins. To minimize the pool's height, builders dug the pool 2 feet into the ground. Then they put a raised redwood deck level with the rim around the entire pool. Wide steps with low risers were built into the deck corner nearest the house and garden. Because each step functions almost like a landing, with room for a large, flower-filled pot at each end, there is a visual merging of the raised deck and the lower lawn. Of course, this treatment costs far more than a bare-bones aboveground pool, but it should add to the value of the house and be a real pleasure to look at and use.

A less expensive option is to plant around the perimeter of an aboveground pool. By layering plants, beginning with the tallest ones closest to the pool and moving out in descending height, you can merge the plantings into the rest of the garden and create an effective screen that hides the pool's sides. For this project, it is worth doing some research at a good local nursery where the employ-

Reasons to Choose an Aboveground Pool

For the money, aboveground pools provide a refreshing oasis where people can cool off from the summer heat as well as a delightful recreational activity for children. Often considered starter pools, many families begin with an inexpensive aboveground pool, then move on to an in-ground pool as their budget allows. Other reasons to buy an aboveground pool include:

- You really want a pool but are living in rental property.
- You would like to try swimming-pool ownership to see how much you actually use it — and how much work and cost it is to maintain — before committing to the expense of an in-ground pool.
- Your budget will not expand to the large expense of an in-ground pool.
- You will be moving soon and don't want to pour money into an in-ground asset you cannot take with you. You *can* take an aboveground pool.
- You'd like a pool for the children, but once they move away from home, you'd like to use the space for a garden.
- You don't want your property taxes to increase due to a capital improvement.
- You want to set it up when the grandchildren come to visit in the summer, but then put it away for the rest of the year.

ees really know plants and are willing to spend time sharing their knowledge with you. It's important to find out which plants are well suited to your region and will thrive in the environment you have in mind for them. One question to ask is how resilient the proposed shrubs and flowers will be to chlorinated water splashing on them. If possible, visit the nursery on a weekday when the staff is less busy. You're unlikely to get the time and attention you want if you turn up on a hectic Saturday.

POOL DECKING
AND COPING

The decking or paving around a swimming pool serves many important functions, both practical and aesthetic. From a practical standpoint, the decking is a buffer zone between the pool and other parts of the garden. A large deck can help prevent leaves, grass clippings, and dirt from finding their way into the water. It can also be a beautiful feature of the poolscape. For people who do a lot of outdoor entertaining and want a lot of living space around the pool, it's nearly impossible to have too much decking. Others may want the minimum paving required to frame the pool, putting the emphasis on the garden setting, with the pool as merely one feature. If you want as much green around the pool as possible and plan to devote a minimum amount of space to pool decking, orient the paved area to the south or southwest, where the sun is strongest. This allows those who want to sunbathe a suitable space to do so.

In addition, you'll want the deck to be easy to maintain and able to tolerate the rigors of pool chemicals splashing onto it and, in colder regions of the country, freeze/thaw cycles. Also keep in mind that the surface should not become too slippery when it is wet, and it should be comfortable for bare feet. Most people prefer a light-colored material that reflects heat so the paving doesn't become too hot.

Because you don't want water runoff from the house or garden flowing into the pool, it is essential to grade the paving so it slopes away from it. Furthermore, you don't want water to collect on the decking. The puddles look messy, and the standing water promotes the growth of moss and algae and creates a slipping hazard. Generally, a slope of ⅛ to ¼ inch per foot is adequate. If the paving is made of bricks or flagstone laid on a sand base without mortar, water can percolate between the joints. In that case, you may need subsurface drains to remove excess water from underneath.

On a level property, a gentle grading away from the pool is usually enough; however, if the pool is positioned at a low point on the property, you will need additional drains. These drains don't have to be intrusive. For example, you could incorporate a drainage system that is hidden under the overhang of each step of paving.

The World of Paving Materials

Poolside paving extends living and entertaining space, and it definitely sets the tone for the entire pool area. There is a wealth of materials with which to surface a swimming pool deck, including wood, natural stone, concrete in various colors and finished surfaces, brick, tile, and interlocking pavers. Choose a material that ties in with other features of the house and garden. You can even match or coordinate the flooring used inside the house with that used for the patio and pool paving.

Learn about the many paving possibilities and choose one that fits your budget and style. When figuring out the cost, keep in mind that although most paved surfaces are expensive to install, they are virtually maintenance-free and most have little or no upkeep costs. In the long run, they may be less expensive than lawns and other plantings.

WOOD

Wood is a warm, natural material that is appealing around a swimming pool because it makes one think of a lakeside dock. A versatile material, it can easily be cut and pieced together to make an infinite variety of pleasing patterns. In addition, wood is cooler on the feet than many other paving materials, as it doesn't absorb heat so readily. Because it has a certain "give," it is comfortable to walk on and even lie on, and the nonreflective surface means there is less glare than from a bright paving surface.

You can have fun designing different patterns for a wooden surface. For example, in addition to simply laying the planks parallel or perpendicular to the house or pool, you can lay them at angles to create a herringbone design, or make a series of concentric squares, a V shape, or a parquet pattern with alternating squares of boards running parallel and perpendicular to the edge.

For an aboveground pool, a wooden deck is a great asset. It provides a place that's level with the pool rim to sun and watch people in the water, and if properly designed, it can disguise the fact that

▼ The blues and pinks of lavender and cosmos spilling onto this flagstone paving are echoed in the natural colors in the stone.

the pool is on top of the ground, rather than sunk into it. Manufacturers offer reasonably inexpensive wooden decks to go with their aboveground pools, but those structures are often barely wide enough for a chaise lounge, and they wrap only partway around the pool. They do not address the problem of the pool being plunked down in the middle of the landscape. If you can afford the extra cost, your garden and aboveground pool will look much more attractive with a custom-made deck that wraps around the entire pool and merges with ground level through a series of steps and platforms (see chapter 1, page 19 for more ideas).

Wood has a downside, however. It is prone to splintering, a real nuisance in an area where people are likely to have bare feet. It also needs to be sealed regularly against water and UV-ray damage. But the main disadvantage of wood is that eventually it rots. There are insect- and rot-resistant woods available, including teak, redwood, cypress, cedar, and larch; however, even these are vulnerable to rot in areas that remain warm and damp for extended periods. In a hot, humid climate, wood may not be the best option.

WOOD COMPOSITES

To address wood's problems of splintering, rot resistance, and toxic chemical additives, manufacturers have created composite woods made from recycled wood fibers, polymer trash bags, and recycled bottles. These products have taken the market by storm in the past few years. Although composites are 30 to 50 percent more expensive than natural wood, they do not warp or splinter, are slip resistant when wet, and provide greater longevity; most come with a 10- to 20-year warranty. Composites also do not need sealing, though some people use a sealer to add color because the material ages to gray. If you want to apply a sealer or paint, you must

▲ Set at an angle, wooden planks create a pleasing pattern near a swimming pool. The diagonal angle also increases the sense of space in this tight area.

Wood Safety

For years, pressure-treated lumber was considered a viable alternative to the more expensive rot-resistant woods. Lately, though, it has come under question because of the toxic chemicals used to treat the wood. You certainly don't want the chemicals in the wood to find their way into the swimming pool, and you may have second thoughts about you or your children lying on the bare wood.

wait 10 weeks after installation to allow the material to off-gas. When you apply the pigments, use an oil-based paint or a solid-color stain.

There is also the issue of environmental responsibility. A popular view is that wood composites are environmentally sound because they are made of recycled materials. Of course, the energy used to produce the product must be weighed against the practice of growth management of forests targeted for logging.

STONE

Stone, with all its natural variations in shape, color, and texture, is an especially beautiful paving material to use around a pool. Many types of stone are suitable, and each one has unique properties that make it more or less ideal, depending on where you live and the overall effect you want to achieve. When making your decision, take into account appearance, durability (especially in climates with freeze/thaw cycles), slip resistance, heat radiation (darker colors will be hotter), and, of course, budget.

The primary stones used for paving are flat flagstones, which are typically sandstone, limestone, granite, quartzite, slate, or porphyry. You can buy flagstones in random shapes or uniform squares, rectangles, and other geometric shapes. Depending on the stone and the depth where it is found, flagstones are quarried by either splitting the stone along the lines of its natural cleavage or sawing solid masses into flat sheets. Split stones have an irregular surface because they are broken along natural fracture lines. As a result, they are less slippery than completely smooth flagstones, but the slight changes in surface level also make for toe-stubbing hazards. However, sometimes the surface of sawn flagstones is "dressed" to give a more natural-looking finish that approximates the look and feel of cleft stones.

Although there are notable exceptions, you will generally get the best price if you choose stone that is quarried within a few hundred miles of where you live, rather than stone that has been shipped across the country or around the world.

▼ At a stone yard, you'll find row upon row of flagstones, such as this Tennessee flagstone, left, sorted by size and type and bundled on flats. The slightly uneven surface of split Pennsylvania bluestone, below, has a pleasing texture and helps reduce slipping hazards around a pool.

Sandstone. This is a popular choice for poolside paving. It comes in several colors, ranging from cream, pink, and crimson to greenish brown and blue-gray. In general, the paler-colored stones tend to be stronger; the reddish or brown stones are softer and easier to cut.

Depending on where it is quarried, sandstone can be more or less ideal for your situation. For example, Pennsylvania bluestone (which is also quarried in New York and the Delaware River valley) is prized for its blue-gray color. It may look most at home when incorporated into landscapes in its native region. Tennessee sandstone comes in shades of brown and rosy, rusty red. Compared to bluestone, it is softer, more porous, and more prone to flake due to freeze/thaw cycles. Sawn pieces quarried from deeper in the ground are more durable because they don't have the cleft seams. They cost 15 to 20 percent more than natural cleft stones, however, because of the labor involved in cutting them. Homeowners who live in a frost-free area can also consider Arizona sandstone, which comes in a rainbow of hues, as well as other stones from the western part of the country.

In addition to local varieties, there also are imported sandstones, such as "Teakwood" and "Rainbow," both from India. "Teakwood" is a yellow striated stone, and "Rainbow" has purple and burgundy against a tan background. These stones run about the same price as Tennessee sandstone and are of similar durability.

Limestone. Because limestone is a porous stone that is prone to breaking under the duress of freeze/thaw cycles, it is more suitable for use in mild climates where weather extremes do not occur. It also tends to pick up stains from leaves and other debris. Depending on the variety, it may be cream colored or slightly red or yellow with a hint of gray. It does not split into layers naturally, so it must be sawn, making it more expensive. Some pieces have shells and fossilized animals and plants embedded in the surface.

Granite. A hard stone that doesn't naturally cleft into sheets, granite must be cut with diamond

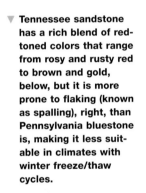

▼ Tennessee sandstone has a rich blend of red-toned colors that range from rosy and rusty red to brown and gold, below, but it is more prone to flaking (known as spalling), right, than Pennsylvania bluestone is, making it less suitable in climates with winter freeze/thaw cycles.

blades. Hence, it is an extremely expensive stone for outdoor paving. In the past few years, however, Chinese producers have begun exporting their wares to the United States. Imported granite sells for about one-third the cost of domestic granite, making it a budget-friendlier possibility for homeowners.

Quartzite. Harder than granite, quartzite cannot be scratched even with a knife. As a result, it is extremely durable. It is composed of tightly interlocking grains of quartz, often with a little feldspar or mica, which makes the stones glisten. Because it is so dense, it doesn't absorb water, making it highly resistant to freeze/thaw cycles. It also resists stains, salt, and acids and doesn't reflect heat. Quartzite has an even cleft; is slip resistant when wet; and comes in shades of white, gray, gold, pink, and salmon, often with variations running through each piece.

Slate. In the United States, slate is mined primarily in New York and Vermont. There the unique chemical and mineral composition produces a huge variety of colors, including green, mottled green, gray, charcoal gray, purple, and red. Nowhere else in the world does slate come in

such diverse colors. Ribbon slate, which is less expensive than uniformly colored slate, is striped with two colors. Slate is a fine-grained rock with a natural cleft that splits easily into smooth sheets. This strong, weatherproof, slip-resistant stone is suitable for both indoor and outdoor use.

The main disadvantage of using slate near a swimming pool is that many of the available colors are dark, so they absorb and retain heat, raising the temperature on the decking significantly. Nevertheless, it is a handsome stone that can be used in combination with other, lighter-colored materials to reduce the heat-retaining effect.

Porphyry. The word *porphyry* means "purple" in Greek, and the name refers to the purplish red or greenish brown swirled patterns that characterize this distinctive stone. Renowned for its hardness, porphyry was used by the ancient Romans to pave their famous roads. Many of the streets of Paris are paved with porphyry. It is more dense than granite and absorbs almost no water, making it impervious to cracks caused by freeze/thaw cycles. This water-resistant quality means that porphyry dries quickly and is naturally

▲ **Because of lower labor costs, granite imported from China, top left, is much less expensive than granite quarried in North America. Slate typically comes in very dark colors that absorb and radiate heat, making them uncomfortably hot around a swimming pool; the Brazilian blue Montauk slate, above, however, is not quite so dark in color.**

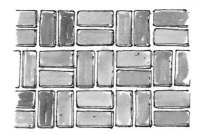

Basket weave

Pinwheel

Running bond

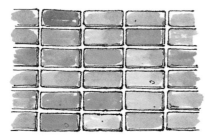

Jack-on-Jack

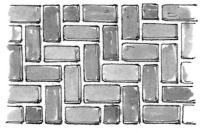

Herringbone, 90°

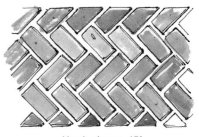

Herringbone, 45°

▲ **These are just a few of the many patterns that you can create with brick. Don't forget that you also can combine patterns, such as a running bond or Jack-on-Jack edge around a pinwheel or basket-weave center.**

slip resistant. Couple all these positive qualities with its rich coloration, and you have an ideal paving stone for poolscapes.

Until recently, porphyry was an expensive, hard-to-get stone in North America. It is extremely heavy, making the shipping costs from European quarries prohibitive. Now Mondial Porfidi, an Italian company that is a major porphyry supplier in Europe, has begun quarrying the stone in Mexico. Although there is still shipping involved, the distances are much less than the transatlantic journey. The Mexican quarry has been operating since 1995, and various American distributors are gradually tapping into the resource, making porphyry more readily available in the United States. Although it is still more expensive than locally quarried stone, the price is not that much more

than that of bluestone. As Jim Fraccaroli, a porphyry distributor based in Chestertown, Maryland, says, "People want something different, and porphyry doesn't look like anything else."

BRICK

A warm, traditional paving material, brick allows you to create all sorts of patterns, such as basket weave, herringbone, pinwheel, running bond, and jack-on-jack, as well as freeform swirls and waves. You can combine patterns, too. For example, a grid of herringbone or basket-weave squares would look nice with an outline edging of bricks. Brick also combines well with other materials. Use it to edge concrete squares to add interest to a large, plain surface or subdivide stone paving with brick. Finally, consider combining different-color bricks to incorporate a colored pattern into a design.

Although most people usually picture bricks as an earthy terra-cotta color, they actually come in a wide range of earthen tones, depending on the mineral oxides in the clay. You will find bricks within the red range, from rust to burgundy, as well as in various shades of yellow and dark gray. Some bricks are a uniform color; others are streaked and mottled with different shades and tones. Whatever the color, it will not fade over time, though in shady areas it may develop a layer of moss or lichen.

Should you opt for brick, visit a supplier to look at the choices, and if possible, take home samples to see which ones blend most successfully with other colors and elements in your house and garden. Do not use glazed bricks around a swimming pool. They're slippery when wet, and the glare of reflected light off the shiny surface can be exhausting to the eyes when you're out in the sun. Select a texture that provides a little traction without being too rough on bare feet.

Most bricks are graded to indicate their ability to withstand freezing temperatures. The most expensive are those graded SW (severe weath-ering). They're baked longer than other types of bricks to reduce the amount of water they'll absorb. They are suitable in any climate, but are essential in regions where winter temperatures drop well below freezing. Bricks graded MW (moderate weathering) are much less expensive than SW bricks. They can take light freezes, but will chip and flake if exposed to subzero temperatures. If you are thinking about using salvaged bricks, have them tested to make sure they meet the SW-grade requirements. According to the Brick Industry Association, most used bricks do not meet those standards.

Besides choosing a brick graded for outdoor use in your climate, the next most critical element in a brick patio is the foundation. An improperly laid base — or one that is not thick enough — can lead to cracking, heaving, or undulations in the brick paving. The minimum recommended concrete base thickness is 4 inches. In very cold climates, where frost heave is pronounced, or on top of soil that is not well compacted or is often saturated with water, you'll need an even thicker foundation. If you are laying the bricks over an existing concrete patio or decking, make sure it is sound. Fill any

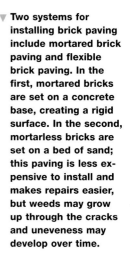

▼ **Two systems for installing brick paving include mortared brick paving and flexible brick paving. In the first, mortared bricks are set on a concrete base, creating a rigid surface. In the second, mortarless bricks are set on a bed of sand; this paving is less expensive to install and makes repairs easier, but weeds may grow up through the cracks and unevenness may develop over time.**

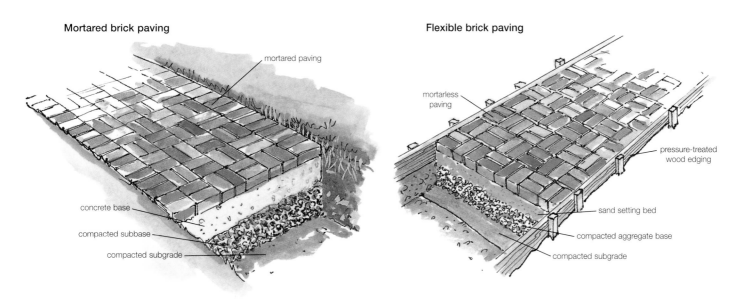

Mortared brick paving

mortared paving

concrete base

compacted subbase

compacted subgrade

Flexible brick paving

mortarless paving

pressure-treated wood edging

sand setting bed

compacted aggregate base

compacted subgrade

Terra-cotta tile, top left, is suitable only in frost-free climates, but porcelain tiles, center, are durable in any climate and are made in an enormous selection of colors and designs. Glass mosaic tiles, top right, often come with premade, color-coordinated borders in a variety of patterns.

major cracks with concrete or mortar.

TILE

Although unglazed terra-cotta tile is suitable for outdoor use only in regions that get little or no frost, there is a wide array of vitreous and water-impervious porcelain tiles that are completely durable in even the harshest climates. These tiles are graded for slip resistance, and many have a special finish incorporated into the surface to improve traction. The selection of tile colors, designs, and motifs is enormous. Some are designed to look like stone, others are printed with patterns, and still others are solid colors. Yellows and reds tend to fade in the sun; browns, blues, and grays are more colorfast.

Glass mosaic tile is a popular trend in outdoor tile. The material is strong and impervious to water, making it perfectly resistant to freeze/thaw cycles. On the standardized scratch-hardiness scale, where diamonds are given a 10, these glass tiles are graded 5. They come in a wide range of colors, as well as in clear, iridescent, and milky forms. Venetian glass tiles are often streaked with metal pigments. In addition to solid-colored and streaked tiles, manufacturers provide a selection of premade border designs, with motifs such as Greek keys, single and double diamonds, waves, argyles, harlequins, and serpentines.

If you select glass mosaic tile for a portion of your pool decking or for a pool or wall surface, you will not receive a box of loose tiles that must be hand laid. These tiles arrive from the manufacturer face-mounted on sheets. All you need to do is set the tile in a properly prepared base, then peel back the sticky mounting paper and fill in the spaces with grout. Of course, manufacturers provide detailed instructions on preparing a proper base for the tile as well as the best bonding mortar to use and how to apply it. Any application that will be submerged in water requires a minimum 14-day cure time before it can be exposed to water.

MOSAIC MEDALLIONS

Several manufacturers make prefabricated stone or tile mosaic medallions that you can insert into a plain paved area to add a bit of visual spice. A good tile shop should have one or two samples on display, as well as other choices in a catalog. If you have a bigger budget and want a personalized motif, ask about custom designs.

POURED CONCRETE

Simple, versatile, and relatively economical, poured-concrete decks around swimming pools are built with expansion joints or seams that protect them from cracking due to freeze/thaw cycles. These joints also provide a runnel for water to drain away from the pool. Concrete can be worked into just about any shape. For a little extra money, you can improve the appearance of a plain slab by tinting the concrete with special pigments before it's poured. You also can incorporate other materials, such as marble dust and crystal aggregates, in various colors. Another approach to beautifying concrete is to treat a clean, dry slab with chemical stains that can be mixed and diluted to produce almost any desired color. Finally, you can paint concrete, though it will need to be repainted every few years to keep it looking its best.

Landscape architect Pamela Burton colored the concrete paving around a Malibu, California, swimming pool in a combination of grays and greens to coordinate with the yuccas, aloes, and cacti in the garden. In addition, tiny black flecks of silica carbide were incorporated into the concrete. When the sun and reflected light of the pool hits them, they sparkle "like little diamonds," according to Burton.

Concrete also allows for various surface finishes. You can create a textured surface by brushing a stiff broom over the concrete before it sets, or hand-trowel the wet concrete to produce an interesting swirled finish. Colored concrete also can be stamped into patterns that resemble stone, tile, and brick. Although the pressed design lacks the color variation and natural irregularity of the actual materials, it is a much less expensive alternative. Another attractive surface option is called seeded or aggregate. While the concrete is still wet, pea gravel or another fairly fine material is pressed into the top layer. The result is a finish that looks like a gravel surface, which disguises the ordinary concrete underneath. To create a pitted surface, builders roll rock salt into the wet material. The salt dissolves and washes away, leaving an interesting pocked appearance that also provides good traction. Unfortunately, this finish is not suitable in climates where temperatures drop below freezing; the water collects in the recesses and can cause cracking when it expands.

INTERLOCKING CONCRETE PAVERS

These pavers may be a more interesting choice for patios and decks than plain poured concrete. As the market for interlocking concrete pavers has grown, so has the variety of choices for colors, textures, sizes, and shapes. Some resemble traditional bricks; others masquerade as terra-cotta tile, cobblestones, or granite blocks. Because they lack the random color variations that are typical of natural

▼ Prefabricated mosaic tile medallions are a striking focal point when set into plain tile or concrete paving. For an additional cost you can have custom designs made to order.

brick or stone, however, they can look institutional.

Putting them together is a bit like building with Lego bricks. Within a style range, the units are designed to interconnect with each other in a wide array of geometric patterns, giving extraordinary design flexibility. The old standbys are pavers that interlock in a honeycomb pattern and provide an exceptionally tight join; other paver series come in various square and rectangular sizes, as well as a pointed, diamond edge that fits together with the more standard geometric forms. Still others are round or wedge-shaped. With those, you can create star, sunburst, and diamond patterns, and other shapes that suit your fancy.

Manufacturers encourage buyers to mix and match pavers to create a unique design that suits their individual project. Do bear in mind, however, that in a large area, such as the decking around a swimming pool, a pattern formed from lots of small units can look terribly busy. Take into account the final area of the paving when you choose your materials.

Even though it will cost more, be sure to purchase pavers permeated with pigment throughout. When the pigment is in only the top coating, it can eventually wear off, exposing the bare concrete underneath. In addition, any chips or other damage will expose the less desirable material inside. The higher up-front cost is worth it to avoid the paving looking chipped and dingy after a few years. Also, according to manufacturers' claims, interlocking concrete pavers are frost-proof when installed properly. They come with a lifetime guarantee and are touted as being at least twice as strong as traditional poured concrete.

◄ **Pitted paving, such as the one shown here, is suitable only in regions where winter freeze/thaw cycles won't break up the surface.**

Planting between Paving Stones

It's a life-affirming experience to see a solitary plant growing out of a tiny crack in an expanse of paving. Clearly, the urge to live and grow is supreme. Try breaking up the monotony of an expanse of paving by leaving intentional gaps and filling them with low-growing plants. You can create just one planting gap or make a pattern of open spaces for plants.

If you're starting from scratch, consider leaving occasional planting gaps in the paving around the pool. If the paving is loose and laid on sand rather than set in mortar, the spaces among the pavers, stones, or bricks also provide a planting opportunity. The minimum space needed between stones is about 2 inches; if you sow seeds, you can get by with less. Many of the recommended plants are spreaders that will take up a lot more space at maturity than when they are first planted, so make sure you leave enough room for walking and sitting. You should also amend the soil — at least where you'll be planting — before installing the paving.

Low-growing, mound-forming plants and ones with a compact, spreading habit are ideal to grow among pavings. If the plants are in full sun, they will need to be able to endure high temperatures, as the heat reflected off paving can get intense. On the other hand, the surrounding slabs keep the roots cool and prevent moisture from evaporating, so you'll need to water less often than you would for container plants.

As a bonus, choose aromatic plants, such as creeping thyme, chamomile, and prostrate rosemary, that release their scent in the hot sun or when crushed underfoot. For a pleasing mixture, combine plants with contrasting colors, textures, and shapes, and include some that will spill out onto the surrounding paving. Buy plants in the smallest pots you can find — they'll cost less and be easier to plant in tight spaces. Finally, mulch the plantings with pea gravel, being careful to tuck gravel under creeping and rosette plants. The gravel provides a tidy, finished look to the area, improves drainage around the necks of plants, helps keep out weeds, holds in moisture, and cools the roots.

Acaena spp. (New Zealand bur), Zones vary

Alchemilla mollis (lady's mantle), Zones 4–7

Antirrhinum, dwarf varieties (snapdragon), usually grown as an annual

Arabis caucasica (wall rock cress), Zones 4–8

Armeria caespitosa (miniature thrift), Zones 5–7

A. maritima (sea thrift), Zones 3–9

Calendula officinalis (pot marigold), annual

Chamaemelum nobile 'Treneague' (chamomile), Zones 6–9

Cistus spp. (rock rose, sun rose), Zones 8 or 9–10, depending on variety

Corydalis lutea (yellow corydalis), Zones 5–8

Cymbalaria muralis (ivy-leaved toadflax), Zones 4–8

Dianthus spp. (border pinks, pink), Zones vary

Diascia, Zones 8–9

Erica (heather, heath), Zones vary

Erinus alpinus (alpine liverwort), Zones 4–7

Festuca glauca (blue fescue), Zones 4–10

Geranium incanum, Zones 5–10

G. sanguineum (bloody cranesbill), Zones 4–10

Helianthemum (rock rose), Zones 6–8

Iberis (candytuft), Zones vary

Juniperus horizontalis (creeping juniper), Zones 3–10

J. procumbens (Bonin Island juniper), Zones 5–9

Lobularia maritima (sweet alyssum), annual

Mazus reptans, Zones 5–8

Phlox subulata (creeping or moss phlox), Zones 3–8

Rosmarinus (rosemary), Zones vary with variety

Sedum spp., Zones vary with variety

Sempervivum spp. (hen-and-chickens, houseleeks), Zones vary

Thymus herba-barona (caraway thyme), Zones 6–9

T. serpyllum (mother of thyme or wild thyme), Zones 4–9

Tropaeolum (nasturtium), annual

Veronica prostrata (prostrate speedwell), Zones 5–8

Viola tricolor (Johnny-jump-up), Zones 4–10

V. x wittrockiana (pansy), Zones 4–10

Coping with the Edges

The rounded, bull-nose edge on this pool's coping is less likely to snag swimsuits and swimmers than is rough material, such as square-cut brick or flagstone.

The traditional coping around the perimeter of a pool is the bull-nosed concrete sections that slope away from the pool for drainage. That approach is practical and economical. The rounded edge is less likely to cause severe injury should someone fall against it, and the water drains away from the pool easily. The slightly raised edge also keep leaves from drifting under the pool cover in winter. With a cover cut to fit the shape of the pool and resting on the bull-nosed coping, you should have little or no debris collecting in the pool over the winter months.

Another advantage of traditional coping is that it is easy on bathing suits. Stones and other materials that overhang the rim of the pool look very stylish, but anyone who scrambles out of the pool over the edge is likely to tear or fray his or her suit. As pool owner Rebecca Allen, of

Vienna, Virginia, puts it, "The old-fashioned concrete coping is the cheapest option — and also the most practical."

For homeowners hankering for something different, there are other possibilities for edging a pool. In many modern pool designs, the edge of the pool is interrupted with boulders — either real or man-made — to create a more natural appearance. This look is particularly effective when the pool has an organic form, rather than a geometric one, and is situated on a wooded lot. With a black bottom and the occasional rock breaking up the edge, such a pool can resemble a woodland pond in a clearing. Flagstone, either as coping alone or as an extension of the overall pool decking, is another beautiful option.

For a sleek, modern look, consider cantilevering a wooden deck or paving slabs about 4 inches over the edge of the pool. That treatment makes the pool appear to float, as if it were in another dimension below the plane of the decking. The overhanging edge should not be sharp. You can install rounded tile strips, for example, or soften the edge of the stone with mitering or a bull-nosed finish. Brick edges are also distinctive. To solve the problem of rough, sharp edges, manufacturers offer a special bull-nosed brick that is rounded at the water's edge.

▲ **Beautiful, large stones and mounding conifers rim the perimeter of this swimming pool, creating the illusion that it is a natural, rather than man-made, body of water.**

ENCLOSING THE POOL

The English word paradise comes from the old Persian word *pairi-daeza,* which means a walled park or pleasure garden. By enclosing your swimming pool with a fence or wall, you create a space set apart from the outside world, giving it the potential to be paradise indeed. Because a high fence or wall blocks the surrounding view, the pool is freed from the local setting and refers to nothing except itself. Instead of being tied to designing a swimming pool that is in harmony with the local surroundings, you can make your own fantasy space. In addition, a solid wall — and even a fence that doesn't have gaps — makes an excellent sound barrier, an important consideration if the pool area backs onto a busy road. Many municipalities and communities have regulations regarding enclosing a pool with a fence or wall, so it's important to check with local building codes and authorities before you begin making your plans.

Regardless of whether a fence or wall is required, it is good insurance. The last thing you want is a stray child wandering into your pool area and getting hurt. In addition, high fences and walls create privacy, so you can enjoy the pleasures of the pool without the intrusion of prying eyes.

You may decide to fence or wall the entire perimeter of the back of your property, or simply enclose the pool area. For example, a wooden fence surrounds the perimeter of Gordon and Lisa Tudor's garden in Encinitas, California. In addition, an attractive wrought-iron fence separates the swimming pool from the rest of the property. With the gate to the pool area closed, children can play safely in the garden without their parents worrying about a mishap in the pool.

In western Massachusetts, the Edgertons' pool is in the middle of a large lawn that is an important play space for their two children. When the children were small, the Edgertons were concerned that they could easily fall into the pool. For an inexpensive solution to the problem, they surrounded the pool area with wire farm fencing, then planted vines on the fence and a narrow perennial

"When we first bought the house, I was really nervous about our small children near the pool, so we put up a chicken-wire fence around the pool and grew flowers and vines all over it. It was really inexpensive, and you can hardly see the fence at all."

Mary Edgerton, Williamstown, Massachusetts

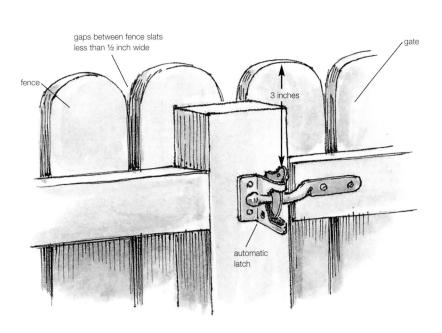

gaps between fence slats less than ½ inch wide

fence

gate

3 inches

automatic latch

and shrub border around the perimeter. With the vines clambering over the fence, and the small shrubs, perennials, and annuals adding interest in the border, the unattractive wire is almost invisible.

Licia and Michael Conforti's pool in Williamstown, Massachusetts, is also in the middle of a large open space. They set it apart from the rest of the garden by enclosing it with a mixed hedge of burning bush (*Euonymus alatus*) and hardy rugosa roses, creating a swimming pool–garden room. The roses add pretty color in the summer and are followed by large, decorative hips. In fall, the euonymus lives up to its common name and turns a flaming red. For spring color, they planted Manchurian lilac (*Syringa pubescens* ssp. *patula* 'Miss Kim') on each side of the entrance to the pool area.

In situations where your property slopes away from the pool, consider placing the fence or wall below eye level along a lower portion of the slope. This approach is particularly satisfying if you have a view you want to preserve. It also takes the pressure off spending large amounts of money for an attractive fence or wall, as it won't be visible from the pool and garden.

While codes vary by community, most experts recommend that fences or walls around swimming pools be at least 5 feet high. In the case of a fence, the vertical spaces should be no wider than 4 inches. In addition, 18 inches on either side of the gate latch, the vertical space should be narrower — no more than ½ inch — so it's impossible to reach through the gap to unlatch the gate. To prevent children or animals from crawling underneath, the space between the bottom of the fence and the ground should be no more than 2 inches.

No matter how high the fence or wall is, a determined child — or adult — may climb over if it is equipped with toeholds or is made of a material that is easy to climb. Design the enclosure so there's nowhere to get a purchase for scaling the heights. In the case of a chain-link fence, choose a mesh with holes no larger than 1¾ inches. By the same token, avoid storing garbage cans, garden furniture, or anything else near the wall or fence that can serve as a perch for leaping over. Nearby trees, especially ones with nicely stair-stepped branches that overhang the fence or wall, are another way of foiling the barrier. Be alert to any possible way that an intruder could enter the pool area.

Once you've taken into account the nuts and bolts of regulations and safety issues for enclosing your swimming pool, then you can focus on the fun part: choosing a design that complements the architecture of your home and the style of your pool.

Fences

Because it is an architectural feature, a fence's design should also relate to the house. A picket fence is charming for a moderately sized, Colonial-style home, but it looks silly around an opulent house. Wrought-iron fencing suits Victorian architecture and very grand houses in parklike settings. Post-and-rail fences harmonize well in farmland or wooded situations. When you plan for a fence, be sensitive to how the style will relate to your home and the other features in the garden.

Sometimes budget must take precedence over all other considerations. In that case, chain link, however dreary, may be the necessary choice. If you are forced into opting for a chain-link fence, consider covering it with a dense-growing vine. Ivy is excellent for this because it will grow in sun or shade and is tolerant of almost any soil. In frost-free climates, bougainvillea, with its vivid-colored flowers borne for months throughout the summer and into autumn, makes a dense evergreen curtain

▼ **The perennials and shrubs planted in front of this discreet fence blend with the garden beyond, making the transition from the pool to the rest of the property almost seamless.**

that completely hides an unsightly fence underneath. Other good evergreen vines to disguise an unattractive fence include cross vine (*Bignonia capreolata*) and *Clematis armandii.* In cold regions, the selection for vigorously growing vines is greater if you are willing to accept a deciduous plant. You also can hide a chain-link fence by planting a hedge in front of it. See page 60 for more information on hedges.

In communities where fences around swimming pools do not have to be as tall as 5 or 6 feet, split-rail or post-and-rail fences are acceptable if they are covered with wire mesh so that small children cannot slip underneath. This is an inexpensive option that suits an informal setting, and is visually less intrusive than a standard paling fence. From a distance, the wire mesh almost disappears. The informality of split rail is ideal in a farm setting or where the pool backs onto a meadow or woodland.

In a small setting, a tall fence may be out of scale with its surroundings. One way around that, if allowed by local codes, is to top a shorter fence with latticework or a trellis. Either provides the necessary extra height but allows light and air to pass through, and the result is less visually dominant.

FENCES ON SLOPES

Although a swimming pool needs to be level, the land around it may be sloping. This topography presents homeowners with several choices for how a fence will work its way down or up a hillside. The three solutions are step fencing, contour fencing, and sloped fencing.

As the name suggests, step fencing is installed in sections to stair-step down the slope in uniform segments. Each panel is parallel to the perpendicular fence post so there are gaps at the bottom of the sections of the fence where the land slopes away. Around a swimming pool, local code

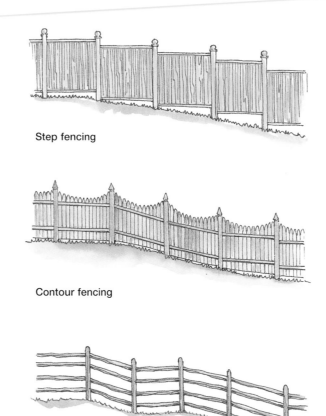

Step fencing

Contour fencing

Sloped fencing

may require that you add wire mesh or other material to prevent people and animals from crawling through the gaps underneath.

Contour fencing follows the contours of the land. Each picket or paling is attached to the horizontal support rails individually so that they are in close contact with the ground. The top of the fence is uneven, echoing the pattern created by the slope of the hillside.

Finally, sloped fencing follows the grade of the hillside. In this design, the top of the fence slopes in the direction of the grade if all the upright boards are the same length. Alternatively, the boards can be cut so the top is level and the bottom follows the slope. In that case, each paling or fence board will be a different length.

◄ A wrought-iron fence is particularly attractive, especially when it is softened and partly hidden by layers of plants in front and back. Here, daylilies, ornamental grasses, catmint, and coreopsis provide a long season of interest.

Walls

The standard materials for walls are concrete block, brick, stone, adobe, and poured concrete. You can cover concrete-block walls with stucco, paint, or a veneer, such as stone or brick, to make them more attractive. Stone and brick are the classic materials for garden walls because they are of the earth and so blend comfortably in a garden setting.

Besides being a safety and security feature, a wall is a strong architectural feature in your swimming pool and garden design. To make the most of it, opt for a design that relates to the style of your house and the rest of your yard. Ideally, the material and style of your wall should be in harmony with the region where you live, thus adding to a sense of place. Stone walls made from rocks unearthed during each spring's plowing are a feature of the New England landscape. Adobe walls are indigenous to the Southwest; in the South, brick walls often have a perforated design that looks decorative and allows for cooling air circulation.

To minimize any oppressive, overhanging feeling, avoid building a high wall too close to the swimming pool. A good rule is to make sure the wall is at least 4 feet from the pool area. One possible solution to a wall that risks being too dominant is to break up the solid mass by combining it with wrought-iron panels or placing lattice on top.

BUILDING A BRICK WALL ON A BUDGET

Brick walls are costly to build in terms of both labor and material. A new technique introduced by the Brick Industry Association, however, makes it possible to build one for a fraction of what it would cost using traditional methods. The technique creates what is called a pier-and-panel wall.

Normally, a straight wall must be thick enough to provide lateral stability, with enough strength to resist wind and impact loads. To make it structurally sound, you must build a concrete foundation, or footing, that is twice as thick as the wall it supports or two-thirds the height of the wall, whichever is greater. In cold climates, the footing must be thick enough to be below the frost line. The footing runs the entire length of the wall. Digging it, disposing of the dirt, and pouring the concrete represent a significant percentage of the construction cost.

▼ **This brick wall is a natural continuum of the house wall, blending perfectly to make a harmonious whole. The low, billowy plants along the pool and wall soften the line and merge the two elements beautifully.**

With the pier-and-panel construction technique, the wall can be as narrow as 3 or 4 inches (one brick thick), and the panel sections are laid directly on bare earth or on top of pressure-treated 2- by 4-inch lumber. Structural support comes from the piers, which are built on standard footings, and narrow ribbons of galvanized reinforcing wire embedded in the mortar joints of the panels.

A pier-and-panel wall requires about half the number of bricks needed for a standard 8-inch or wider wall, thus significantly reducing the cost of materials. In addition, builders estimate that the time spent on labor is almost cut in half because the footing does not have to be dug. In the end, you'll probably save at least 30 percent of the cost of building a traditional brick wall.

Building a brick wall without footings goes against everything masons have ever been taught. You're likely to encounter skepticism if you approach a bricklayer with the project. However, it does work. For specifications on building a pier-and-panel wall without footings under the panels, contact the Brick Industry Association (see Additional Information on page 197).

SCREENS AND WINDBREAKS

A cooling breeze may be welcome on a hot day, but for wet swimmers that breeze may be a bit chilly. If your swimming pool is in the line of prevailing winds or situated where you may be exposed to the curious eyes of outsiders, consider screening the area. In addition to fences and walls, rows of shrubs or trees make an excellent screen both for protection from the wind and for privacy. If you are in a setting where you want protection from wind but don't want to block a beautiful view, opt for a transparent wall made of heavy-duty glass. Glass walls are generally installed in sections and supported by posts spaced about 10 feet apart. These modular sections allow for great flexibility in layout and design.

▲ **Glass walls are ideal in places where you need protection from wind but don't want to block a spectacular view.**

▲ This simple, inexpensive gate meets local codes for swimming pools and blends comfortably with the split-rail fence. Note the fine wire mesh attached to the fence to keep out small children and animals.

▶ This wide, double gate is a perfect complement to the fence and allows plenty of room for bringing in pool furniture or even large garden equipment.

When designing a fence or wall, usually the structure should connect to itself or to some other end point to make an enclosed area. A fence left floating in the garden with no logical end point is unsettling and ineffective. That rule does not apply to glass walls, however. Because they are a see-through block rather than a solid barricade, it is less critical that it connect to another fence or structure. You may decide to place a short length of glass screen in just one spot to create a protected area for sunbathing, or you can run the wall across the entire length of your property.

GATES

The opening in a fence or wall is as important as the structure itself. A gate is the transition from the outside world to the "inner sanctum." You communicate a message with your gate. For example, a tall, solid gate provides privacy and security. People cannot see beyond the gate, and the message is clearly "Keep out unless invited in." A gate with an open pattern encourages glimpses into the garden or pool area. It is less private but also more welcoming.

The possible styles of gates are limited only by your imagination. Iron and aluminum can be custom made into almost any shape, design, and pattern. Wood also has huge scope for design choices, from a basic grapestake or stockade to louvered board or pickets. In addition, you can set fretwork wood patterns into a cutout area of the gate or incorporate a spherical opening near the top for an oriental "moon."

Your gate can be a dramatic feature or an unobtrusive element. Put an arch over it, and the gate becomes a special entryway. If you don't want to cause an unattractive break in the fence line, you might opt for a design that blends with the fence so the gate almost disappears. Whatever you decide to do, make sure the design is harmonious with the surrounding structures.

In addition to the emotional and aesthetic considerations of designing your gate, don't forget practical matters. Think about what sort of traffic will pass through the gate. Make sure the gate is wide enough to accommodate garden equipment, such as mowers and wheelbarrows, garden and poolside furniture, and other large items. Also make sure the gate can be locked and that the latch's design meets your community's safety codes for swimming pool areas. To keep people from reaching over the top to open the gate, the latch should be at least 3 inches down from the top of the gate and fence. Some codes require self-closing gates equipped with a spring mechanism that pulls the gate shut and a latch that closes automatically when the gate swings against it.

Landscaping a Fence or Wall

A naked fence or wall is stark, but either one makes a wonderful background for a wealth of planting arrangements. If you want to spend a lot of time working in the garden — with interruptions for refreshing swims in the pool — a perennial border looks fantastic when backed by a fence or wall.

For less work, consider planting a shrub border. Choose shrubs that require similar growing conditions (type of soil, light, and water requirements) and that will blend to create a pleasing picture. Factors to consider include the ultimate height and spread, foliage texture, foliage color, and flowering season. Place the tallest plants in the back row and shorter ones in front. Combine shrubs with different foliage textures and colors to create an interesting tapestry-like effect. Remember that dark colors, such as deep

green and red, appear to recede, making them look farther away; paler colors, such as gold, appear visually closer.

We think of plants growing up, but many cascade down. Take advantage of this attribute by growing plants with cascading or spreading habits in planter boxes placed on top of a wall or fence. Aggressive performers, such as New Wave and Surfinia petunias, will give you an almost uninterrupted, summerlong display of brightly colored flowers spilling down the face of the wall. Other good plants to cascade out of boxes include the prostrate or spreading varieties of rosemary, nasturtium (*Tropaeolum majus*, not the dwarf, bushy hybrid types, such as the Jewel and Alaska Series),

scaevola ('Blue Wonder' has larger blossoms than the common, garden-variety version and flowers almost continuously throughout the summer), variegated *Vinca major*, and sweet potato vine (*Ipomoea batatas*). For extra drama, try 'Blackie', a sweet potato vine with near-black foliage.

An alternative to putting planters on top of a fence or wall is to hang them on the face. There are all sorts of decorative planters designed with one flat side to hang on walls or fences. Arrange them in clusters or place one in the center of each wall panel between support piers. Make sure the containers are in scale with the length and height of the wall. A tiny pot affixed in the middle of a large wall will look silly.

▲ **Large planters placed on top of this wall are filled with cascading 'Purple Wave' petunias that clothe the wall from the top down. Hydrangeas add color from the ground up.**

ESPALIER

Still another option for disguising a fence or wall is to espalier plants along it. *Espalier* is the art of training a tree or shrub to grow flat against a surface. The term comes from the Italian *spalla,* which means "shoulder" or "support." Almost any tree or shrub can be trained in this way, as long as you begin when the plant is young enough.

Traditionally, fruit trees were espaliered along the walls of kitchen gardens. The trees benefit from the extra warmth radiating from the walls, and the owners enjoy an extra harvest without taking up any significant additional planting space. As a bonus, because the angle of growth of the branches is systematically controlled, fruit trees tend to bear two or three years sooner than trees planted in the open. (It was in the third century B.C.E. that the Greek mathematician Euclid noticed that tree branches growing anywhere from horizontal to a 45-degree angle produced fruit sooner than those growing more vertically.)

Other good candidates for espalier are forsythia and flowering quince (which lend themselves to informal, freeform training), Southern magnolia (*Magnolia grandiflora*), cotoneaster, and pyracantha. In temperate climates, follow the lead of the Spaniards and grow oranges and other citrus trees against walls.

Another idea is to train a small-leaved ivy in a geometric pattern on a wall or fence. A living trellis is a fascinating feature, and most varieties of ivy are easy to grow. For a quick and easy-to-train ivy trellis, attach wires to the structure in a diamond pattern, then tie the ivy along the wires. Prune as necessary to keep the pattern clearly visible, and continue to tie up the new growth.

You can use a trellis to support an espalier, or install a system of wires laid out in the pattern you want to achieve. Because white walls reflect a lot of heat, arrange the wires about 1 foot away from the wall to prevent radiated heat from stimulating new growth too early in spring. On dark walls that absorb heat, supports can be as close as 4 to 6 inches. Do leave some space, however, to allow for air circulation.

A basic knowledge of the principles of pruning will go a long way in helping you train an espalier. Pruning is a way of communicating with the plant, telling it how you want it to grow. If you want to remove growth so it won't come back, instead of cutting from the tip back to a growth bud, remove the branch at its growing source, at either the trunk or the main branch. The message you deliver is clear: Don't send out extra shoots; there are enough here already.

What time of year you prune also communicates a definite message. If you want to increase the plant's vigor, prune in winter. If you hope to slow growth temporarily, cut back in summer. The exception to this rule is plants such as California natives that are dormant in summer and actively growing in the winter rainy season.

▼ Ivy trained along wires in a diamond trellis pattern transforms an unattractive wall into an eye-catching garden feature. Once the ivy grows thicker, it should be trimmed periodically to maintain the pattern.

Training an Espalier

You can either grow a freeform espalier, where the plant spreads randomly over the wall and is allowed to follow its own pattern, or train the plant into a formal design. Choose a pattern that is well adapted to the natural growth habit of the plant you want to train. For example, magnolias, althaeas, forsythias, cherries, peaches, and plums grow in an upright form that suits a fan shape. Pyracantha adapts easily to a horizontal cordon.

To train an espalier into a formal pattern, begin with a young plant. If you can find an older plant that already has branches where you want them, that will save you time. Otherwise, purchase a 1-year-old, unbranched tree, called a "whip" or "maiden." If you are beginning with a whip, prune off the central, vertical leader at the point where you want side branches to form.

When the new shoots are long enough, choose two to train to the side and a third branch to train vertically as the central leader. (The exception is a Belgian fence design, which requires just a pair of branches growing in a V-shape at a 45-degree angle.) Tie the side branches firmly but loosely (you don't want to constrict a branch with a tight band) at the angle at which you want them to grow, top right. Because vertical growth is more vigorous than horizontal growth, let branches that you want to train horizontally grow at a 45-degree angle for their first summer. They'll grow faster, and they'll still be supple enough to bend into a horizontal position at the end of the growing season. Check the ties periodically to make sure they haven't become too tight.

If you are training an espalier with multiple levels, allow the central leader to grow until it has reached the point where you want it to branch off again. Cut off the tip at a growth bud, then repeat the training process for the new shoots that develop, center.

Once your espalier is established, trim back excess foliage along each branch to keep the pattern tidy and clearly visible, bottom right. To encourage abundant fruit or flowers, research pruning recommendations for specific plants.

Although most fruit trees are pruned only during the dormant season, espaliered fruit should also be pruned in summer to limit foliage growth and encourage more fruit production. Timing is important. Midsummer, when the new wood has become woody at its base, is the best time to do the job.

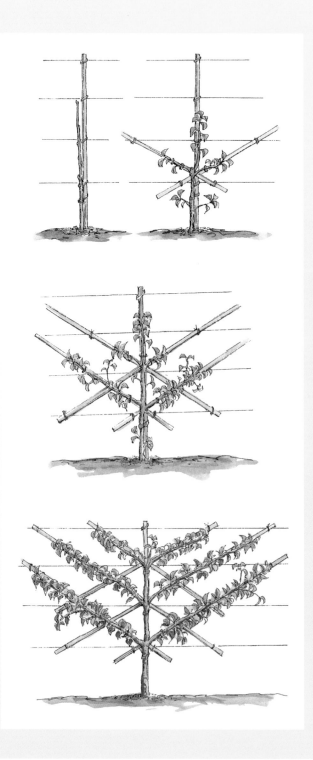

Hedges around the Pool

In municipalities where fences are not required by law, a hedge is an attractive way to enclose a pool area. In addition, in most communities, the height regulation for walls and fences does not apply to hedges, so you have an opportunity to have a taller screen from neighbors, if that is necessary. Should your local codes require a fence and you want a hedge, install an inexpensive chain-link fence, then plant an evergreen hedge right up against it so the foliage grows through and hides it on both sides.

Almost any shrubs planted in a row will grow into a hedge. If you want a traditional, pruned hedge with a tailored appearance, opt for shrubs that tolerate shearing well. Plants traditionally used for hedges include yew, boxwood, hornbeam, holly, and privet, all of which grow slowly and require pruning less often. Many of the deciduous shrubs, though bare in the winter months, have the bonus of flowers, berries, and autumn foliage, making them more interesting than shrubs used for a typical evergreen hedge.

Choose hedge plants that are suited to your growing conditions. Notice how much sun or shade the spot receives, whether the area is low-lying and soggy after a heavy rain, and what kind of soil (clay, sand, or loam) you have. Visit a local nursery and talk with a qualified professional to find out which plants will do best in your region and in the specific site you've selected for them.

PLANNING A HEDGE

To determine how many plants you need for a hedge, find out the expected mature width of the shrub. To ensure that the plants will intermingle to form a continuous, uninterrupted line, reduce the average expected width of each plant by about one third. Then divide the length of the hedge by the reduced expected width of the plant. For example, Japanese boxwood (*Buxus microphylla* var. *japonica*) typically grows 5 feet tall with a 4-foot spread. For your hedge calculations, reduce the projected optimum spread to about 3 feet. If the length you want to plant is 30 feet, then you will need 10 plants. It wouldn't hurt to add two or three more shrubs for good measure.

If you want to save money and are willing to be patient, start the hedge with small plants.

▼ **This hedge separates the swimming pool from the rest of the garden, while the arched opening provides a tantalizing glimpse of the blue water beyond.**

There is a significant difference in price between a 1-gallon shrub and one growing in a 3- to 5-gallon container. After all, the extra soil in the larger pot is heavier to transport, and the nursery had to look after the plant for a much longer time before bringing it to market. All that adds to the cost.

Many retailers are backing off on stocking plants in smaller containers because most of the buying public wants immediate gratification with a larger plant, and the profit margins are bigger on the larger specimens. If your nursery doesn't carry the plants you want in a small size, ask whether the store will order them for you. Although that may mean waiting another season before you get the plants, the savings should be worth it. Curiously, in many cases smaller plants quickly catch up in size to larger ones planted at the same time because they experience less transplant shock. With deciduous shrubs, you can save money by purchasing bare-root plants.

You can boost the growing rate of your hedge by mulching the plants with well-rotted

▲ A low-growing rhaphi-olepis hedge surrounds this Spanish-style spa, giving it a sense of privacy and enclosure without hovering over the space.

manure. Writing in the March 1996 issue of *Traditional Home* magazine about his garden at Highgrove, Prince Charles extolled the virtues of manure for stimulating plant growth: "I took one look at the small yews we planted and thought they would never grow, but Lady Salisbury assured me that as long as we put on lots of well-rotted cow manure they would grow by at least a foot a year. She was absolutely right, and ever since then I have had the greatest possible faith in the properties of well-rotted cow manure." Left to its own devices, yew grows at a rate of 6 to 8 inches a year, so manure can make a huge difference!

When you are ready to begin planting, set the shrubs along the line of the hedge, spacing them evenly. Don't forget that the plants will spread at the end of the row as well as in the middle; inset the first plant in the row by half the expected mature width, measuring from the center of the plant. To ensure that the hedge line is straight, you may find it helpful to run a string tied between two stakes as a guide. If the hedge will go in front of a fence or wall, bring it forward from the structure by half the mature size of the shrub. In the case of Japanese boxwood, the center of the plant should be spaced 1½ feet in front of the fence or wall.

PLANTING SHRUBS

The procedure for planting shrubs is the same whether they are planted singly or in a row. The old wisdom for planting trees and shrubs was to dig a hole twice the width of the rootball, then add amendments to the backfill to improve the local soil. Recent research has determined that you're better off planting directly in the native soil. That way, the soil won't settle, sinking the plant deeper into the ground than it should be. Also, the plant's roots are likely to extend much farther than the amended hole. If the soil in the hole is too rich, the roots will be loath to venture out into a less hospitable environment. Ultimately, they may become rootbound in their own hole. Having said that, you're wise to choose plants that are suited to your soil type. For example, if your soil is heavy clay, it wouldn't make sense to plant honey locust tree (*Gleditsia triacanthos*), which prefers sandy soil.

Container and balled-and-burlapped stock. For container-grown trees and shrubs and balled-and-burlapped stock, dig a hole large enough to contain the rootball. Check that the crown of the plant, where the trunk or stem joins the roots, is slightly above ground level. A good way to measure this is to set the plant in the hole with the roots resting on undisturbed soil. Lay the shovel handle across the hole to see where the crown is relative to the surrounding soil. Adjust the depth of the hole (either dig deeper or backfill) until it is right for the plant. If your soil is heavy clay, plant a little higher,

▼ To ensure that a hedge is planted in a straight line, stretch a string along the row to use as a guide. Also be sure to space the plants equidistant from each other. When available, bare-root plants are less expensive than those growing in containers.

with the crown about 2 inches above soil level. That will help prevent root rot.

Once the hole is the right size, fill it with water and allow it to soak in. This step ensures that the roots will have a nice, moist environment in which to grow. While the water is being absorbed, water the plant in its container. Then remove it from the container or unwrap the burlap. Real burlap will rot away quickly, so it's fine to leave it around the rootball, but nowadays nurseries often use a synthetic material that's almost indistinguishable from burlap, except that it doesn't decompose. If you leave on the synthetic material, the plants will rapidly become rootbound and die. Rather than second-guessing whether or not the wrap is made from a natural fiber, you're better off removing all root coverings.

If you notice that the plant's roots wrap around the perimeter of the rootball or are a tight mass of kinks, unwrap them or cut away the outer tangle of roots. Most plants will take this roughing up of their roots quite happily. In fact, the pruning will stimulate the growth of new feeder roots, which help establish the new plant.

▲ **Carefully remove a plant from its container, top left, by holding it and slipping the stem between two fingers. If the roots are a tight tangle, slice through the roots to butterfly the rootball, top right. Fill the basin around the newly planted shrub with water, allowing it to soak in thoroughly, bottom left.**

Place the plant in the middle of the hole, making sure the top of the soil ball is slightly above ground level. Then backfill the hole with the original soil, pressing down firmly to remove air pockets. Use the extra soil to build a berm around the plant to create a basin to hold water. Water thoroughly several times, filling the basin and allowing the water to soak in each time. Many balled-and-burlapped plants have been grown in heavy clay soil. If your garden soil is lighter than the soil around the plant's roots, the clay soil will absorb water more slowly, so make sure the water is being soaked up by the soil immediately around the roots.

Bare-root stock. The technique for planting bare-root stock is nearly the same as that for container plants. To prevent the roots from rotting or drying out, get the plants into the ground as soon as possible after you bring them home. If you cannot plant them right away, find a shady, wind-

▼ A true garden wonder, shredded bark mulch helps discourage weed growth, maintains soil moisture, makes the beds look tidy, and ultimately breaks down to improve the soil quality.

protected spot in your garden and bury the roots temporarily, tilting the trunk at an angle to discourage new root growth. Called "heeling in," this step gives you a little extra time before you must get the new plants properly in the ground.

When you're ready to plant, stick the roots in a bucket of water while you dig the holes. Make each hole big enough to contain the roots without folding them over or bunching them up. Fill the hole with water and allow it to soak into the surrounding soil. Then mound up soil in the bottom of the hole and spread the roots over the mound. Lay a shovel across the hole to make sure the growing crown is 2 inches above ground level. When the plant is settled at the correct level, backfill the hole, firming the soil around the roots. Water again, allowing it to soak in slowly.

Bare-root trees and shrubs are dormant when they are shipped. Once you have planted them in a permanent site, water again only when the soil becomes dry. As soon as you see new growth sprouting, water more frequently.

MULCHING A HEDGE

Any tree or shrub, whether planted from a container, balled-and-burlapped stock, or bare-root stock, will benefit from being mulched to retain soil moisture and deter weeds. A substantial layer, 3 to 4 inches thick, is very effective. Spread mulch the length of the hedge to provide all the horticultural benefits and give it a tidy look. If you use an organic mulch, such as shredded bark, it will also nourish the soil as it breaks down. Be careful not to push up the mulch against the trunk or stems of the shrubs.

Experts used to recommend pruning back trees and shrubs at planting time to create a balance between roots and foliage. Recent research has shown that the extra foliage actually benefits newly planted trees and shrubs, because it produces hormones that encourage root regeneration. You can tidy up a tree or shrub by removing any broken or dead branches, but otherwise leave it alone.

MAINTAINING A HEDGE

Pruning actually stimulates growth. Botanists have found there is a concentration of growth hormone in the branch tips of plants. When you cut back a branch, you redirect those hormones to the growing buds just below the cut. As a result, a pruned plant will send out two or three shoots from each bud, ultimately doubling the plant's fullness. Therefore, to encourage your hedge to fill out and grow up, give it a light shearing. Then allow the plants to grow for a year without interference.

As necessary, trim the hedge to even out the size of the plants and encourage denser growth. Slow-growing shrubs traditionally used for hedges, including yew and boxwood, generally need to be pruned just once a year. If you chose a faster-growing plant, you may need to do the job twice yearly to keep the plants looking neat and tidy.

Always prune a hedge so the sides flare out slightly, making them wider at the bottom than at the top. That way, the entire surface of the hedge will receive even sunlight, encouraging healthy, dense growth. If the hedge tapers outward from the top to the bottom, the top of the hedge will shade the bottom, and you are likely to get unsightly bare branches where light cannot reach.

Small-leaved hedges comprising plants such as Japanese or Chinese hollies, boxwoods, or yews, are ideal for shearing. For hedges with coarser leaves, you'll achieve a more attractive finish if you shape the hedge with secateurs or loppers, rather than shears, and cut back each individual branch to a growth bud. If you shear plants with large leaves, the shrubs will end up with a lot of leaves chopped in half.

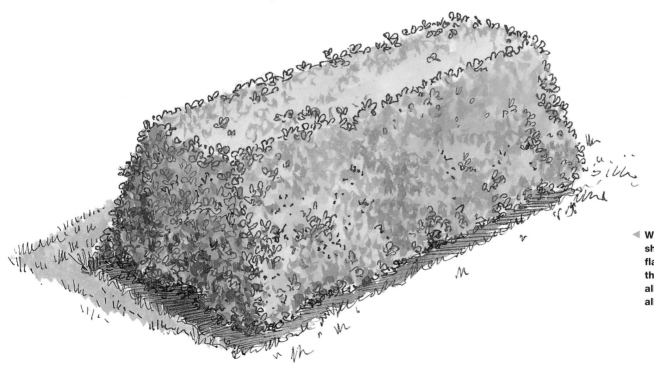

◀ **When pruning a hedge, shape the sides so they flare out slightly from the top to the bottom, allowing light to reach all the foliage.**

Trees and Shrubs for Hedges and Windbreaks

Almost any shrub planted in a row will grow into a hedge. If you want a pruned hedge with a tailored appearance, opt for shrubs that tolerate shearing well, such as yew, boxwood, hornbeam, holly, and privet. For flowering hedges, consider lilac, rugosa roses, camellia, hibiscus, abelia, or pyracantha.

Ilex aquifolium

DECIDUOUS TREES

Alnus cordata (Italian alder), Zones 5–7, fast-growing

Arbutus unedo (strawberry tree), Zones 8–9, slow to medium growth rate

Carpinus betulus (European hornbeam), Zones 4–8, slow-growing

Crataegus monogyna (English hawthorn), Zones 5–7, slow to medium growth rate

Fagus sylvatica (European beech), Zones 4–7, slow to medium growth rate

Ilex aquifolium (English holly), Zones 7–9, slow-growing

Laurus nobilis (sweet bay), Zones 8–10, medium growth rate

Melaleuca quinquenervia (broad-leafed paperbark), Zone 10, strong-growing

Metrosideros excelsus (New Zealand Christmas tree), Zone 10, robust growth

Olea europaea (olive), Zones 9–10, slow-growing

Populus x canadensis (Canadian poplar), Zones 4–9, fast-growing

Prunus lusitanica (Portugal laurel), Zones 7–9, medium growth rate

Zelkova serrata (Japanese zelkova), Zones 6–8, medium growth rate

Chamaecyparis lawsoniana

CONIFERS

Abies grandis (giant fir), Zones 5–6, slow to medium growth rate

Cedrus deodara (deodar cedar), Zones 7–9, medium growth rate

Cephalotaxus fortunei (Chinese plum yew), Zones 6–9, slow-growing

Chamaecyparis lawsoniana (Lawson false cypress), Zones 5–9, medium growth rate

Cupressocyparis leylandii (Leyland cypress), Zones 6–9, very fast-growing

Juniperus chinensis (Chinese juniper), Zones 4–10, slow to medium growth rate

J. communis (common juniper), Zones 2–10, slow-growing

J. scopulorum (Rocky Mountain juniper), Zones 4–10, medium growth rate

Larix decidua (European larch), Zones 3–6, medium to fast growth rate

Picea omorika (Serbian spruce), Zones 5–8, slow-growing

Pinus nigra (European black pine), Zones 5–8, medium growth rate

P. radiata (Monterey pine), Zones 7–9, medium growth rate

Pseudotsuga menziesii (Douglas fir), Zones 5–7, medium growth rate

Taxus baccata (English yew), Zones 7–8, slow-growing

Thuja plicata (Western red cedar), Zones 6–8, slow to medium growth rate

Tsuga canadensis (Canada hemlock), Zones 4–8, medium growth rate

Abelia x grandiflora

SHRUBS

Abelia x grandiflora (glossy abelia), Zones 6–9, fast-growing

Berberis spp. (barberry), Zones vary, slow to medium growth, depending on species

Buxus spp. (boxwood), Zones vary, slow-growing

Camellia **spp.,** Zones vary, slow-growing

Cotoneaster **spp.,** Zones vary, slow-growing

Dodonaea viscosa (hop bush), Zones 9–10, fast-growing

Duranta erecta (golden dewdrop), Zone 10, medium growth rate

Elaeagnus x ebbingei, Zones 7–10, medium to fast growth rate

E. pungens (silverberry), Zones 7–9, very fast-growing

Euonymus **spp.,** Zones vary, growth rate varies with species

Griselinia littoralis (broadleaf), Zones 8–9, fast-growing

Hibiscus **spp.,** Zones vary, medium growth rate

Ilex cornuta (Chinese holly), Zones 7–9, slow-growing

I. crenata (Japanese holly), Zones 6–8, slow-growing

I. glabra (inkberry), Zones 5–9, slow-growing

Lavandula **spp.** (lavender), Zones vary, slow-growing

Ligustrum **spp.** (privet), Zones vary, fast-growing

Lonicera nitida (box honeysuckle), Zones 6–9, fast-growing

Osmanthus **spp.,** Zones vary, slow to medium growth rate

Photinia x fraseri (red tip), Zones 7–10, medium to fast growth rate

Pittosporum **spp.,** Zones 9–10, slow-growing

Prunus laurocerasus (English laurel), Zones 6–9, medium growth rate

P. lusitanica (Portugal laurel), Zones 7–9, medium growth rate

Pyracantha coccinea (scarlet firethorn), Zones 6–10, medium to fast growth rate (beware of thorns)

Rosmarinus officinalis (rosemary), Zones vary, medium growth rate

Tamarix ramosissima (five-stamen tamarisk), Zones 2–10, fast-growing

Rosa rugosa

ROSES FOR HEDGES AND SCREENS

Unlike modern hybrid tea roses, many of the old-fashioned shrub and species roses are vigorous growers that make excellent hedges and screens. They are hardy and pest- and disease-free. Many are tolerant of salt-laden sea air. With all these points in their favor, the flowers are a bonus.

Rosa x alba **'Celeste';** Zones 4–9; pale pink, fragrant flowers; vigorous spreader

R. x alba **'Great Maiden's Blush';** Zones 3–9; fragrant, double, pinkish white flowers

Rosa **'Felicia';** Zones 4–9; hybrid musk rose with double, fragrant pink flowers; vigorous grower

R. gallica **'Tuscany Superb';** Zones 4–9; strongly perfumed; semidouble, velvety dark red flowers with gold stamens

R. gallica **'Versicolor'** (Rosa mundi); Zones 3–9; pale pink flowers striped reddish pink

R. gallica **var. officinalis** ('Apothecaies Rose'); Zones 3–9; bold pink flowers

R. glauca; Zones 2–8; single, cerise pink flowers with cream centers and gold stamens; orange-red hips in autumn

R. moyesii **'Geranium';** Zones 5–9; single, carmine red flowers with yellow stamens; red hips

R. moyesii **'Marguerite Hilling';** Zones 4–9; soft rose pink flowers with gold stamens

R. moyesii **'Nevada';** Zones 4–9; creamy white flowers with gold stamens

Rosa **'Penelope';** Zones 4–9; hybrid musk with fragrant, double, pink-cream flowers

R. pimpinellifolia **'Frühlingsmorgen';** Zones 4–9; cherry pink single flowers with primrose centers and gold stamens

R. rugosa; Zones 4–9; cupped, single, white or magenta flowers; large orange hips; tolerant of salt spray

CHAPTER FOUR

POOLSCAPE
PLANTINGS

Like the frame for a painting or the setting for a jewel, the garden around your swimming pool is key to the overall effect you create. A well-designed planting around the pool will show the entire pool setting to best advantage, while ragged, uncared for beds or those that are poorly designed and planted will detract from the scene. Your choice of poolside plantings also contributes to any theme you may have for the design. For example, Mediterranean plants, such as lavender, rosemary, and cistus, evoke images of southern France, Italy, Spain, and Greece. Architectural plants such as *Dracaena marginata,* with its multiple stems topped with clusters of spiky foliage, create a spare, dramatic effect in a minimalist design. For a lush, tropical, Hawaiian look that provides floral interest and color throughout the year in frost-free climates, plant impatiens, wax begonias *(Begonia semperflorens),* and tropical hibiscus *(Hibiscus rosa-sinensis).*

▲ Native ferns thrive in the crevices of the granite rock that abuts this pool in western Massachusetts, giving the garden a pleasing sense of place.

decking will reflect heat and cut down on water that is absorbed into the ground.

Plants that litter excessively, either with leaves, berries, spent flower petals, or splattering sap, are a nuisance around a pool. Because you won't want to spend more time cleaning the decking and the pool than swimming and relaxing, you would be wise to avoid untidy specimens. Of course, in much of the United States, cleaning up the fallen leaves of deciduous trees is accepted as an annual rite of passage. Don't exile a tree or shrub from your pool just because it's deciduous, as long as it remains reasonably tidy the rest of the year. However, you'll want to choose small trees and shrubs to plant near the pool. Larger trees should be far enough away that they don't block the sun on the water, but you may want a shade tree in one corner to provide a haven from the heat of the decking and the glare of the pool.

In tropical climates, palm trees are excellent poolside choices because the roots grow straight down and have a narrow spread. But beware of willows, ficus, and silver maples (*Acer saccharinum*), which have extensive, aggressive roots systems. The roots of such trees can heave up huge concrete slabs, cracking and buckling them, and willow roots, which seek out water, can find a tiny crack in a pipe and work their way inside, wreaking havoc in the process. Opt for trees with noninvasive root systems. Cindy Benoit, a landscape architect in San Diego, California, recommends planting trees — even ones with roots that are unlikely to push up paving — at least 10 feet away from the pool.

Add bird-of-paradise (*Strelitzia regina*) and lantana to provide spring color, and plant some star jasmine (*Trachelospermum jasminoides*), geraniums (*Pelargonium*), agapanthus, and *Mandevilla* 'Alice du Pont' for summer color.

Qualities to look for in plants immediately near the pool include tidiness, no objectionable odors, no thorns or other plant parts that can cause injury, and restrained root systems that don't intrude where they aren't wanted. Also look for plants that are heat- and drought-tolerant. Although the pool is a large body of water, the surrounding

Sweetly scented flowers and foliage are a great asset near a pool, but some plants smell better than others. Avoid plants that produce unpleasant odors that may put people off. In some cases, response to scent is a very personal matter. For example, some people love the smell of boxwood

(*Buxus sempervirens*); others find it deeply offensive because it reminds them of the odor of cat urine. There you'll have to make a judgment call.

Some people may be concerned about plants that are active bee magnets because of the possibility of someone getting stung. If you leave a bee alone, it won't bother you; however, if you, or someone in your family, has a strong allergy to bee stings, then definitely avoid plants, such as yarrow and autumn-flowering sedum, that are known to attract bees. In areas where children — and adults — are playing with abandon, don't plant specimens with large thorns or sharp, spiky leaves nearby. That's not to say you shouldn't have any roses or other armored plants, but it's best to grow them out of the way of the immediate pool play area.

▼ Close enough to attractively frame the view of the swimming pool, these honey locust trees (*Gleditsia triacanthos* 'Sunburst') are planted far enough away so that their roots don't disturb the paving.

Useful Design Principles

Whether your poolscape is modern or traditional, formal or informal, evocative of a style from abroad or rooted in your local vernacular, certain time-honored design principles will help ensure a successful composition. As you design poolside plantings, aim to achieve a sense of unity and harmony among the plants and the various components in the landscape. Also, pay attention to proportion and scale, and a balance between mass and space. Use plants to create a pleasing combination of texture and shape. Truly great gardens use all these principles to evoke a delightful balance between restful and stimulating. Such gardens are harmonious without being repetitive and boring. A well-designed garden is balanced and unified, and at the same time surprising.

UNITY AND HARMONY

A garden that has unity and harmony comprises many components that blend together as a cohesive whole, free of any jarring elements. One way to achieve a sense of unity in a poolscape is to select a

▼ Large swaths of ornamental grasses, shrub roses, lavender, and other easy-to-care-for perennials merge happily with the landscape beyond, creating a harmonious scene.

theme, then stick to it. For example, if you opt for a tropical, South Seas motif, plant lush, large-leafed specimens that conjure up the tropics. On the other hand, those same opulent-looking plants will look out of place in a streamlined, minimalist setting. Unless your pool is walled off and completely set apart from the garden, make sure it is in harmony with the rest of your property and, if you have views beyond the boundaries of your land, with the greater environment. If your pool is right next to open fields, for example, you may want an informal landscape that blends harmoniously with the view beyond.

Repetition and rhythm contribute to a garden's sense of unity. Everyone has seen gardens that feature a lot of different plants plunked into a bed or border with no rhyme or reason to the arrangement and no apparent relationship among individual plants. The result is unattractive and unsettling — even jangling to the nerves. A more successful approach is to combine compatible plants in pleasing clumps, then duplicate those combinations along the length of a border to create a sense of rhythm. To keep the composition from looking repetitious and boring, make some minor variations, such as reversing two plants in a group or changing the spacing between the repetitions. You also can create rhythm by repeating a motif, such as a series of raised beds, or by planting a row of uniformly spaced trees or shrubs.

It's also important to unify all the elements in a poolscape by visually linking them. When architectural features are all the same style, they create a sense of unity. With plants you can connect and unify different areas with ground covers or hedges, or by repeating colors or plants in different areas. For example, if you have flashes of pink in a

▲ Roses in complementary shades of pink surround this poolside patio. Clumps of blue-flowering catnip add variety and spice to this well-balanced composition.

The multistemmed trees at the left and the large market umbrella add welcome vertical elements to the horizontal composition around a pool.

Although shorter in stature, the Sabal palm provides greater visual mass than the feathery queen palm *(Syagrus romanzoffiana).* Together the two palms give the small planter a sense of balance.

border on one side of the pool, use that same pink in a couple of containers on the opposite side.

Pruned trees and shrubs can support or detract from a garden's sense of unity and harmony. Certain plants, such as yew, holly, boxwood, and hornbeam, look marvelous in a formal setting when they are tightly pruned. In an informal setting, those same plants look better when they are allowed to grow in their more natural form with perhaps just a little judicious trimming to keep them in bounds. In addition, plants that grow in a distinct, appealing, natural form look inharmonious when they are severely pruned. An example is forsythia, which grows in a fountainlike form when left alone. To keep forsythia in bounds, many people prune it into boxes or balls, spoiling its natural shape.

By the same token, healthy plants contribute to an overall sense of harmony in a landscape. It is painful to see plants struggling to survive because

they have not been planted in the right kind of conditions. Once you get to know plants and their habits, it is also jarring to see plants grown together that come from very different habitats, such as a moisture- and shade-loving primrose next to a drought-tolerant, sun-loving lavender.

PROPORTION AND SCALE

Based on the findings of early Renaissance mathematicians and artists, there are specific guidelines for achieving pleasing proportions in any design. To create a comfortable balance between the depth of a garden border and the height of the structure or hedge behind it, make the border one-third taller than it is wide. For example, if the border is in front of a 6-foot-tall fence, it should be about 4 feet wide. To keep the display from being overwhelmed by exceptionally tall plants, make sure the tallest plant in the border is no taller than half the border's depth. Foundation plantings against a house or other building are the exception. In that case, experts recommend that the foundation planting be about as wide as the tallest shrub or plant in the bed.

When you plan your garden and swimming pool area, look with a critical eye to determine whether the plants you put together are in a pleasing scale among themselves as well as with the rest of the garden and that the various elements have attractive proportions.

MASS AND SPACE

Just as objects have physical weight, so too do they have visual weight. A large, dark item takes up more space visually than something pale in color, and a solid object generally looks larger than one with open spaces. For example, a dark-colored, solid table will look like it takes up more space than a glass-topped one of the same size.

Plants create the same visual effect. A dark green yew that is 5 feet tall and wide looks much more bulky or massive than a lacy Japanese maple tree of the same proportions. When designing with plants, try to achieve a balance of heavy and light, not only in the composition of a bed or border, but also in the overall landscape. Plants that have mass are important to define and fill space and provide visual resting places.

Space also provides a visual resting place. In a poolscape, the pool itself is a dominant, uninterrupted flat surface. Provide contrast to the open space with a combination of plants that provide height and mass. Ideally, you want a balanced mix of mass and space: Too much blank canvas — or flat water — will make the garden feel empty; too much mass will make the space feel dark, cramped, and heavy. Of course, there are successful poolscapes that celebrate the horizontal aspect

with little or no vertical elements, but most have at least one tall focal point, such as a single tree centered on the far end of the pool or a pair of trees or shrubs to draw the eye and provide contrast.

TEXTURE AND SHAPE

A common mistake most homeowners make when choosing plants for a garden is to select varieties that are similar in height and size. You can add interest to your beds and borders by introducing plants of different sizes, textures, and shapes. Experiment with different effects by combining contrasting textures, planting a spiny-leafed specimen next to a feathery one, for example, or combine straplike foliage of plants such as daylilies with broad-leafed varieties. Large-leafed plants are bold in texture, creating a strong, assertive look; small-leafed plants appear more delicate. Too much of either makes a less successful design than a balanced blend of different leaf textures.

Flower forms also contribute to texture in the garden. For example, a garden consisting of only daisylike blossoms will look monotonous; instead, mix spiky, round-headed, cuplike, and trumpet-shaped flower forms. Spikes and spires are among the strongest shapes in flower design. They reach boldly upward, giving excitement and even a spiritual lift to the design. If plants were punctuation marks in a sentence, spiky flowers would be the exclamation points. Visually, globe-shaped flowers tend to be more earthbound; umbelliferous and flatheaded flowers, such as yarrow, provide a horizontal element. The plateau of such flower forms provides a place for the eye to rest. Such a variety of textures, blended into an attractive whole, is part of a garden's visual appeal.

◀ **Contrasting textures, dominated by feathery flower panicles of fountain grass and dense, rounded sedum flower heads, make an appealing poolside planting.**

Planning a Design

efore you begin planting around your pool, think carefully about your goals for the overall landscape. Your choice of plants and how you use them are important in setting the tone for your swimming pool. Clipped hedges, symmetrical layouts, and simple color schemes all contribute to a formal appearance. Introduce bright colors, curved beds, and plants spilling onto paving, and you have a more informal design. Some pool owners opt for a minimalist look, putting the focus on architectural elements; others choose to have lush plantings surrounding the pool area.

▼ Curved planting beds echo the irregular shape of this swimming pool, contributing to a relaxed, informal look. The planting motif is repeated in both beds for pleasing repetition.

▲ Landscape designer Phillip Watson filled the perennial border next to his pool, top left, with summer-flowering, easy-care phlox, coreopsis, daylilies, and black-eyed Susans. At top right, Carol Paul opted for a repeating mix of peonies, daisies, dianthus, and Salvia 'May Night' for floral interest from early summer until first frost.

▶ This perennial bed follows the curve of the pool, bringing floral color right up to the edge with a generous planting of perennials and annuals that provide summerlong interest. The brick edging helps contain the bed and adds to the strong lines.

For example, Allen Mushinsky's pool in Potamac, Maryland, is in the middle of a clearing in the woods. He planted eulalia grass (*Miscanthus sinensis*) and fountain grass (*Pennisetum alopecuroides*) as a transition between the forest area and the pool. The soft, billowing forms of the two grasses look attractive in a cultivated setting, and they also blend comfortably into the wild forest beyond. In contrast, Phillip Watson's pool in Fredericksburg, Virginia, is set in the middle of a cottage-style garden. He planted a perennial border right at the edge of the pool and filled it with heat-tolerant, summer-flowering plants, such as *Phlox paniculata*, daylilies, and black-eyed Susans.

In western Massachusetts, Barney and Pat Shine's swimming pool is tucked up against a hillside of exposed granite rock. Instead of trying to fight the situation, the Shines let the native ferns have their way. These plants thrive in the clefts of the rock, creating an attractive, very low-maintenance planting near the pool.

The pool at Dick and Carol Paul's home, also in western Massachusetts, has a spectacular backdrop of mountains. An ornamental metal fence protects the view while at the same time adhering to local ordinances, which require that the pool be enclosed. Carol Paul maintains a low perennial border along the fence's length. To minimize care, the border is kept fairly simple, with a repeating combination of peonies interspersed with daisies, lower-growing dianthus, and salvia 'May Night'. The repetition creates a pleasing rhythm along the border, and the combination of plants ensures flowering interest throughout the season. The peonies and dianthus bloom in early summer, followed by the daisies and sage, which bloom for most of the summer months.

If you don't have the flower border of your dreams, there are plenty of creative ways to remedy the situation. To revive a flat, scruffy, and sparsely planted border that follows the curve of the swimming pool, you can add topsoil, then raise the level of the bed to form a low, gently mounded enclosing wall for this special garden room. In the back of the border, plant a mixture of shrubs and large perennials. Place the large shrubs toward the back of the border to anchor the design, then layer in front with different plants of descending height. As the border curves closer toward the pool, plant a wide assortment of lively perennials and annuals to provide color throughout the summer.

These examples of poolside flower beds display a range of maintenance requirements — some call for more upkeep than others. Be realistic about how much time you are willing to spend tending the garden. The gorgeous perennial borders pictured in many books and magazines are tempting, but they require a lot of planning as well as regular maintenance to keep them looking their best. A shrub border composed of a pleasing mixture of bushes with different leaf colors and textures generally needs much less upkeep. Annuals, many with perpetual summer blooms, are generally less work than are other plants. Once you've gone to the trouble to plant them, they pretty much look after themselves. Just give them water as needed and an occasional boost of fertilizer to keep them flowering.

In addition to planning the design, work out a budget for your poolside plantings. If money is tight, you may want to draw up a master plan so you know where you are ultimately going with the design, then implement the scheme as money allows. In that case, the first stage of planting should focus on structural plants, such as trees and large shrubs, that need time to become established and which define the bones of your landscape. Consider splurging on one major tree or shrub to be a focal point in the design. During the first year or two, when the plantings are less full, you may want to fill in with inexpensive annuals.

MAKING A LIST

In the world of plants, we are spoiled by choice. Selecting plants from the tens of thousands available can be an overwhelming task. Add to that the fact that you're working to artistically combine living things that have different growth patterns, habitat requirements, flowering times, textures, and sizes, and some people freeze in fear. To overcome this understandable paralysis, many people find it helpful to take a systematic approach to developing a garden design.

First, generate a list of plants you think you'd like to include in the landscape, making a separate list for each bed or area around the pool. Designate columns to include useful information about each plant, such as its height and spread, season of bloom, and foliage and flower texture and color. Plant catalogs, especially lushly illustrated ones, are a great resource for identifying plants you'd like to have. If you're working with several catalogs, add a column on your plant list for the catalog and page number where you found the plant so you don't have to keep leafing through multiple pages and booklets to recheck a plant of interest.

After you've generated a long list of plants, begin to narrow it down to the ones that will make attractive combinations and grow well in your specific situation. Also bear in mind that you'll be using the pool area mostly in summer, so you may want your selection of plants to look their best during the summer months.

CREATING A PLANTING MAP

The next step is to measure each planting area around the pool, then draw the outline of each one to scale on separate pieces of paper. Choose paper that is large enough so the scale is comfortable to work with and you have room to write. Once the bed is drawn to scale, add a diamond grid pattern over it, spacing the lines to scale so they are 2, 3, or

▼ To help select plants for a perennial border, create a plant wish list with columns for flower color and bloom time, foliage texture, plant height, and special features.

PLANT NAME	BLOOM TIME				DESCRIPTION		
Perennials	Spring	Early Summer	Summer	Fall	Foliage	Height, Width	Special Features
Alstroemeria 'Redcoat'						2' tall, 2' wide	unusual color
Aquilegia 'Robin'						2' high, 1' wide	spurred, good spring color
Heliopsis helianthoides scabra 'Summer Sun'						4' tall, 2' wide	daisylike, long bloom
Mentha 'Himalayan Silver'					downy gray	1½–2' tall, 1' wide	spikes, good foliage contrast
Veronica 'Goodness Grows'						1' tall, 1' wide	spikes, long bloom

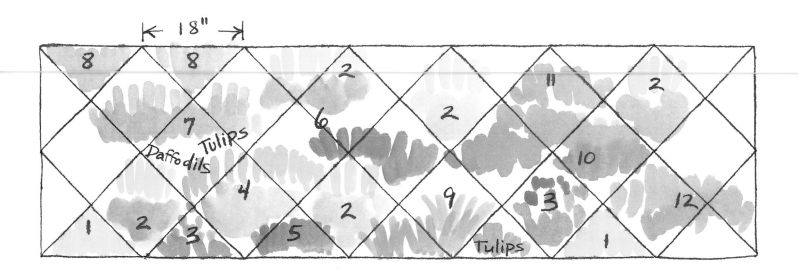

18"

8 8 2 11 2

7 2 10

Tulips

Paffodils 6

4 9 3 12

1 2 3 5 2 1

Tulips

1. *Alchemilla mollis*
2. *Ligularia dentata* 'Desdemona'
3. *Pulmonaria saccharata*
4. *Spiraea japonica* 'Goldflame'
5. *Hedera* spp.
6. *Angelica archangelica*

7. *Ligularia przewalskii*
8. Ferns
9. *Hemerocallis* hybrids
10. *Clerodendrum bungei*
11. *Viburnum opulus* 'Sterile'
12. *Rubus phocenicolasius*

4 feet apart in the actual bed. At this point, you may want to make several copies of each planting map so you can experiment with different groupings.

Now choose plants from your list to fill in the spaces on your planting map. If each diamond in your grid represents 18 inches, for example, and the chosen plant ultimately grows to 4 feet wide, then fill in two and a half diamonds. If a plant is small and you want to use several to fill in a larger space, note how many you'll need. Use colored pencils to distinguish each plant, and assign each one a number that corresponds to the final plant list.

When you've worked out a design that satisfies you, calculate how many plants you'll need to fill in each block of color and add them up. Don't forget to take into account the mature size and spread of the plants. You'll save yourself a lot of money if you accept that a newly planted bed will

have spaces among the plants for the first year or two, until they begin to fill in. You'll also save yourself a lot of work digging out overcrowded specimens later on if you don't plant them too closely in the beginning.

TRIAL AND ERROR

Even when you've planned carefully and made informed decisions, you may find that some of your choices are problematic. There are all sorts of reasons why you may not be completely happy with what you decided. Some of the plants may not do as well as you expected, or you may discover that you put an aggressive grower next to a meek plant that is overwhelmed by its neighbor.

Sometimes external conditions interfere with your success. That was the case with a border planned by John Nickum and Linda Lear, of Bethesda,

▲ **A drawn-to-scale map of the bed to be planted is a valuable design tool. The diamond grid on top helps you place plants so they flow in natural-looking groups. Use colored pencils to indicate where plants will go, and match each plant to its name with corresponding numbers.**

Maryland. Not wanting to replant every spring, the couple decided to have only shrubs, perennials, and bulbs in the border next to their swimming pool, but they found that the plants along the edge became damaged in winter by the pool cover, which stretches over part of the bed and is attached by heavy lugs to big metal columns in the ground to pull it taut. The area where the pool cover overlapped the border didn't receive adequate moisture, and the movement of the columns during freeze/thaw cycles damaged the perennials closest to the pool.

"I resisted the move to annuals," admits Lear, "but both Karen Rexrode of Windy Hill Plant Farm in Aldie, Virginia, and Tony Avent of Plant Delights Nursery in Raleigh, North Carolina, helped push me to tropicals that were easy to over-winter." To achieve a tropical-style planting near the pool, they created a layered border with large, hardy flowering shrubs, such as oakleaf hydrangea (*Hydrangea quercifolia*), smoke tree (*Cotinus*), nandina, and magnolia, as a background. Although not truly tropical, these shrubs, with their opulent leaves, fit the image.

In front of the shrub border they planted Canna 'Wyoming', which has black-maroon leaves and orange flowers; several species of acanthus; dwarf palmetto (*Sabal minor*); joe-pye weed (*Eupatorium purpureum*); a banana with large, red-tinged leaves (*Ensete ventricosum* 'Maurelii'); and a black-leafed taro (*Colocasia esculenta* 'Black Runner'). In the foreground, the border is filled with Coleus 'Copper Glow'; a black-leafed sweet potato vine (*Ipomoea batatas* 'Blackie') that echoes the color of the taro leaves; and tassel flower (*Emilia coccinea*), which bears sprays of fluffy, orange-red flowers about ½ inch in diameter.

The resulting color palette of orange canna flowers, coppery red coleus, and tiny red tassel

▼ **The Nickum-Lear family achieved a sophisticated, exotic look in their poolside border by combining a mixture of tender tropical perennials with hardy flowering shrubs.**

flowers, along with the dark black foliage of the tall taro plants, canna, and low-growing sweet potato vine, is sophisticated and dramatic. The repetition of plants along the border and the use of color echoes create a pleasing rhythm and sense of unity, while the unexpected color contrasts add that stimulating element of surprise and tension. It is an exciting border, stabilized by good bones and structure. The perpetual color interest that the annuals and tropicals provide throughout the summer has convinced the couple that their new direction is the right one.

Like Nickum and Lear, you'll find that trial and error is part of the garden design process. As the renowned Edwardian gardener and writer Vita Sackville-West wrote, "Gardening is largely a question of mixing one sort of plant with another sort of plant, and seeing how they marry happily together; and if you see that they don't marry happily, then you must hoick one of them."

SCREENING UNWANTED VIEWS

Plants are a great resource for blocking an unwanted view. Lower-growing evergreen shrubs can help camouflage the view of pool equipment or soften the blatant presentation of an aboveground swimming pool. If a neighbor's house is closer than you'd like and a tall fence or wall would be too unfriendly, unsightly, or against local codes, then plant tall shrubs, trees, or noninvasive bamboo along the border instead. If you opt for bamboo, remember that even the clumping varieties can spread quite vigorously. Depending on the type you choose, you may want to install an underground barrier to stop the roots from spreading too far.

When space is at a premium along a narrow side of the house, look for trees with a fastigiate form, meaning they typically grow with a tall, narrow crown, rather than a spreading canopy. Another

Bamboo Suitable for Hedges

The following list represents just a few of the many varieties of bamboo that make superb screens or hedges. For more information on bamboo, search the Internet for nurseries that specialize in bamboo. Their expert employees should be able to advise you on the best selection for your region and specific landscape situation.

Fargesia dracocephala; clumping, plum-purple, ¾-inch-thick stems; grows to 16 feet tall and 12 feet wide; Zones 5–9

F. murielae (umbrella bamboo); clumping, yellow-green stalks; grows to 12 feet tall and 5 feet wide; Zones 8–10

F. nitida (fountain bamboo); clumping, slow-growing, dark purple-green culms (stalks) ½ inch in diameter; grows to 12 feet tall by 5 feet wide; Zones 7–10

Phyllostachys aurea (fishpole or golden bamboo); clumping form; as they mature, culms turn from green to yellowy brown; grows to 6 feet tall but spreads indefinitely; Zones 6–10

P. nigra (black bamboo); clumping, slender green culms turn shiny black in second or third year; grows 10 to 15 feet tall with 6- to 10-foot-wide spread; Zones 7–10

Semiarundinaria fastuosa (Narihira bamboo); running rhizomes; green culms striped purplish brown; grows to 30 feet tall and spreads to 6 feet or more; Zones 6–9

way to gain more space is to plant a tree or shrub that takes well to severe pruning. The obvious choices are traditional boxwood, yew, and holly, but there are other possibilities as well. For example, you can prune fast-growing Leyland cypress into a formal hedge, and in frost-free climates Eugenia is an attractive choice. Another surprising candidate is Canadian hemlock, which fills into a very dense, formal hedge when sheared regularly. If you don't want to eat up all your ground space with a tall hedge, create a hedge on stilts. Simply prune off the lower branches to the desired height, then trim the remaining foliage on top as a hedge.

White Plants for a Nighttime Garden

A white garden is ideal for working couples, who often aren't home until after nightfall. If a busy schedule keeps you away from home during the day, consider planting a white garden near the swimming pool or filling containers with white-flowering plants and white-variegated foliage. Except on the darkest nights, the pale-colored flowers and foliage will be visible, unlike deeper colors, such as blue and red, which disappear at dusk. There are even a few flowers that remain closed until the cool of the evening, when they open to release a heady fragrance designed to attract night-flying, pollinating insects. Other plants, such as heliotrope and nicotiana, that are billed as having sweetly scented flowers actually don't begin to scent the air until evening draws near.

It is impractical to name the hundreds of plants with white flowers. Instead, the following list focuses on night-blooming flowers and white blossoms that are fragrant after sunset. Also included are plants with silver or white-variegated foliage to perpetuate the opalescent theme even when flowers are past.

FLOWERS THAT OPEN AT NIGHT

Datura inoxia (angel's trumpet), grown as annual in cold climates

Ipomoea alba (moonflower), fragrant annual vine

Mirabilis jalapa (four-o'clock), annual

Nymphaea spp. (water lily), some tropical varieties

FRAGRANT WHITE OR CREAM FLOWERS

Cestrum nocturnum (night jessamine); vine; night-scented flowers; Zone 10

Choisya ternata (Mexican orange); Zones 8–10

Convallaria majalis (lily of the valley); ground cover perennial; Zones 2–7

Freesia lactea syn. *F. alba* (freesia); corm; Zones 10–11

Gardenia augusta (gardenia); shrub; Zones 8–10

Hedychium coronarium (white ginger lily); Zones 9–10

Heliotropium arborescens 'Alba' (heliotrope); tender perennial

Hesperis matronalis var. *albiflora* (sweet rocket); Zones 4–9

Hosta plantaginea (plantain lily); Zones 3–8

Hymenocallis spp. (spider lily); Zones vary with species

Jasminum officinalis (jasmine); woody climber; Zones 9–10

Lathyrus odoratus (sweet pea); annual vine

Lilium candidum (Madonna lily); Zones 6–9

Lilium 'Casa Blanca'; Zones 4–8

L. longiflorum (Easter lily); Zones 7–9

Lonicera spp. (honeysuckle); Zones and flower colors vary with species

Matthiola incana (stock); Zones 7–8

Nicotiana sylvestris (tobacco plant); annual or short-lived perennial; night-scented flowers

Nymphaea spp. (water lily); 'White Delight' and others; tropical

N. caroliniana 'Nivea' and others (hardy waterlily)

Philadelphus spp. (mock orange); Zones vary with species

Phlox paniculata 'David' (garden phlox); Zones 4–8

Pittosporum tobira (Japanese mock orange); Zones 9–10

Polianthes tuberosa (tuberose); temperatures above 59°F

Primula alpicola (moonlight primrose); Zones 4–8

Reseda odorata (mignonette); annual

Rosa (rose); many white-flowering, fragrant varieties; Zones vary with species

Stephanotis floribunda (Madagascar jasmine); Zone 11

OTHER WHITE-FLOWERING ANNUALS AND PERENNIALS

Cleome hasslerana 'Helen Campbell' (spider flower); self-sowing annual

Cosmos 'Purity' and 'Sonata White' (cosmos); self-sowing annual

Echinacea purpurea 'White Swan' and 'White Lustre' (white-flowered purple coneflower); Zones 3–9

Helianthus annuus 'Italian White' (sunflower); annual

Impatiens spp. (impatiens); any white variety, self-sowing tender perennial (below 40°F)

Lavatera trimestris 'Mont Blanc' (mallow); annual

Lilium martagon var. *album* (turk's-cap lily); Zones 3–7

Malva moschata 'Alba' (musk mallow); Zones 4–8

Nierembergia caerulea 'Mont Blanc' (cup flower); Zones 7–10

Nigella damascena 'Miss Jekyll Alba' (love-in-a-mist); annual

Papaver orientale 'Black and White' and 'Perry's White' (Oriental poppy); Zones 4–9

Petunia spp.; white-flowered cultivars; annuals

Platycodon grandiflorus f. *albus* (balloon flower); Zones 4–9

Zantedeschia aethiopica (calla lily); Zones 8–10

SILVER, GRAY, AND CREAM VARIEGATED FOLIAGE

Artemisia absinthium (wormwood); Zones 4–8

A. arborescens; Zones 5–9

A. ludoviciana (western mugwort); Zones 4–9

A. stelleriana (dusty miller); Zones 3–7

Cornus alba 'Elegantissima' (variegated red-stemmed dogwood); Zones 2–8

C. alternifolia 'Argentea' (pagoda dogwood); Zones 4–8

C. controversa 'Variegata' (giant dogwood); Zones 6–9

Cotoneaster horizontalis 'Variegatus' (rockspray); Zones 6–9

Eryngium variifolium (Moroccan sea holly); Zones 5–9

Euonymus fortunei var. *radicans* 'Silver Queen' (wintercreeper); Zones 5–9

Fragaria vesca 'Variegata' (alpine strawberry); Zones 5–9

Hedera canariensis 'Gloire de Marengo' (Canary Island ivy); Zones 7–10

H. colchica 'Dentata Variegata' (Persian ivy); Zones 5–10

H. helix 'Glacier' and other variegated cultivars (English ivy); Zones 5–10

Holcus mollis 'Albovariegatus' (ornamental grass); Zones 5–9

Hosta albomarginata; Zones 3–8

H. fortunei 'Marginata-alba'; Zones 3–8

H. sieboldiana 'Francee'; Zones 3–8

Hydrangea macrophylla 'Variegated Mariesii'; Zones 6–10

Ilex aquifolium 'Ferox Argentea' (English holly); Zones 7–9

I. aquifolium 'Silver Milkboy' (English holly); Zones 7–9

Lamium maculatum 'Beacon's Silver' and 'Silver Pewter' (spotted dead nettle); Zones 4–8

Osmanthus heterophyllus 'Latifolius Variegatus' (false holly); Zones 7–9

Philadelphus coronarius 'Variegatus' (mock orange); Zones 5–8

Rhamnus alaternus 'Argentovariegatus' (Indian buckthorn); Zones 7–9

Saxifraga stolonifera (mother of thousands); Zones 6–9

Stachys byzantina (lamb's ears); Zones 4–10

Verbascum spp. (mullein); Zones vary with species

Vinca major 'Variegata' (periwinkle); Zones 7–11

Organic Swimming Pools

Picture in your mind's eye a swimming pool that looks like a natural pond, where the swimming area merges with a bog garden that grows along the margin and water exchanges freely between the two spaces. In this setting, a pool and its landscape are inextricably entwined and mutually dependent.

Such pools do exist, and they are a growing trend in Europe, where they were first developed in 1985 by an Austrian ecologist named Pieter Peitrach. To avoid the chemically based water-cleaning systems typical of standard pools, Peitrach designed a self-cleaning ecosystem in which the water is purified by the natural regenerative and cleansing properties of plants rather than by chemicals and metals. One of his challenges was to figure out a way to combat the natural occurrence of algae, which thrive in warm environments with a high (alkaline) pH. Zooplankton is the microorganism that controls algae, but it prefers cooler waters and a lower pH. When water temperatures rise, the zooplankton sinks to the bottom and waits for conditions to shift. The imbalance allows algae to multiply rapidly, turning the water green.

In a balanced, natural pond environment, bog plants growing along the margin of the pool shade the water, keeping it cooler and encouraging zooplankton growth. Bog plants also consume nitrogen and phosphates, winning the competition against algae for the same nutrients. Bog plants do raise the pH level because they consume carbon dioxide from the water; however, the decaying plants and other organic matter that nourish the living marginals produce carbon dioxide. When the pond has reached homeostasis — a balance between living and decaying plants — algae are kept to a minimum.

To give the system an extra boost and ensure an algae-free swimming environment, Peitrach patented the Biotop Catalyzer, which draws carbon dioxide–heavy air from the ground and passes it through granulated rock, binding it with such nutrients as phosphate, then circulates it back into the pool. The catalyzer lowers the pH through increased carbon dioxide.

Perfectionists who want crystal-clear water can add a Biotop plant filter, a filter substrate placed under bog plants in the regeneration zone. The filter sifts out even the smallest particles, including bacteria and germs, without destroying the beneficial zooplankton. In this self-maintaining

▼ **Instead of using chemicals and metals to keep swimming pool water clean, this natural swimming pond employs the purifying properties of marginal bog plants.**

REGENERATION ZONE

PLANT FILTER

PIPE TO AIR PUMP

AIR PUMP

DIVIDING WALL

SWIMMING AREA

DOCK

system, the plant roots keep the filter substrate permeable and draw up the freed nutrients, so the filter never needs to be changed.

This ideal ecological balance does not happen overnight. Owners should not swim in a newly built organic pond for 2 months in order to allow the plants to settle and establish their root systems. Even then it takes time for the plants to fill in and begin performing their balancing functions effectively. A newly established pond may develop some algae in the early stages. Once the ecosystem is ticking over properly, however, the pond should need just an annual spring cleaning.

These natural swimming ponds require more space than do traditional swimming pools because the planted regeneration zone must be almost as large as the swimming area. However, the pond and the garden are one entity, and they

remain an attractive landscape feature even in winter, when most pools are closed down. In fact, in climates where water freezes, owners use their swimming ponds as ice skating rinks!

More than 1,000 organic pools have been built in Europe. The ponds meet the strict European Union guidelines for cleanliness in public pools. Although interest for them is growing in the United States, as of late 2002, none has been built in North America. Because no one has tried it here, it's not known for certain whether these pools will be successful in all regions of the United States, particularly where both days and nights remain hot for much of the summer. In regions where nighttime temperatures drop (giving the water a chance to cool off), there shouldn't be a problem. It's an exciting frontier, breaking new ground in the concept of what a swimming pool can be.

▲ A natural swimming pond is a revolutionary pool design based on a balanced ecology that allows homeowners to have a clean, chemical-free swimming pool.

CHAPTER FIVE

PLANTERS AND CONTAINERS

Containers and built-in planters are an ideal way to bring color and greenery to the paved surface around a swimming pool. In addition, they break up the horizontal monotony of the poolscape and put smaller plants at eye level. There are thousands of plants that can thrive in containers — almost anything, from tiny alpines to substantial trees and shrubs — if they are given enough space for their roots. The scope for combining plants in creative, dynamic ways is enormous, and in the case of annuals, you can experiment with different plant and color combinations each year. Besides being a home to plants, built-in raised beds and planters also provide an opportunity to echo architectural elements of the house or pool. For example, a stucco planter may be painted to match the house, or the sides could be tiled with the same material used in the pool.

Bringing the Garden Up Close

An open expanse of patio or deck cries out for a planter or raised bed to break the horizontal lines and add a splash of greenery in the midst of paving. If you run a planter along the edge of a deck or patio, it doubles as a low wall, helping to define the space. Use it as a partition, creating a space, for example, for outdoor dining that's part of the pool area, yet separate. If you have an arbor or pergola near the pool, consider building planters around each post. Plant a vine in each bed, and train it to grow up the post. Excellent choices include wisteria, honeysuckle, grapes, bougainvillea, star jasmine (*Trachelospermum jasminoides*), *Stephanotis floribunda* (Madagascar jasmine), and mandevilla 'Alice du Pont'.

▶ A tall, classic urn is a desirable vertical feature near a pool, and it brings floral and foliage interest to otherwise stark paving.

▼ The soft, "pillowed" edge of this planter mirrors the rounded edges of the stucco wall behind it, unifying the architectural elements around the pool.

Raised planters can double as seating on a deck or patio. If that is your plan, build the support walls to a comfortable height for sitting (the standard bench seat height is between 15 and 18 inches) and make the rim wide enough to serve as a bench. If you fill the bed with fragrant plants, the planter/garden seat will provide an additional sensory pleasure.

Whether the raised bed or planter serves as a low wall, garden seat, or both, its design should blend attractively with its surroundings. Build it from materials that complement the house, decking, and pool. In a formal setting, brick is probably your best option. Other possible materials include stone, poured concrete, and wood. To tie the structure to the pool design, incorporate tiles that match the ones used in the pool.

SOIL, DEPTH, AND DRAINAGE

Plants growing in raised planters are easier to tend because you don't have to bend over or kneel on the ground, and the rim of the walls is a handy perch from which to work. If your soil is extremely poor, or if you want to grow plants that need a soil different from what is naturally available in your garden, planters are an easy solution to the problem. Rather than going to all the trouble to amend the local soil, simply fill raised beds with soil appropriate to what you want to grow. Soil in a raised bed generally isn't walked upon, so it is less likely to become compacted. Water, air, and roots all have difficulty moving through compacted soil.

The depth of a planter is governed largely by what you want to plant. Small trees require from 1½ to 3 feet of soil; most annuals can get

by with as little as 6 to 8 inches. Perennials and vegetables with deeper root systems, including cabbage, broccoli, carrots, eggplant, tomatoes, and cauliflower, need a minimum of 10 inches, though a depth of 18 inches is even better. If you don't want the sides of your raised bed to be too tall, consider cultivating the native soil inside the bed to increase the effective planting depth.

Don't forget that planters need to drain. If you've made yours out of landscape timbers, railroad ties, or wooden sides with unsealed seams, water should seep out just fine. On the other hand, a raised bed or planter will need drainage holes if it is built with solid sides made of material such as stone or brick held together with mortar. While building a solid-sided raised bed, insert pipes into the wall near the bottom of the bed for the water to drain through. Place a pipe at each end of the bed, and if it is large, in the middle as well.

CONTAINER GARDENING

In some cases, containers may be the only way to get color around the pool. John Alioto, of Del Mar, California, particularly wanted flower beds around his swimming pool, but because the house is near a cliff, landscape architect Gary Stone was concerned that the water the flowers required could cause a landslide. "I was almost willing to risk it," said Alioto, "but my wife wouldn't let me." As a compromise, they have planted 20 large ceramic pots with blooming annuals and perennials and placed them around the pool.

Too often, containers planted for a sunny location contain just the usual pelargoniums and marigolds. Break the mold and think about other, more unusual plants you can combine for a sophisticated, dramatic presentation. For example, in a 24-inch pot, consider planting the center with three canna lilies, such as 'Pretoria' (also sold as 'Bengal

a burnt orange zinnia flower or copper-colored 'Copper Glow' coleus.

Don't overlook the dramatic potential of foliage texture as well. Try combining the spiky foliage of a cordyline, New Zealand flax (*Phormium tenax)*, or *Hakonechloa macra* 'Aureola' with the round-headed flowers of a *Pelargonium hortorum.* The feathery plumes of fountain grass contrast beautifully with flowering maple (*Abutilon),* canna lilies, bacopa, and sweet potato vine. Or fill a container with purple, frilly leafed ornamental cabbages, such as *Brassica oleracea* 'Redbor', mealy cup sage (*Salvia farinacea* 'Victoria'), and the catmint *Nepeta* 'Walkers Low' for a delightful blend of blues and purples.

Use container-grown vines to add a vertical element near a swimming pool. Choose a large pot or tub, such as one of the square wooden Versailles planters. The container should be large enough for the plant's roots yet be in scale with the ultimate height of the vine. Use a pyramid trellis to provide three-dimensional support for vines planted in pots that will be out in the open; a flat trellis will suit a pot set against a wall. For extra pizzazz, paint the plant support a color to coordinate with the flowers.

You can plant any number of annual vines, such as sweet pea, morning glory, and clock vine, in a container. Also consider a perennial vine that doesn't grow too tall, such as a large-flowering clematis variety. Good choices are 'Bees Jubilee', 'Comtesse de Bouchard', 'Hagley Hybrid', 'Henryi', 'Lasurstern', 'Miss Bateman', 'Mrs. N. Thompson', 'Nelly Moser', and 'Silver Moon'. Another pretty option is a honeysuckle vine.

Plant the vine, then insert the legs of the pyramid trellis into the soil, working them in firmly and securely. Tie the vine to the trellis so they are arranged as you wish. As the vine grows, you will probably need to tie in new lengths. If you

▲ **Bring floral color up to eye level with a matched set of densely planted hanging baskets. Watering is easy with drip irrigation lines attached to an automatic timer. Note the color echo in the pink-flowering crepe myrtle on the opposite side of the pool.**

▶ **The spiky foliage of ornamental grass is in fun contrast to the petunias planted around the pot's rim. As a bonus, the purple petunias complement the dark purple-black foliage.**

Tiger') and 'Striped Beauty', which have stunning, green-and-yellow-striped foliage. Echo the yellow color in the canna leaves with a collar of yellow-flowering *Coreopsis verticillata* 'Moonbeam' planted around the base of the cannas. Then contrast the yellows with a ruffle of scaevola 'Blue Wonder' spilling over the pot's rim in a blue-flowering cascade. As the cannas grow through the summer, cut back the stems to keep them in bounds. You'll sacrifice the flowers, but the foliage (which is the reason for choosing these cannas) will be bushier.

Another option is to experiment with unexpected, bold color combinations. A glazed, cobalt blue container is a striking background to lime-green flowers and foliage and bright orange flowers. Combine the almost black foliage of the sweet potato vine *Ipomoea batatas* 'Blackie' with like, you can underplant the arrangement with low-growing annuals or trailing plants.

Large specimens are another great candidate for a good-sized container. If you live in a region that has freezing winters, treat yourself to a tender tree or shrub, such as a citrus tree or bay laurel. Grow it by the pool during the summer, then move it indoors for the winter. For added color and interest, plant low-growing or trailing annuals around the base of the plant.

A greenhouse or an unheated sunroom is a useful asset for overwintering tender trees, but most trees in containers will do fine in a sunny spot indoors during the winter months. Wait as long as possible to bring tender potted plants inside. Ideally, you want to overwinter a tender tree in a very sunny area in a cool room away from heating vents. If the plant must be near a heat vent, close it. Dry air blowing on a plant and warm nighttime temperatures stress tender trees. Most trees brought indoors for the winter want daytime temperatures around 68 or 70°F, with nighttime temperatures in the 50°F range.

Even away from heating vents, the humidity indoors during the winter is significantly lower than what most plants enjoy. To increase the humidity around a plant, set the pot on top of stones in a water-filled saucer. The stones keep the plant from standing in the water, and the evaporating water lowers the humidity slightly. Be sure to top up the water as needed. To add even more moisture, mist the plant daily.

Many parts of the country experience periodic warm spates in winter, when temperatures, even at night, stay well above 40°F. If the weather report predicts a series of warm days, consider taking the tree outside for those days and nights. All but the extremely cold-sensitive tropical plants will appreciate the boost of fresh air and natural light.

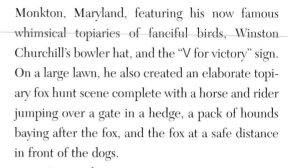

TOPIARY SCULPTURE

Another idea for dramatic presentation is to create topiary sculptures by pruning plants into geometric or fanciful shapes. Topiaries trained on forms are well suited for containers — a great asset if you want to accent your pool decking with green "statues." In addition to the enjoyable challenge of shaping a plant into a specified form, topiary has the advantage of being much less expensive than many sculptures, yet it serves the same design function.

Historians believe the technique was first practiced by the Romans. During the first century A.D., Pliny the Elder wrote of "hunting scenes, fleets of ships, and all sorts of images" cut from cypress trees. Pliny attributed the invention of topiary to Julius Caesar's friend Cnaius Matius. Writing in 1712, Dezallier d'Argenville dubbed the art of creating topiary "the richest and most distinguished in the whole Business of Gardening."

Just about anything you can conceive as a sculpture can be created out of topiary. In the 1930s, Harvey Ladew created extensive gardens in Monkton, Maryland, featuring his now famous whimsical topiaries of fanciful birds, Winston Churchill's bowler hat, and the "V for victory" sign. On a large lawn, he also created an elaborate topiary fox hunt scene complete with a horse and rider jumping over a gate in a hedge, a pack of hounds baying after the fox, and the fox at a safe distance in front of the dogs.

You might want to create a topiary to tie into the water theme of your pool. Why not create a fun shape, such as a voluptuous mermaid or a dolphin leaping over the crest of a wave? Plant a monumental form in a large container to create a prominent, arresting poolside feature, or plant a small form in a pot that will fit comfortably on a nearby tabletop to fashion a striking centerpiece.

Generally, topiaries are created from slow-growing plants and shrubs, such as holly, boxwood, and yew. Although a slow-growing topiary will take longer to reach completion, it will need less frequent pruning once it is established, and all your work will be rewarded with a longer-lived specimen. To ease the job of creating and maintaining a topiary form, choose a plant whose natural growth habit is compatible with the shape you'd like to create. If you want to carve a tall form, for example, a layered "cake," an obelisk, or a tall animal such as a giraffe, select a plant with an upright habit. For a low form, such as a cube, sphere, or small animal, choose a plant with a spreading habit. If you want a topiary with a lot of detail, choose a fine-textured plant, such as yew.

For complicated shapes, such as animals, or for forms where perfect symmetry is essential for a successful effect, you may find it helpful to place a wire frame around the plant to serve as a pruning guide. Position the frame over a young plant and anchor it firmly to the ground. Commercially made frames are equipped with spikes designed to sink

▶ A variegated, small-leafed ivy has been trained over a wire form to create this swan topiary nesting comfortably in a concrete basket planter.

▼ One way to make a topiary, bottom left, is to grow a shrub through a wire frame. When the foliage begins to protrude from the frame, bottom right, trim it to shape.

into the soil. Start pruning when the tips of the plant begin to grow beyond the edge of the frame. Ultimately, the plant should completely hide the wire structure.

Topiaries from vines. A shortcut to the traditional pruned topiary is to grow a vine over a wire form. Choose a fine-leafed, vigorously growing vine, such as a small-leaved ivy cultivar ('Pixie' is a good choice) or creeping fig (*Ficus pumila*). Creeping fig is not frost-hardy, so in colder climates you'll need to bring the topiary indoors for the winter.

Insert the wire form's stakes into the soil, then plant the vine at the base of the form. Depending on the size and shape, you may need to start with several plants. Tie the newly planted vines to the form, stretching them as far as they will comfortably go. As a vine grows, continue to train it onto the form. Once the form is completely covered, keep the topiary trimmed so the shape looks tidy and is easy to recognize.

Topiary standards. There are all sorts of standards in this world, but in the terminology of the garden, a standard refers to a plant that is trained to resemble a miniature tree. The foliage along the stem or stalk of the plant is removed, allowing only the leaves remaining at the top of the plant to grow so it looks like the crown of a tree. Depending on the nature and growth habits of the plant you train into a standard, you can either leave this "tree crown" to grow freeform or prune it into a sphere, mushroom, cone, or pyramid. One fanciful variation is the "poodle," which features multiple crowns or pompoms spaced along the stem at regular intervals. Whether the standard is growing in a pot or in the ground, consider underplanting it with low-growing plants to carpet its "feet."

Standards are not difficult to train, and the stylized result can be very effective in the right setting. They look particularly good flanking a

Plants Suitable to Train as Standards

You can train almost any plant with a woody stem into a standard. The following list includes just a few of the many plants that lend themselves to this treatment. Many of the plants listed are not frost-hardy, though most will tolerate near-freezing temperatures. In cold climates, bring frost-tender standards indoors during freezing periods or store them in a cool greenhouse where the temperatures stay above freezing. To help keep house-bound tender perennials healthy over the winter, put them outside on days when the temperature is above freezing. They'll appreciate the exposure to fresh air and direct light. Just don't forget to bring them inside again if freezing weather is predicted.

Aloysia triphylla (lemon verbena), Zones 8–11

Cuphea hyssopifolia (false heather), frost-tender

Euonymus alatus (burning bush), Zones 4–9

Fuchsia, upright varieties, Zones 8–10

Helichrysum italicum sub. *serofinum* 'Nana' (curry plant, dwarf), Zones 7–10

H. petiolare (licorice plant), Zones 10–11

Hibiscus syriacus (rose of Sharon), Zones 5–9

H. rosa-sinensis (Chinese hibiscus), frost-tender

Lantana, upright varieties, frost-tender

Lavandula dentata (fringed lavender), Zones 8–10

L. stoechas (French lavender), Zones 8–10

Leptospermum scoparium (New Zealand tea tree), Zones 9–10

Myrtus communis (myrtle), Zones 8–9

Pelargonium spp. (geranium), Zones 8–10

Prostanthera rotundifolia (round-leaf mint bush), Zones 9–10

Rhododendron spp. (azalea), Zones vary

Rosa (rose, grafted), Zones vary with hybrids

Rosmarinus officinalis (rosemary), Zones 7–10

Salvia elegans (sage), Zones 8–10

S. officinalis (sage), Zones 7–10

Santolina chamaecyparissus (lavender cotton), Zones 6–10

Syringa vulgaris (common lilac), Zones 4–8

Thymus vulgaris (common thyme), Zones 4–10

Viburnum opulus (European cranberry bush), Zones 4–8

classic-style doorway or the beginning of a path. In a formal setting, place one pair at the base of a stairway and a matched set at the top. Large-scale standards are particularly useful near a swimming pool because they add a vertical element to a generally flat space.

To make a topiary standard from scratch, select a young plant with a straight, central stem that has never been pinched off at the top. If the plant has multiple stems, cut away all but the central one you want to keep. Insert a stake into the soil next to the plant. Then remove any side shoots from the main stem, leaving just the little primary leaves growing out of the stem and the cluster of leaves near the top of the stalk. Loosely tie the stem to the stake at regular intervals. As the plant grows taller, tie the new length of stem to the stake. Check periodically to make sure the ties are not too tight. If necessary, replace the original stake with a taller one.

When the plant approaches the desired height (you want a nicely proportioned balance between the height of the plant and the diameter of the crown), pinch off the tip of the central stem. Allow the sides branches near the top of the plant to continue growing; when they're about 4 inches long, pinch each one just above a node to encourage vigorous, bushy growth. Continue pinching as needed to keep the head of the plant well branched and full.

Once the top growth has filled in, remove the primary leaves growing along the stem. Pinch or prune as needed to maintain the shape of the crown, and remove any unwanted sucker growth. As the plant matures, the woody stem will harden; when it is firm, you can remove the stake. Protect a container-grown standard from winter weather by wrapping the container in bubble wrap, a blanket, straw, or some other insulating material.

▼ To train a standard, begin with a young plant. Tie the stem to a support stake, left, and remove the lower leaves. As the plant grows, tie in the new growth, center left, and pinch off unwanted foliage from the stem, center right. Wrap insulating material around the container and base of the plant, right, to protect it during the winter.

Choosing Containers

The options for containers are as vast as your imagination. You can find pots in terra-cotta, glazed clay, plastic, carved or cast stone, polyethylene (which resembles terra-cotta or stone) and wood. Choose containers that are compatible with the other elements in your poolscape. For example, if your pool is sleek and modern, select pots that contribute to that look. Plastic containers would look out of place near a formal, classically designed pool but may be suitable in a more informal setting.

The larger the container, the more visual impact it will have on your design. In addition, a large pot gives you plenty of scope for creative planting. Cluster several large containers with some smaller ones in front to fill in the lower level, and you've created an instant garden in the middle of paving.

IDEAS FOR UNUSUAL CONTAINERS

Many found objects or items around the house and garden have the potential to be fun, unique containers to use around the pool or in the garden. You can waterproof permeable containers, such as baskets, by lining them with plastic, and protect or dress up rusty items by giving them a coat or two of paint. Unless you are planting a water garden in the container, be sure to drill drainage holes in the bottom. In many cases, an unusual container can contribute to the theme of your setting or relate to the previous history of the land. For example, at Butchart Gardens on Vancouver Island in Canada, an old mining cart has been transformed into a large planter, reminding people that the garden has been created out of a former strip mine. Use the following list as a starting point for more creative ideas.

- Old kitchen sinks and bathtubs
- Saucepans, kettles, buckets
- Old watering cans
- Wheelbarrows
- Old wagons
- Chimney pots (group different heights for a striking display)
- Old boots
- Large shells
- Troughs
- Baskets, barrels (lined with plastic)
- Hayracks and wire baskets
- Old boat (great for a seaside pool)
- Driftwood
- Carpenter's toolbox

▼ **A painted pig trough makes an eye-catching water garden container to house ornamental rice plant (*Oryza sativa* 'Red Dragon'). Notice how the container picks up the color of the rice foliage, which also is echoed by the *Coleus* 'Copper Glow' across the pool.**

PROTECTION FROM WINTER FREEZES

Unglazed clay pots absorb moisture, putting them at risk for cracking and flaking in climates where they are exposed to freeze/thaw cycles. You have several options for protecting them during the frigid months. One possibility is to store the pots in a dry place, such as a shed, cellar, or garage. If you don't have enough room in a covered storage area, empty out the soil (put it on your garden beds or compost heap) and turn the pots upside down so the water drains away. To allow for even more air circulation and drainage, set them on wooden slats. Another way to keep them dry is to wrap them in plastic for the winter.

Many plants that are hardy in the ground may be tender in pots because the roots have less insulation from the cold through the thin walls of the container. In addition, you may want to keep a tender plant, such as a bay tree or myrtle, alive for more than one growing season. There are several possible ways to deal with the problem. If you have storage space in a garage or shed with windows — or better yet, a greenhouse — move tender plants there for the winter. While dormant, they can get by with a lot less light and water than they need during the growing season. Periodically refresh them outdoors — and give them a good watering — when the weather will be mild for a few days at a stretch. Do not fertilize during this time. By spring, they may look a little peaked, but they will return to vigor once they are outside in the warm air again.

Alternatively, you can insulate the containers to keep the plants' roots warm. Possible ways to do that include wrapping the pots in bubble wrap and grouping them together with stacked hay bales around them.

Making a Three-Tiered Container

To add drama and height to her swimming pool area, Laurie Connable built a three-tiered stack of containers, then planted it with a beautiful medley of tender perennials that bloom perpetually for much of the year in the mild Southern California climate where she lives. Here's how to accomplish what she did:

At a nursery that has a good selection of containers, choose three matching shallow, wide-based pots in descending sizes. For Connable's stack, the bottom pot is 40 inches in diameter, the middle one is 30 inches, and the top pot is 26 inches. Then select two upright pots, with one proportionately smaller than the other, to use as pedestals to hold up the structure's next layer. Connable picked one pot that is 12 inches tall and 10 inches in diameter at the mouth and one that is 18 inches tall and 16 inches in diameter.

Position the bottom pot where you want the structure to remain. (Once completed, it will be too heavy to move.) Fill it with potting mixture to within ½ inch or 1 inch of the rim, then water well so the soil can settle. Top up with more soil, if necessary. Center the larger pedestal pot on top of the soil, then place the middle container on the stack, making sure it's securely balanced on the pedestal base. Fill it with potting mixture, water well, and then position the second, smaller pedestal pot and top it with the final tier. Fill it with potting mixture, then plant up the tower.

Connable planted her stacked pots with trailing verbena, petunias, and bacopa in shades of pink. Other good choices are scaevola, sweet potato vine, trailing nasturtiums, trailing geraniums, vinca, sweet alyssum, and creeping zinnias *(Sanvitalia procumbens)*.

Potting Mediums

As a rule, soil from the garden is not a good choice for containers. It tends to inhibit root growth because it is heavy, often with too much clay, and can harbor weed seeds, harmful insects, and diseases. Look for a well-aerated mix that is highly nutritious, retains moisture, and drains freely.

If you want a soil-based mix, use bagged topsoil purchased at a garden center. Those soils have been sterilized to remove unwanted weed seeds, pests, and pathogens.

There is a wide selection of commercially prepared potting mixes on the market. Some are designed for a specific type of plant, such as orchids or cacti; others are general purpose. You'll find premium mixes fortified with slow-release fertilizers; others contain moisture-retentive polymers that keep the mix from drying out too quickly. Any mix with these beneficial additives will be more expensive. Avoid commercial mixes that use polystyrene to make the mix lighter. A nonorganic material, polystyrene will not break down in your compost heap (where spent container mixes should be recycled). The preferred ingredient is perlite, a natural material created from volcanic glass.

The primary ingredients in soilless potting mixes are peat moss, sterilized compost, perlite, and vermiculite. Here are their characteristics:

Peat moss, though it is essentially inert chemically, is valued in potting mixes for its ability to absorb and retain moisture, suppress disease organisms, and bulk up the mix. There are two types of peat: peat humus and sphagnum peat moss. A stickier material used for making soil blocks, peat humus is darker, heavier, and more moisture-retentive than sphagnum peat moss. Gardeners concerned about the environmental ramifications of using peat moss (it renews itself much more slowly than the rate at which it is harvested) are experimenting with well-rotted leaf mold and hardwood as alternatives to peat.

General-Purpose Potting Mix Recipes

Many homeowners prefer to make their own potting mix from scratch. The cost is generally low, and you have control over the quality of the ingredients. Following are a few of the many recipes available. Most of these recipes are variations on a theme. Experiment to find the mixture that satisfies your plants' needs best. In addition, give your homemade mix the same nutrient and mineral enhancements recommended for store-bought potting mixes.

3 parts compost
2 parts perlite
2 parts sphagnum peat moss
2 parts vermiculite

1 part horticultural perlite
1 part packaged potting soil
1 part peat moss
2 tablespoons dolomitic lime (per 12" pot)

1 part horticultural perlite
1 part peat moss
1 part vermiculite
2 tablespoons dolomitic lime (per 12" pot)

Compost is rich in microorganisms and nutrients that are beneficial to plant growth. It's essential, however, that the compost used in containers be finished, meaning all the ingredients have broken down completely.

Perlite, which is heat-expanded volcanic glass, is a prime potting mix ingredient because it is lightweight, promotes drainage, and keeps the mix well aerated.

Vermiculite, similar to perlite, is a thin material made from mica deposits. Like perlite, vermiculite helps with drainage and aeration. It also holds nutrients in the mix.

Although the professionally designed, bagged potting mixes are convenient, they are costly if you are filling a lot of pots. You can save some money by purchasing the least expensive mix and boosting it with bagged sterilized compost at a ratio of 2 parts potting mix to 1 part compost. Another valuable amendment to improve the fertility of an inexpensive commercial mix or your own homemade blend is a handful of greensand per bushel of mix. A good source of potassium, greensand also stimulates mineral release, so it's available to plants, and it helps retain water in the mix. Other additives you may wish to use include:

- A handful of rock or colloidal phosphate per bushel of mix
- A handful of bonemeal per bushel of mix
- A sprinkling of blood meal or alfalfa meal, for a natural nitrogen boost
- Kelp meal, rich in trace minerals, makes phosphorus available to plants
- Hardwood ashes, for potassium
- Worm castings, an excellent source of calcium and trace nutrients

- Water-retentive polymers, which hold more than 100 times their weight in water. The plant roots can tap into the reservoir of water stored in the polymer, and as the soil mix dries, polymers release their water back into the mix. Follow the package instructions for how much to add.

RENEWING OLD POTTING MIX

Even with regular fertilizing, eventually potting mix will grow old and tired. The lightweight perlite tends to migrate to the top of the mix, and the nutrients are leached out by frequent watering. Every two years or so, you should plan to renew the potting mix in your containers.

When it's time to begin again with fresh potting mix, empty the old mix onto a garden bed as top dressing, or put it in your compost heap. Because the pots will be empty, take the opportunity to clean them, scouring any accumulated moss, algae, and fungi with a nylon scrubbing pad under cold, running water. To eliminate the possibility of a pest or disease infestation, disinfect the cleaned pots by soaking them for several hours in a mix of 1 part bleach to 5 parts water. Rinse the pots well before you replant.

If the residue from alkaline water, known as white salts, persists after scrubbing clay pots, try soaking them for a day or two in undiluted vinegar (buy it in gallon containers to save money). After soaking, scrub them with a nylon pad and rinse them. You may need to repeat the process for stubborn stains. Alternatively, empty, salt-stained pots that are left outside for several months will eventually be rinsed clean by the rain. If you know you will be renewing the potting mix in spring, leave the pots outside during the fall and winter.

Caring for Container Plants

Soak brand-new unglazed terra-cotta or other clay pots in water overnight before you plant them. When you're ready to plant, cover the drainage hole in the bottom with a square of wire mesh, a pebble, or a pottery shard. If you are using a pebble or shard, set it over the hole so that water can still drain out but the soil will be kept inside.

Partially fill the container with your potting medium, then arrange the plants so the soil level of each one is just below the rim of the container. The extra space between the pot rim and the soil level gives you space to fill with water so it can soak in properly, and it keeps the soil mix from splashing out.

Slide a plant out of its container. If you notice that its roots are growing in a tight ball, tear them apart a little, shave off the tight outer layer of roots, or "butterfly" a large root ball by cutting it up the center a few inches from the bottom and spreading the halves over the soil in the pot. These

▼ To prolong the years that a tree or shrub can stay in the same size container, prune the roots and tops when it begins to outgrow its space, then replant it with fresh potting mix.

seemingly heartless actions will encourage new feeder roots to grow and allow them to spread into their new environment. Most plants take well to having their roots pruned or roughed up a bit.

When your plants are positioned at the right depth and where you want them in the pot, fill in the spaces between the roots with soil mix, tamping it down firmly to remove any air pockets. Water two or three times, allowing the water to flow through each time, so the potting mix can settle. Add additional mix, if necessary.

REPOTTING CONTAINER PLANTS

Perennials that live permanently in containers will eventually outgrow their homes, becoming rootbound. If you notice that water isn't soaking through the soil properly, or that roots are sticking out the bottom of the container, it's time to take action. The plant either needs to be potted up into a larger pot or its roots and top should be pruned to keep the plant in bounds.

The best time to repot most plants is in spring, when they are about to embark on a growth spurt. Then they will have plenty of time during the summer months to reestablish themselves. Autumn and winter are the worst times to repot because plant growth is slowing for the cold season, and it will take a plant much longer to generate new roots.

For the plant to be in pleasing proportion with its container, choose a new pot that is about 2 inches larger than the previous one. Prepare the larger pot for planting, partially covering the drainage hole and adding potting mix, then carefully slide the overgrown plant out of its old

container. Loosen the rootball (if it has grown very tight, you may want to butterfly it, then place the plant in the new container so it will sit at the same level as before. Add more planting mix to fill the gaps and water well.

If you want to keep a growing perennial small so it is in scale with the setting you've chosen for it, you can "bonsai" it by pruning the roots and top growth. Remove the plant from its container, and trim away the outer layer of roots. Depending on the size of the rootball, cut off anywhere from ½ inch to as much as 2 inches of roots all around. An old, sharp kitchen knife is the best tool for this job. Repot the plant, using fresh potting mix, and water well. Then prune back the foliage so the plant is slightly smaller than the ideal size you want.

WATERING CONTAINER PLANTS

Plants growing in containers dry out much faster than those growing in the ground. In hot, dry climates, especially where there is a wind, you may find you need to water potted plants as often as twice a day. To make the job easier, have a spigot and hose as handy to the containers as possible. The pleasure of watering your pots, grooming the plants, or just thinking thoughts as you do becomes an onerous task if you have to drag a hose over great distances and then wind it up again when you're finished.

Most gardeners water their containers directly from the hose. Although not essential, a watering wand with a rose nozzle is a helpful tool to make the job a little easier. The extended rigid arm makes it simpler to reach hanging baskets or pots in out-of-the-way corners, and the rose nozzle provides a gentle spray that won't dislodge the soil or damage the plants. If you don't have too many containers, or if you plan to feed the plants with a liquid or water-soluble fertilizer, you may opt for a bucket or watering can.

Each time you water, thoroughly soak all the soil. Fill the pot until water runs out the bottom of the container. If the plant is rootbound or became very dry between waterings, water may run straight through without soaking into the soil. When in doubt, burrow 1 inch into the soil with your finger or a pencil to see whether the soil is properly moist. If water isn't soaking in, set the pot in a tub of water and let it soak from the bottom.

Techniques to Reduce Watering

Busy schedules and summer travel make it difficult to water container plants as often as necessary. Here are ways you can reduce watering frequency.

- Add water-retentive polymers to the planting mix.
- Choose plastic, fiberglass, metal, and glazed ceramic containers, which have the least evaporation through their sides; porous materials such as clay, wood, and concrete have the most.
- Avoid dark-colored containers. They absorb heat, causing the soil to dry out faster.
- Use larger pots. The greater volume of soil will dry out less quickly.
- Mulch the soil in pots to hold in moisture. In addition to pebbles and bark, consider using nutshells, decorative marbles or colored glass beads that coordinate with the color of the pot and plant.
- In large pots with tall-growing plants, underplant with low-growing ground covers, such as ajuga, sweet alyssum, and lobelia, to slow evaporation.
- Protect pots from drying winds and the intense heat of midday.
- During the summer growing season, use saucers under pots to provide a reservoir of water. Remove the saucers during cooler weather or when it rains for several days in a row.
- Install drip irrigation lines and put the system on an automatic timer.
- Use self-watering containers that have a "false bottom" with a reservoir underneath. The water wicks up into the soil, and eventually the roots grow down into the water.
- Group containers. The larger mass will reduce evaporation.
- If you have a plant that likes being rootbound, bury the smaller pot in a larger container to slow evaporation.

CHAPTER SIX

THE POOL
AT NIGHT

During the day, your swimming pool is a cheerful, sunny playground. By lighting the area at night, you extend the use of the pool, and with the special lighting effects available today, you can create a magical, lit-up oasis in the middle of a dark desert. Even with just a standard underwater spotlight, a pool glimmers like an opal or moonstone. There is something enchanting about a garden and swimming pool lit at night. Outdoor lighting creates a welcoming atmosphere that enhances the unique features of your landscape, home, and pool. Just as on a stage, you can use lights to create almost any effect you like — from dramatic and theatrical to romantic, mysterious, subtle, or subdued. You can opt for decorative fixtures that are a feature in themselves or hidden lights placed unobtrusively on the ground or up in trees, working their magic from a seemingly invisible source. In the "old days," landscape lighting was 120 volts.

Cables and wires had to be buried in waterproof pipes, and the complicated and involved installation generally required an experienced electrician. Because of the buried wires, the lights needed to be in permanent positions, leaving little flexibility for any changes in the layout or lighting needs as the landscape evolved.

Today, all that has changed. Low-voltage systems are easy to install and designed to create the same illuminating effects as their predecessors. They are inexpensive to operate as well. One homeowner in Maryland estimates that it costs him $150 a year to run the lights for his one-acre garden. Such systems are also flexible. Because the electrical wires do not need to be buried, it is easy to move the fixtures, a feature that is particularly useful in an ever-changing garden setting where plants grow. Eventually, a light fixture may be covered by the foliage of a nearby shrub or no longer be in the best position to show off a now-enlarged plant's features. When that happens, you simply upstake the fixture and move it to a better position.

"A well-illumined pool in the middle of a dud landscape means nothing. The primary characteristic of a pool is its reflective qualities. It's not uncommon for homeowners to leave the pool unlit, and to let it reflect the surrounding garden lights."

Skip Phillips,
Owner of Questar Pools and Spas in Escondido, California

Principles of Design

Designing with lights is an art form akin to painting or sculpture; however, instead of paint or clay, you use light as your medium. The same elements of design and composition apply to lighting as they do to any other art. The qualities you want to achieve for the most visually pleasing results are harmony and unity; proportion and scale; mass and space; and pattern, texture, and color.

> "Lighting is an enhancement and should not make a bold statement. Our design is successful if you are not sure that the lighting is there — until you miss it when it is turned off."
>
> **Mark Oxley, Outdoor Illumination, Inc., Washington, D.C.**

HARMONY AND UNITY

A successful composition, whether a painting or a garden design, must be in balance, so the entire picture hangs together as a cohesive whole. When balance is successfully achieved, the composition feels harmonious. The same is true for designing effective lighting for your landscape. You want to create a harmonious whole. If the lighting design is spotty, say with brightly lit areas broken up by dark holes that don't lead the eye to a focal or resting point, the result is jarring and inharmonious. A design is more cohesive if there are soft layers of light between brightly lit areas. This soft "transition" light helps the eye move smoothly through the composition to the different points of interest rather than leapfrogging unassisted over dark gaps to the next bright spot.

Balance can be either symmetrical or asymmetrical. Symmetrical compositions tend to be more formal, offering visual stability. If a daytime landscape is strongly symmetrical, you probably want to reflect that in your nighttime illumination. For example, if your garden features a pair of trees as a focal point, you may want to give equal weight to lighting both trees at night. To achieve symmetry in lighting design, you generally need to create equal brightness from one side of the composition to the other.

Asymmetrical designs are less visually stable. Done well, they can be exciting and dynamic because they encourage the eye to move through the picture, evoking a series of emotional responses as the eye settles on an object and then moves on. Generally, asymmetrical designs will be more harmonious if you feature odd numbers. One, three, or five points of interest are more stable — more unified — than two or four focal points that are given equal weight. In the case of even numbers, the eye tends to bounce back and forth between the objects, never knowing where it's meant to rest. Because the eye is drawn to bright light, it will skip back and forth between two lit-up areas.

If you want to feature more than one focal point in an asymmetrical lighting design, consider how each will interact with the entire composition. It helps to assign degrees of importance to each feature. A star item should be more brightly lit than lesser features. Bear in mind that you do not have to include all the daytime focal points in your nighttime composition. For the sake of your design, you may decide to leave an object dark that is a major feature during daylight. A pool is transformed at night, so you can make the most of that fact by creating a space that feels completely different from its midday self.

The exception to preferring odd numbers in clusters to even groupings is when you want to create a sense of rhythm by repeating a series of lighting effects, perhaps to link two focal points. You can create rhythm with garden lights by illuminating a row of trees, each with its own spotlight, or by highlighting each support post of a vine-covered pergola next to the pool. A row of equally spaced lights grazing the wall of the pool house or cabana is another example of rhythm.

PROPORTION AND SCALE

To achieve a sense of pleasing proportions, make sure objects properly relate to each other by size. Some people have an instinct for pleasing proportions, always knowing the perfect-size couch to combine with two side chairs so they all fit comfortably in a room or the right shrub to fill a space without being too dominant. Others will find assistance from objective standards of proportion established by mathematicians in the thirteenth century.

The Italian mathematician Leonardo Fibonacci discovered a series of numbers that represent visually pleasing combinations. The series is created by adding together the two numbers that precede the next. For example, add 1 and 2 to get 3; 3 plus 2 (the previous number) equals 5, which is the next number in the series. You can continue this series (1, 2, 3, 5, 8, 13, 21) forever. Interestingly, the Fibonacci sequence is found in many plants and animals, including the spiral of

the chambered nautilus, the seed cones of fir trees, and the arrangement of seeds in a sunflower. To find pleasing proportions for a space, use adjacent numbers as the dimensions. For instance, a room that is 8 feet by 13 feet feels right, as does one that's 13 feet by 21 feet.

Proportion comes into play when lighting a swimming pool area because it is an outdoor room where you play and entertain. You create the "walls" of your room with garden lights, which visually define the perimeter of the space. On a lot with plenty of trees, you can use them to create the illusion of walls by focusing some spotlights up at trees growing near the pool area and hanging other lights to shine down through the branches. At night, if you want your pool area to feel larger, you can make it so by lighting a plant or feature that's beyond the property line, thus borrowing from the surrounding view.

▲ **The chambered nautilus is a classic example of the proportion revealed in the number series discovered by the Italian mathematician Leonardo Fibonacci. The area of each successive chamber is the sum of the two immediately preceding it.**

You'll also want to achieve pleasing proportions among the plants, structures, and garden ornaments you plan to illuminate. Think in terms of relationships among objects — their comparative sizes, shapes, and densities — and look at them as units, with an eye to how their proportions interact with each other. For example, if you highlight too many diminutive features, you risk making the lighting scheme appear busy and lacking in focus.

MASS AND SPACE

In the language of garden lighting, *mass* is evoked by areas left dark and *space* is evoked by regions that are lit. If you leave too much dark, a nighttime pool will feel unwelcoming and unsafe. If everything is flooded with light, the harsh glare and lack of contrast also will be unappealing. The goal is to strike a balance between features and areas that are lit and those left in darkness. See "Designing

▼ **Discreet light fixtures built into a stone wall illumine the decking at the end of the pool and shine in reflection on the still, dark water.**

with Photographs" on page 128 to help you visualize how different combinations of dark and light, mass and space, will work in your proposed lighting scheme.

Even when well lit, a large, bulky plant also projects a sense of mass in a design. In contrast, an uninterrupted area of pool decking and the pool itself are swaths of open space. Trees with an open, lacy canopy have less visual mass — even if they are extremely tall and large in diameter — than a short, tubby white spruce. Plants with dark foliage appear more massive than do plants with pale leaves. Use lighting to make a pleasing picture that includes a sense of mass from plants and pool structures, as well as a sense of space from open areas and lacy plants.

PATTERN, TEXTURE, AND COLOR

You'll find patterns, textures, and colors (even different shades of green) throughout the pool and garden. Look for the branching pattern on a tree or the trunks of multistemmed specimens, such as crape myrtles. A spray of palm fronds and the spiky leaves of dracaena have both pattern and texture. Tree bark, foliage, and the surfaces of structures all have texture that you can highlight or minimize with your lighting design. Large-leaved plants are bold in texture, creating a strong, assertive look. Small-leaved plants have a finer texture that gives them a more delicate appearance. You might use a spotlight to create the silhouette of a spiky-leafed plant against the pool house wall or the fence surrounding the pool, or use downlighting to capture the dancing shadow pattern of fine-textured tree foliage on the lawn or pool decking.

At night, the eye tends to see things in black and white, but lights bring back the color. Nevertheless, each color, depending on how dark or pale it is, reacts differently to being lit. Certain

▲ Uplighting from a spotlight tucked into hostas shows off the beautiful mottled bark and multiple stems of a crape myrtle tree.

colors come alive under artificial light. Salmon-colored flowers, such as azaleas and impatiens, look more brilliant at night than during the day. Shiny or pale colors reflect light; dark colors tend to absorb it. Silver maples (*Acer saccarinum*) and some of the poplar and birch species have silvery undersides that almost sparkle when lit from below. In contrast, the tan-colored woolly underleaf of some Southern magnolias (*Magnolia grandiflora*) make the plant look dead if it is uplit. Some leaves are thick and opaque, while others are translucent and look fantastic when light shines up through them. To brighten your nighttime poolside plantings, use garden lights to illuminate a large pot or tub with salmon-colored impatiens, and uplight nearby trees, especially if the foliage has pale undersides, so you can enjoy the magical effect of the light while you float on your back in the water.

▲ The salmon-colored flowers of giant hyssop (*Agastache rupestris*) are particularly effective when lit at night.

▶ The "floating fire" created by pool designer Skip Phillips, is a dramatic feature of this La Jolla, California, pool. Such features provide warmth, light, and pretty reflections.

MOOD MAKERS

In addition to touching our visual sensibilities, pool and garden lighting evokes various moods or atmospheres. Bright lights are exciting. That's why amusement parks, especially the midway, are so brightly lit. There you'll see white lights, colored lights, and many that blink on and off. The result is a charged atmosphere where exciting things are bound to happen. Fairy lights strung through a tree add sparkle to a scene, another dynamic, upbeat mood inducer.

For drama, design with high contrast. A single sculpture spotlit in the middle of a dark area is dramatic. There it is — a visual POW! — in the middle of a void. On the other hand, that kind of high-contrast lighting isn't suitable for a space where people will be moving around, as it's too dangerous (the eye cannot adjust quickly enough to extremes of light and dark), but it's great for a set-apart feature viewed from a distance. If you have a specimen plant or sculpture visible from the pool but set apart, you could leave all around it dark with just a single spotlight focused on the feature. Alternatively, during the winter months when you're looking at the pool from the house but not worried about safety issues stemming from people walking around the space, you can use a light to pick out one stunning feature of the pool, leaving the rest of the area dark.

Everyone knows that soft light evokes a romantic or mysterious mood. Moonlight filtered through trees or reflected on still water is calming. You can create the same effect by mounting downward-facing spotlights in trees or on buildings. Soft lighting is flattering; years drop from faces when the lights are low. Dim lights also add a pleasing air of mystery because everything cannot be seen at once. For example, a no-nonsense garden path that runs straight and true takes on a mysterious aspect at night when the far end of the path is left unlit so it gradually disappears from view as the eye follows it into the darkness. At night, no one knows where it goes or what lies at the other end.

Around the pool, you may want some areas of decking lit more brightly than others. The corners that are dimmer become private — perhaps romantic — retreats, while the brightly lit spaces may be where people gather for lively conversation, poolside barbecuing, and other festivities. Perhaps there is a path that leads away from the pool to an unlit part of the garden where you don't want people going at night. If the path disappears into darkness, people are unlikely to venture down it, but they will enjoy the sense of mystery it provokes.

Special Effects with Lights

here are all sorts of techniques and "trade tricks" that lighting designers use to create various effects in a landscape. The three most important variables are the position of the fixture, the amount of light shining on an object, and the direction of the light. These factors affect how shape, color, and detail will be perceived, as well as the flat or three-dimensional appearance of an object. By using these techniques, you can achieve just about any effect you want.

MOONLIGHTING OR DOWNLIGHTING

Downlighting creates a very natural appearance because we are already familiar with the sun as a source of light. Instead of the sun, floodlights pointing downward from high in the trees create the illusion of moonlight — even on cloudy nights. It is particularly effective if the trees have a lacy canopy that casts an intriguing shadow on the ground. If trees aren't convenient, place the light high on a wall to illuminate objects from above.

▼ A central overhead light illumines the table in this arbor, while downward-pointing spotlights highlight each classical column.

In large spaces, downlights should ideally be at least 25 feet off the ground. If you have tall trees, it's worth it to hire an arborist to place the light fixtures as high as 55 feet up in a tree. Before settling on their permanent location, make sure the lights don't shine in anyone's eyes (on either your property or your neighbors'). Also, avoid having large lower limbs in the way of the light beam. The chunky shadow it will create is not as appealing as a lacy pattern of leaves and small branches, especially if the shadows will be clearly visible on a swath of lawn or paved surface. Choose fixtures that provide the maximum light spread for an even wash of light over the ground.

For small spaces, lights don't need to be placed so high up because the scale is reduced. In that case, mount downlights from arbors or trellises or lower down in trees. For a pleasing effect, try to position the light so it filters through leaves to make pretty, dancing shadows. If there isn't a vine nearby, plant one for future enjoyment.

Because downlighting from a high source bathes an area with even light, it is also the ideal way to illuminate paths and steps leading to and from the pool, rather than with traditional ground-level path lights. It is hard on the eye, and confusing to the brain, to move from bright pools of light interrupted by dark areas. In addition, if properly placed, the light source is less obtrusive, shedding soft illumination in a way that feels completely natural on pool decking. The light is noticeable only when it isn't there.

▶ **Three lighting techniques: Spotlights aimed directly at a building facade, top, flatten the perspective and wash out architectural details. Uplighting, center, emphasizes texture on the wall by creating shadows. A side-aimed spotlight, bottom, washes the building in light but also creates shadows, highlighting architectural features.**

UPLIGHTING

Light focused up from the ground on trees and walls gives a new perspective to the world. Uplighting highlights bark and foliage and accentuates textures and forms. Leaves with pale undersides appear to sparkle when lit from below, and inner veins shine forth on translucent leaves. By uplighting trees around the perimeter of a pool area, you establish the walls and ceiling of the garden room. Whenever you uplight a tree canopy, be sure to include the tree trunk in the light beam as well. Otherwise, you will have the uncomfortable sense of a disembodied form floating above the ground without any structure to support it.

Different trees benefit from different uplighting approaches. For a tree with a tall, willowy form, fine-textured foliage, and an open canopy, use a minimum of three fixtures placed evenly around the tree to show off its full shape. Position the light fixture away from a tall, conical evergreen and set the angle so the entire side of the tree is washed with light. Japanese lace-leaf maple (*Acer palmatum* 'Dissectum'), with its beautifully twisted bare branches in winter and finely lobed leaves in summer, is an ideal candidate for uplighting. Place the light fixture inside the tree near the center so the light shines through the canopy of leaves in summer and shows off the branch structure in silhouette in winter. In the case of an evergreen with a narrow, fastigiate form (columnar or narrow growth habit), place a narrow-beam light directly at the base and aim it straight up (or at a slight angle) so the light grazes the surface of the plant, showing off the foliage texture.

Grazing the surface of tree trunks and building surfaces with light will emphasize their surface texture and pattern. Simply place the light at the base of the object and shine it directly upward. This technique is particularly effective on trees with interesting bark, such as river birch (*Betula nigra*) and paperbark maple (*Acer griseum*), and on stucco, brick, and stone walls, where you'll see the texture of the building material and, in the case of brick and stone, the shadows created by the joints and mortar. Grazing is also a great way to emphasize architectural features, such as columns, but it does not benefit siding.

Ideally, you want the light fixtures to be unobtrusive. Whenever possible, tuck them into ground covers or next to low-growing shrubs so they aren't as noticeable. Some fixtures are designed to be buried in the ground with a protective grate or grille placed over the hole.

Uplighting larger trees around the perimeter of a swimming pool area helps establish the walls and ceiling of the space. If these trees are also close to an entertainment area, downlighting from those same trees will provide a subtle, natural, and uniform light over the locale. When a tree is lit with both uplighting and downlighting, the combination can be quite magical. The tree is highlighted by a beam of light focused along its trunk and up into its branches; at the same time, the general area is softly lit, as if bathed in the glow of the moon.

SILHOUETTING
AND SHADOWING

To make an interesting object stand out in silhouette, shine a light from behind it. Use this lighting technique on a tree or shrub with a simple, striking form to define its outline. The plant will show up best if it is near a fence or wall or in the open, where there aren't other forms to distract from the silhouette. Such backlighting provides no texture or detail — just an object's outline.

Double your viewing pleasure by shining a light in front of an object so that its shape is perfectly reproduced in shadow on the wall or fence behind it. Like silhouetting, this technique is most effective on objects that have a remarkable outline. Front lighting shows the details of an object to dramatic effect, but it also flattens them because it eliminates shadows where the light is focused.

SIDE AND WASH LIGHTING

When you illuminate a building or an object from the side, you increase the awareness of textures because of the shadows created by the angle of light. Experiment with the placement of the light fixture and the focus of the light beam to achieve the most dramatic effect.

When you place a light fixture directly in front of, but some distance away from, a building, plant, or sculpture, you get an even wash of light over the entire surface. The effect shows off the shape of the object being illuminated, but the overall effect is flat because you don't have the shadowing to provide contours.

CREATING A SENSE OF DEPTH

How you use lighting can make a nighttime garden feel deeper and larger or it can minimize the perception of depth to create a sense of mystery. Think of the garden around the pool in terms of three zones: the foreground, the middle ground, and the background. For a strong sense of depth, put the brightest lights in the background to draw the eye to the boundaries of the area. The foreground should be the next brightest area, with the middle ground the darkest. If you want to hide an ugly feature in the background or make the space feel more enclosed and intimate, then eliminate the background lighting and make the brightest area be the middle ground.

▲ Uplighting gives a new perspective on the world, since we generally are accustomed to a light source (the sun or moon) from above. Here, white phlox catches the beam of a hidden light that is aimed up at the paperbark maple tree.

◄ A combination of uplighting and downlighting is magical. Here, uplighting emphasizes the multiple stems of a crape myrtle tree while downlighting bathes the area in a soft glow that mimics the light of a full moon.

MIRROR LIGHTING

With a swimming pool you have the perfect opportunity to create a mirror lighting effect where nearby lit objects are reflected in still, dark water. By leaving the pool dark, or dimly lit, it will work like a mirror, reflecting back nearby light. When a breeze ripples the water, the reflected light shimmers and splits into fascinating patterns.

LIGHTING SCULPTURES

Sculptures can be either two-dimensional wall decorations or freestanding, three-dimensional objects. For murals and friezes, graze the surface with uplights to highlight an interesting texture or use a wall-washing technique by placing a spotlight (or two for cross lighting) some distance from the wall so the light spreads an even glow over the entire surface.

Three-dimensional sculptures require a little more thought. Downlighting illuminates the figure in the same way as the sun does. However, the sun moves across the sky throughout the day, hitting a sculpture at different angles. An overhead light shining down on a sculpture will create an unmoving pattern of shadows on the underside of a protruding feature, such as the nose on a face. If set in the wrong position, downlighting can create some sinister effects, especially on faces.

Generally, when you uplight a sculpture, you want to position the light source away from the object so the light covers it evenly. Otherwise, you'll get dark shadows created by the sharp angle of the light. Experiment with the fixture location until you find the best solution. Even the experts need to do that. When Mark Oxley of Outdoor Illumination in Washington, D.C., set out to light the figure of the little boy fishing shown here, he first tried placing the light fairly close to the sculpture so it would stand out dramatically, but this put the face in deep shadow. After trial and error, he found just the right

▲ Two spotlights focused directly onto the wall from the front wash it in even light, removing all shadows and making the Tree of Life fountain stand out in sharp contrast.

▶ It took some trial and error to find the ideal position of the spotlight to illumine this little boy's triumphant face without casting odd, unpleasant shadows. Landscape light designer Mark Oxley found that the light was best when it was placed further back from the sculpture, illuminating some of the surrounding shrubbery as well as the sculpture.

spot that shows off the triumphant little boy as well as just a little of the shrubbery around him.

In some cases, such as when the foliage texture or pattern behind a sculpture adds to the drama of the setting, a combination of an uplight behind and a spotlight in front may be a good solution. It draws the background into the picture, incorporating it as part of the overall composition.

LIGHTING WATER FEATURES

Water features, such as fountains, ponds, and waterfalls, can be lit either from beneath the water or from above. Lighting from beneath produces the most dramatic effect. Water droplets are transformed into diamonds when the light catches them from below, and the turbulent power of a waterfall is emphasized with an underwater light source. The swimming pool spotlights set into the side walls of the pool accentuate the shape of the pool and the contours of the bottom.

If the underwater light source is a traditional incandescent bulb, it must be watertight and made of the finest materials to withstand the corrosive effects of water over the years. As a result, these fixtures cost three to five times more than above-water fixtures. Changing the bulb is a maintenance challenge. Either the fixture has to be lifted out of the water or the pool or pond has to be drained to get to the bulb. In addition, the hot lightbulb will increase the water temperature significantly. This issue is important if you have a pond full of fish that can be upset or even physically harmed by changes in water temperature. (Fish also may not enjoy having artificial light in their environment. Make sure they have a dark corner to retreat to when the underwater light is turned on.)

Fiber optics is another option available to homeowners. With fiber optics, the light is channeled through tiny fibers to the exact place where the lighting effect is wanted. Because the actual light source is removed from the point where the light is seen, it can be located in a weatherproof room or box. Maintenance is as simple as can be.

Lighting water from above has its own challenges because the water, particularly still water, reflects light, rather than absorbing it. If the light isn't angled carefully, it can be a glaring nuisance. Generally, the angle from vertical should be no more than 35 degrees. Moving, turbulent water, such as a fountain spray or a stream that moves around and over rocks, is full of air bubbles that absorb and diffuse light, so the water glows and sparkles. Low-voltage lights are easy to move, so experiment with various locations and angles until you find the one that looks best for your setting.

▼ **While incandescent underwater light fixtures are three to five times more expensive than above-water fixtures, the dramatic effect of subaqueous lighting is well worth the expense. Here, light reveals the underwater turbulence created by falling water.**

Lighting the Pool and Garden

We're all familiar with the standard underwater spotlight installed in swimming pools. While functional, spotlights glare, and the source of light is clearly visible. In addition, many pool owners find that the bright light attracts bugs. They prefer to swim with the underwater light turned off. Fortunately, there are other, more aesthetic, creative, and contemporary alternatives.

Creative swimming pool designers are looking for nontraditional ways to use incandescent lights under the water and innovative ways to create beautiful light reflections on the water's surface. "We do underwater lighting with no hot spots," says Skip Phillips, of Questar Pools and Spas in Escondido, California. "Hot spots" refers to the jarring glare of traditional underwater spotlights. To avoid glare, Phillips uses lower-wattage lamps on dimmers. In one case, he had the bulb lenses frosted for a diffused light. To capture the reflected light off turbulent water, he also places underwater spotlights at the base of waterfalls.

STRIP LIGHTS

Strip lights are either 120-volt or low-voltage tiny incandescent lamps mounted inside waterproof tubing. When the strip is made, you can specify that the lamps be spaced anywhere from 1 to 12 inches apart. Tucked under the pool coping, strip lights provide a line of lights around the pool perimeter, outlining the shape and reflecting in the water's surface.

There is a risk that strip lights may make a pool look very "flashy." However, lighting designer Jan Moyer, of MSH Visual Planners in Troy, New York, used them effectively on a long, rectangular pool. The parallel row of strip lights down both edges of the pool directs the eye to the far end, where a pair of dramatically illuminated trees and arbors are the focal points of the nighttime garden. Except for the necklace of lights around the pool's perimeter and a dim underwater light in the spa, the rest of the pool is unlit, allowing the still, dark water to reflect the beautifully illumined landscape.

FIBER OPTICS

The latest breakthrough in underwater lighting is fiber optics. Instead of locating the light source directly in the pool, or in a niche designed for housing the fixture, the light is generated at a location away from the pool and then run through fiber-optic bundles to multiple points inside the pool. This approach makes system maintenance far easier because you don't have to get to the fixture from underwater or from behind the pool wall via an access tunnel.

The possibilities for lighting with fiber optics is enormous. Ron Gibbons used the technology to create the impression of a starry night sky in the black, marble-dust bottom of a pool he designed for clients in Westhampton Beach, New York. Gibbons installed more than 2,200 individual fiber-optic lights to provide a pinpoint lighting effect throughout the 900-square-foot pool. Each fiber was coated with epoxy to protect it from any possible chemical reaction with the surrounding gunite, then installed by hand. The lights are about 4 inches apart from each other and appear to spill out from under the bridge into the deep end of the pool. The final plaster layer of the pool — a blend of white Portland cement, marble-dust aggregate,

and three hues of colored crystal aggregates — was hand-troweled around the fiber optics.

Landscape architect Ray Lopez likes to use fiber-optic filaments fitted into the bed of a waterfall to make the cascading water appear to sparkle and dance at night. By using multiple light sources to feed the fibers and a small computer chip to control the circuits, a pool owner can choreograph the lighting by changing patterns and colors. The light source can be a traditional lightbulb or a solid-state laser diode, such as what is used in a computer's optical mouse. The laser diode light source is available in a number of colors, including yellow, green, and red, but not white. In addition, colored filters used with traditional white lights allow pool owners to create unlimited color combinations as well as interesting effects. One homeowner in Woodlands, Texas, has a pool that glows bright pink thanks to red fiber-optic lights.

Using computer-controlled fiber-optic lights opens the door to incredibly creative approaches to underwater pool lighting. For example, you could install a grid of fiber-optic bundles evenly spaced throughout the pool, then generate various images — say, a birthday cake with lit candles — for different occasions. In the same way that strings of Christmas lights flash on and off in different patterns, alternating currents can make an array of fiber-optic lights switch on and off so they appear to dance and move.

At this point, the underwater use of fiber-optic lights is still a relatively new idea. As a result, it tends to be expensive, and many designers have not yet attempted to use them. But as the idea gathers momentum, the technology will be used more and more. Creative designers are breaking new ground to use underwater lights in interesting ways. Eventually, fiber optics will probably become the norm.

▲ **This "starry night" pool designed by Ron Gibbons for a client in New York uses fiber-optic lights in a creative, masterful way. More than 2,200 individual fiber-optic lights installed into the bottom of the pool create this effect.**

OUTDOOR LIGHTING FIXTURES

Here is a selection of outdoor lighting fixtures that are suitable for a pool area and garden. Each is designed to perform a specific function, although in some cases there is some overlap. Make your selections based on your overall goals for design and lighting effects.

Bollard Lights. Cylindrical in shape, bollard lights feature a faceted lens that diffuses light both downward and outward, making them useful for accenting pool areas, walkways, flower beds, and patios. Some come with a removable light shield, giving you the option of full, 360-degree or 180-degree lighting in any direction. Bollard lights have a streamlined, contemporary look that is ideal for a modern-style home.

▼ A clay garden pot makes an effective casing for this in-ground floodlight. The rough plywood behind helps direct the light where it's wanted.

Floodlights or Spotlights. Floodlights, also known as spotlights or bullets, are wonderful for creating a multitude of outdoor lighting effects. They come mounted on a flexible base that allows you to point them in any direction. Some are equipped with a focusing devise that enables you to choose the width of the light beam, with a selection that ranges from a tight to a medium to a flood focus. In addition to being useful for security in such places as the driveway and next to the garage, floodlights are great for artistic lighting. Use one to illuminate a fountain, a sculpture, or another special garden feature.

When pointed downward from high up in a tree, a floodlight can create the ambience of moonlight. For shadow lighting, put one in front of a plant growing against a wall or fence (if the fence is an attractive one) and angle the light to illuminate the plant and cast its shadow on the backdrop. Position two or more floodlights near the ground and angle their beams so they cross high above the subject. This cross-lighting technique sheds a pleasing, soft light on objects and adds depth and dimension to the scene.

The most versatile floodlight currently available is the MR-16 (multimirror reflector). At only about 2 inches in diameter, this compact floodlight allows you to focus the light beam, targeting it exactly where you want it. In contrast, most incandescent bulbs put out an explosion of light that flows in all directions. The MR-16 provides a light spread range anywhere between 8 and 60 degrees. An even smaller fixture that is easier to conceal is the MR-11, although there have been reliability problems with the sockets. The MR-8 is half the size of the MR-16, and it has the same focus-control options and bright light.

All these fixtures take halogen, rather than incandescent, bulbs. Halogen light is generally considered more attractive than incandescent light, and the bulbs are highly rated for long life. A good-quality halogen bulb can burn for 2,000 to 4,000 hours, an important asset if the fixture is in a hard-to-reach spot. Some bulbs are rated for as many as 10,000 hours, though at those high ratings, the reflectors tend to fail before the bulb does, making the light ineffective.

Globe Lights. Like lampposts, globe lights provide general, diffused illumination. They are effective rimming a swimming pool or recreational area, where they provide illumination that covers a large area without annoying glare. The globe may be clear or a translucent white. One available style has a shaded globe for a more downward-directed light.

Lantern Lights. Essentially lidded boxes encased in glass, lantern lights provide illumination from three or four sides, creating an appealing atmosphere around an area. Their one drawback is the potential glare, because light radiates outward at a right angle from the fixture. If you choose a lantern with frosted glass, the glare will be less intense.

Mushroom Lights. Mushroom lights look like their namesake. They stand on a riser stalk with a cap on top that conceals the light source and gives the fixture its mushroomlike appearance. Mushroom lights point downward, but with no outward spread. Models on taller riser stems light a broader area. They're useful to highlight borders, walkways, and low foliage, but because they have no spread, they don't produce any general ambient light. As a result, they are less atmospheric than tier lights (see below).

Surface Deck Lights. These lights have a compact, flat design so they can be mounted on the sides of decks and benches or along stair railings. Designed so they provide a diffused light without glare, they give a welcoming, festive feeling to a deck

or stairway. You can also mount them under eaves and along fences and walls.

Tier Lights. Mounted on a short post or stake, tier lights are fitted with angled shades arranged in tiers along the light source. The shades direct light downward and outward so that pools of light illumine the ground. These fixtures are ideal for lighting walkways and steps; the downward light provides safe footing, while the tiers keep the outward-spreading light from casting glare into your eyes. When lighting a path, position the fixtures to light nearby flower beds as well, thus making the

▲ The surface deck lights mounted into the sides of the stone stairs are discreet when turned off, but they spill light onto the treads at night, when the steps would otherwise be hazardous.

journey down a walkway more interesting. Tier lights are also effective when arranged in a row along a terrace, like a necklace glowing in the night, or for highlighting flower beds and ground covers.

Well Lights. These spotlights are housed in a weather-resistant tube and are buried in the ground so the source of light is hidden. Place them under trees and shrubs to create uplit shadows and to highlight the underside of leaves. They also work well along the foundation of a house, wall, or fence to accentuate textures and shapes.

What to Look For in Lighting Fixtures. There is a wide range of low-voltage lighting fixtures available. Your choice will be governed by four considerations: appearance, function, mechanical features, and cost. Lighting fixtures range in style from purely functional to sleek and modern to specific architectural periods. Many manufacturers have a line of fixtures in different sizes and for different uses, but all in the same style. If you opt for one of these "families" of fixtures, you will create a cohesive look throughout your garden. While spotlights are probably the workhorses of garden lighting fixtures, there is a wide selection of other fixtures, each designed for a particular function.

As is true with most things, you get what you pay for. Inexpensive light fixtures and systems can end up being frustrating because they tend to need frequent maintenance to keep them operating properly, and they may corrode and decay, eventually becoming useless. While top-quality equipment costs more initially, in the long run you'll be happier with better-quality equipment, and the fixtures will last much longer. Quality light fixtures are a good long-term investment. When evaluating lighting fixture quality, try to select equipment that is:

■ **Waterproof.** Insist on fixtures that are totally enclosed. The lens should be sealed and gasketed to the housing in order to be waterproof.

The exception is fixtures designed to use PAR-36 (a 4½-inch-diameter low-voltage bulb in a parabolic aluminized reflector) and PAR-38 (a 4¾-inch standard-voltage bulb) incandescent lamps, because the glass lens on these can tolerate the temperature shocks of cold rain or snow on hot glass.

■ **Adjustable.** Select fixtures that can be adjusted to provide a wide and varied aiming range and beam spread, as well as the ability to accept different bulb wattages. These qualities are particularly useful for highlighting growing plants. As a shrub grows larger and denser, for example, you'll probably want more beam distribution and a higher-watt bulb to light it adequately. Some fixtures are designed so you can adjust the beam spread simply by moving the lightbulb toward the back of the housing (for a wider beam) or toward the front of the fixture (for a narrower spread).

■ **Accessorized.** Fixtures that accept accessories, such as shrouds, louvers, lenses, and color filters, will give you more versatility in your lighting design.

■ **Easy to maintain.** Look for fixtures that accept long-life bulbs and that make it easy to change bulbs or perform maintenance tasks.

■ **Corrosion resistant.** Select fixtures built with corrosion-resistant materials. Copper and brass are particularly good, and they make attractive outdoor lighting fixtures. Unfortunately, they are also expensive. Materials that contain iron are more prone to corrosion. Cast iron is relatively inexpensive, but it is weaker than other metals and prone to corrosion when exposed to high lamp temperatures. Most good-quality outdoor lighting equipment is made of aluminum or aluminum alloys coated with a corrosion-resistant substance. Even with these coatings, however, aluminum does not hold up well in coastal areas with salty air. Extreme desert heat and acidic soil also break down aluminum.

■ **Self-cleaning.** While there is no such thing as a completely self-cleaning fixture, some are better designed to slough off debris than others. Look for design features, such as curved glass and drainage holes, that minimize the ability of water, soil, leaves, and bark to collect in the fixture.

■ **Not made of plastic.** Beware of fixtures made of plastic or that have plastic components. There are many kinds of plastic, some of better quality than others, but most are less durable than metal. Many plastics become brittle when exposed to ultraviolet light. Others experience structural failure when exposed to some chemicals. Pressure, weight, and high heat from lightbulbs can cause deterioration. If a fixture has plastic components, check with the manufacturer about the durability of the plastic used. See Additional Information on page 197 for outdoor lighting manufacturers.

◄ **The frosted cover on this custom-made light fixture diffuses the light, making it easy on the eyes. It's important to choose fixtures and position them so they don't create glare or shine in people's faces.**

▼ **This charming copper light fixture is a pretty garden feature by day and night. Generally, metal light fixtures last longer and are more durable than ones made of plastic.**

Developing a Lighting Plan

Successfully highlighting a nighttime pool area with special lighting effects takes some thought and planning. Before you rush to the nearest home improvement center to purchase an all-purpose kit, take some time to think through what you want to achieve and how you want to illuminate this special space in your garden.

Begin by assessing the pool landscape during the day. Work out how you will establish the visual perimeter of the area so you can define the space with a "wall" and a "ceiling" of lights. Then pick out one or two striking features, such as a dramatic specimen tree, a waterfall, a pool house, a gazebo, an arbor, or a statue, and think about how you'd like to emphasize them. Also, think about how you plan to use the pool at night. If you do a lot of nighttime swimming and outdoor entertaining, you'll need to light it for comfort and safety; you'll probably want the deck surface fairly evenly lit from above. You want to create a natural look, however, such as moonlight filtering through the trees on a bright night, rather than the brightly lit atmosphere of a parking lot. Remember, eyes do adjust to the dark, and it's not necessary to overly light the area unless you're looking to create the excitement of a carnival.

Think about access to the pool area and possible traffic patterns around the decking. The

▼ **A row of tier lights placed on the retaining wall behind the pool makes a necklace of light and defines the boundary of the pool area. An underwater spotlight emphasizes the contours of the bottom of the pool.**

routes from the house and other parts of the garden to the pool should be safe as well as attractive. Walkways and steps are safer to use at night if the light spreads an even glow over them, rather than creating pools of light interspersed with dark patches. Because the eye is always drawn toward movement and light, you can use light to direct people's progress through an area. It's uncomfortable to walk through a dimly lit space to an even darker space, but people will happily walk down the same path toward a visibly lit area.

You probably don't want to light every tree and shrub in the garden. The positive, lit spots will be all the more special and important if they are seen in contrast to negative, dark areas. Also, don't throw too much light onto any one object or plant. Generally, a subtle lighting that leaves some mystery is most effective. For variety, think about using different lighting techniques (see pages 114–119) for different parts of the garden. Otherwise, it will look repetitive if every single garden element is given the same lighting treatment.

In most cases, lightscaping is most effective when you don't see the source of the light. If possible, conceal or camouflage the fixtures behind trees, bushes, or ornaments, in flower beds, or anywhere else that will hide them. If you are putting lights up high, make sure they are angled so they don't shine unwanted light into your neighbors' windows or send a glaring beam into the eyes of someone sitting or walking in your garden. In addition, keep the lights out of the way of lawn mowing and foot traffic. You certainly don't want to be constantly righting a light fixture that gets knocked about by normal garden maintenance or to run wires across areas where they will create a tripping hazard.

When planning a complicated combination of different light fixtures and effects, you may find it easier to visualize the scheme if you draw it on

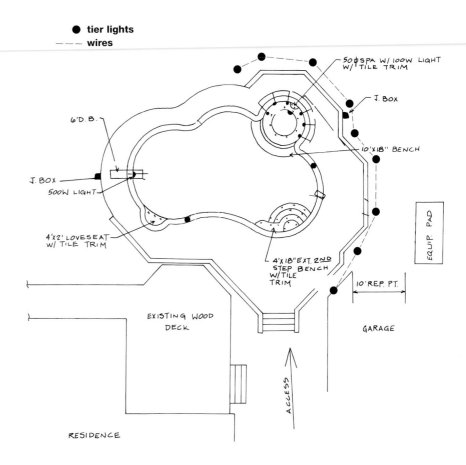

graph paper. If you already have a site plan for your garden, use that. Otherwise, create a worksheet by drawing the footprint of the house to scale and adding the other outdoor features. Don't forget to note the location of the outside, grounded electrical outlets. For more information, see Designing with Photographs on page 128.

Decide where you want to position each light, then work out the most logical and efficient layout for the wire cables. Conside the length and layout of each circuit, along with the total wattage of the lights, when choosing the right cable and power transformer to use. Free do-it-yourself guides are provided by outdoor lighting manufacturers to assist you in mapping out the plan and then selecting the right equipment, including the transformers, for your application.

▲ **Use a copy of the blueprint of your pool area as a worksheet to help you plan where you want your poolside light fixtures to go. Here, the homeowners have opted for a row of tier lights to rim the retaining wall behind the pool (see photo at left).**

DESIGNING WITH PHOTOGRAPHS

Even with a grasp of the principles of garden lighting, some people may find it difficult to visualize what the space will look like with lights. In addition, there may be more than one satisfying lighting solution for any particular space. Despite the flexibility of low-voltage light systems, it's still a lot of work to move lights around while you experiment with different effects. To help you in the design process, grab one of the best, time-tested design aids: your camera.

Take a photograph of the pool and garden from the main viewing point (this example uses the photograph on pages 106–107). If there are several points from which you are likely to view the pool at night, take a picture from each angle. Enlarge the photographs, then place a piece of tissue or tracing paper over each picture. Trace the outline of the various garden features that you want to light. You may single out a prominent tree, then clump a group of shrubs as one unit. When you are finished, each page should be full of shapes representing the

features and plants in your garden. Make several copies of these abstract schemes.

Assign a number to each shape, the lowest number representing a space or feature you want to light brightly, the higher numbers indicating areas that will be darker. Create a key in the corner of the paper to remind you of the lightness and darkness of each number. Then go back and shade in each numbered shape, making the intensity of the shading consistent with your numbers. To see how other plans will look, repeat the process, making different sections of the garden lighter and darker. With several possibilities to choose from, you can pick the one that best meets your needs and aesthetic goals.

WORKING WITH AN EXPERT

It is not at all complicated to design and install a simple set of garden lights, such as tier lights or well lights. Even someone with absolutely no experience with electrical matters can easily follow the instructions to install a simple system. If you want an elaborate combination, however, the job becomes

▼ **To help visualize how lighting will look, photograph the space, then overlay the picture with tissue paper and outline basic shapes. Assign a low number to brightly lit shapes, higher numbers for those left dark, bottom left. Highlight the shapes according to how bright the light will be, bottom right.**

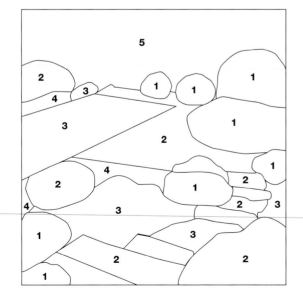

more complex. For some experienced do-it-your-selfers, that's the kind of challenge that satisfies. If you do decide to design and install your own system, consider hiring a professional at least to install the lights that will be mounted in trees. It takes trained people with special equipment to get up that high safely and to position the lights properly.

For those who opt to hire a pool and landscape lighting designer, the next step is finding someone to work with. One source for local people is the Yellow Pages; look under "Landscape Lighting." Another source is referrals from friends and neighbors who have attractive outdoor lighting. Drive around neighborhoods at night and notice homes with effective landscape lighting. If you are uncomfortable knocking on a stranger's door, send a brief letter. Most people will be flattered by your interest and happy to pass on their designer's name.

Once you've found one or more designers, look at their portfolios. During interviews, think about how you enjoy interacting with the person. You are embarking on an artistic project where there are better and worse solutions, but few absolutes. Ideally, you want to work with someone with whom you feel compatible, who listens to your needs and desires, who is willing to work with you to achieve your goals, and who will take an ongoing interest in your property's lighting needs. A good lighting designer must have creative ideas as well as the technical experience to implement them.

Once you think you've found the right person or company, ask for references and check them. Talk to previous clients about how satisfied they are with the finished product. Find out whether the projects came in on budget and whether the agreed-upon schedules were maintained. Photographs don't always tell the real story. Ask to visit their pool and garden at night to see how it actually looks. People who have made an effort to make their gardens more beautiful

Helpful Lighting Pointers

- Angle lights so they don't glare in anyone's eyes, including those of your neighbors.
- When lighting fixtures are simple and utilitarian, rather than ornamental, try to hide them so you cannot see the source of the light.
- Allow a transition in light levels between a brightly lit interior and outdoor nighttime lighting.
- When you look at landscape lighting from inside a brightly lit room, the indoor lights will dilute the effect of the outdoor lights. To compensate for the indoor light, increase the wattage of the outdoor lights.
- The farther away the light is from the viewing point, the more muted it will seem. Increase the bulb wattage to make a distant light shine brighter.
- Consider nighttime traffic patterns when you plan outdoor lighting. For example, decide whether you want to light a path so you have access to it at night or whether you would just as soon leave it dark. You may decide to light it just for visual effect, even though you will never use it at night.
- Anticipate plant growth. The 20-watt bulb in the MR-16 fixture (one of the most used and versatile of the spotlights available on the market) may eventually need to be replaced with a 35-watt bulb as the tree grows. The fixture can take the extra wattage, but the line coming out of the transformer may not be able to. Plan ahead for these variables when you calculate the power you will need for each line.
- As plants grow, you may need to change the lighting fixture. For example, a well light may be fine under small plantings, but as they grow, an out-of-ground mounted fixture may be more suitable. The beauty of low-voltage lights is that such changes are easy to make.
- Think about the changes that the seasons bring. In summer, you may prefer to illuminate a Japanese maple with a light fixture located away from the tree, shining the light on its canopy. In winter, you may want to move the fixture under the plant to accent the bare, twisted branches. Perennials that may block fixtures in summer die back in winter, making it necessary to adjust the location of fixtures from season to season. Leave enough length of wire to accommodate these seasonal changes in fixture location.

are generally pleased to show them off. They can always say no. Finally, ask about follow-up maintenance and even finessing the design. Many designers want to come back once or twice after the lights are installed to make sure everything works as it should.

CHAPTER SEVEN

WATERFALLS AND
FOUNTAINS

Water in motion has an indisputable allure. The splashing, gurgling sound is a balm to the spirits, and watching water, whether it bubbles up in a mass, spills and spreads evenly over objects in its way, or sprays into millions of fine, light-catching particles, can happily occupy people for hours. Once you have a swimming pool, adding a watery accessory, be it a fountain, water slide, waterfall, or combination of them all, is a natural direction in which to go. Water features add drama and beauty to a pool design, and they mask intrusive noise from nearby traffic or neighbors. In addition, a water slide or a waterfall you can swim through enhances the play value of a pool. There are numerous ways to add water features to a swimming pool. Whatever approach you take, make sure the design is in harmony with the overall style of your house and the rest of the pool setting.

Waterfalls

Waterfalls are a natural adjunct to swimming pools, not only because they add to the watery theme of the setting, but also because, in most cases, they can be attached to the existing pool circulation system. From the completely natural to totally stylized, waterfalls come in all sorts of guises, with a wide range of styles and effects you can achieve. For example, when water spills over a smooth surface, it makes an uninterrupted, glistening ribbon. Put an obstacle in its path, and the ribbon is divided into sections. If water drops onto a hard surface from a great height, it will splash into tiny droplets of mist that will catch the sun to form rainbows. For a "falling cloth" waterfall, run a large volume of water over a high ledge so it spreads out like a curtain. It is very special to be able to walk behind these sheets of water and to look back at the world through the watery screen while keeping relatively dry in the cool recesses.

In Asian landscape design, a delicate, slender stream of falling water is known by the poetic name "silver thread." Some designers who specialize in water features that evoke the Far East are masters at directing the course of water so that every part of its journey is an intended, studied picture. Sound is also orchestrated by guiding the water to ripple over pebbles, crash from a great height, or move slowly around obstacles, such as rocks and logs.

Of course, you can combine different effects. An upper fall might split into two where a rock blocks its path or gush between narrow boulders as a white, frothy spume, while a lower fall might glide over a smooth edge in a clear sheet of water. The common denominator for all waterfalls is a change in level, so the water has a place from which to fall.

Properties with a swimming pool at the bottom of a slope have a ready-made opportunity for a waterfall, but there are also ways to create a waterfall on a level lot. Often a spa is built on a level above a swimming pool, so you could install a spillway or waterfall to drop from the spa and circulate warm water into the larger pool. You also can create a natural-looking waterfall by building up an area with soil to make a berm. If your waterfall will be constructed at the same time as your pool, you can use earth excavated from the pool site. Any stones unearthed from the site are ideal to use for the water feature, as they are native to the region and will give the landscape a sense of locality.

It's not easy to replicate nature so that it looks unstudied and spontaneous. A lot of thought and planning goes into designing a mountain-style waterfall that looks completely at home in its setting. Marjorie Casey of La Jolla, California, knew exactly how she wanted her proposed tropical mountain stream to tumble over stones and into the swimming pool, but she needed a way to convey that vision to the builders. She made small stones out of clay and created a model of the waterfall she envisioned. When the model looked exactly as she wanted, the builders located the right stones and constructed the actual waterfall. As Casey planned, the water bubbles out the top, settles in eddies and small ponds, then spills over and around rocks to the next level. Plants tucked among the stones and overhanging the falls add to the illusion of a tropical mountain setting.

Skip Phillips, of Questar Pools and Spas, Inc., took a radically different approach to a waterfall for a swimming pool in La Jolla, California.

Phillips conceived a "rainfall" waterfall. The feature is a monumental vertical rectangle along the far side of the pool. Individual drops of water stream down the face of the box, looking and sounding like a heavy downpour. At night, underwater spotlights fitted with rotating colored filters shine up at the falls, catching the drops and turning them alternately pink, blue, and white.

The bold, geometric design of the rainfall waterfall complements the rest of the poolscape, which comprises a series of repeated geometric forms. The rectangle of the vertical waterfall echoes the proportions of the rectangular pool and spa. Six large, square stepping-stones appear to float in front of the waterfall and match a set of

"The thing that thrills me about the waterfall is that even though we didn't know anything about constructing it, it turned out so well. Everyone told us we were out of our minds because waterfalls can be so tricky, but we haven't had any problems. It's worked perfectly from the first day."

Marjorie Casey, La Jolla, California

stepping-stones in the lawn on the opposite side of the pool. Nearby, a raised bed planted with giant bird of paradise (*Strelitzia nicolai*) repeats the square motif.

In addition to being a striking element and an important focal point in the overall poolscape design, the rainfall waterfall serves a practical function. It screens much of the view from the neighbor's house, distracts from the close presence of the boundary fence, and creates white noise that blocks sound coming from both sides. It is a brilliant, harmonious blend of design and function.

Another example of an innovative, contemporary waterfall was designed by Arabella Lennox-Boyd. She created a garden featuring a series of three waterfalls spilling down a wide flight of concrete stairs. A modern metal sculpture at the rear of the garden is the source of the sleek-looking waterfall; the water then flows through a narrow channel between perennial beds, spreads out into a rectangular holding pool, then spills by steps into a water lily pond. Instead of a pond, the stepped waterfall could just as well have flowed into a swimming pool.

The narrow channel in Lennox-Boyd's design is evocative of the waterways created by the ancient Moors who conquered Spain in the eighth century. At the famous Alhambra Palace in Granada, Spain, visitors can see beautiful courtyards and gardens that feature Moorish fountains and ponds. Particularly characteristic are the long, narrow runnels that look as streamlined and up-to-date today as they did when they were built between 1248 and 1354. If you have a patio at a higher level than the swimming pool, consider building a narrow, Moorish waterway running perpendicular to the pool, with a waterfall at the end spilling into the pool below.

Some pool owners prefer to build a waterfall that looks more like a natural setting, with water tumbling and bouncing down a rock face to a swimming pool below. The rocks lining the waterfall can be excavated from the property when the pool is built, providing a native feel. If the stones for the waterfall are uneven, with some protruding more than others, the water will bounce from stone to stone and be churned into frothy white foam.

Another great waterfall design features a stone lintel strategically placed above a swimming pool. When water rushes over the lintel, it plunges in a wide, smooth sheet into the pool below. This is a perfect setting for the front of an entrance to a stone grotto with a cool, recessed cave inside.

Swimmers must pass through the curtain of water to enter the cave; from inside, they can look back at the scene through the watery film. Needless to say, some of these projects require a generous budget, but homeowners with more modest means can take these ideas from well-known designers and implement them on a less extravagant scale.

Building a waterfall, whether to look like part of a mountain stream or to stand out as a stylized creation, is a special skill that requires not just artistic but also technical expertise. For example, if the soil is mounded high to provide for the fall, it must be properly compacted to avoid any shifting or settling that can crack the concrete holding it together. Leaks are not uncommon, and they are often hard to find and difficult to fix. Unless you have a lot of do-it-yourself experience, particularly working with concrete, electrical equipment, and pipe fittings and routings, you may be better off turning to an expert to design and install your waterfall.

▼ **Although this modern waterfall, created by English landscape designer Arabella Lennox-Boyd, spills into a lily pond, it would work equally well with a swimming pool. Lennox-Boyd used elements of Moorish styling to create a stimulating blend of ancient and contemporary design.**

Water Slides

When I was a young girl, the apex of swimming pool design, as far as I was concerned, was a water slide. Those blue fiberglass chutes accessed from a metal ladder may not have been the most attractive items around a pool, but oh the joy of plunging full speed into the water from what was, relatively speaking, a great height.

Although those ready-made water slides are not a visual asset to a swimming pool landscape, it is undeniable that most children — and many adults — really enjoy the sensation of slip-sliding into water. Of course, there are other ways to have the pleasures of a water slide without the eyesore of a visible ladder and an ugly, eye-arresting sliding surface.

For example, the water slide at Gordon and Lisa Tudor's swimming pool in Encinitas, California, is incorporated with a waterfall into a grottolike structure. Realistic-looking man-made boulders are piled up at one end of the pool. On one side, the water tumbles over these "stones" and into the pool as a splashing waterfall. Next to the waterfall, the large "rocks" enclose the slide, which slips between a "cleft" and spills into the pool. The slide is molded and colored to blend in with the rocky setting. Behind the mounding structure of boulders and falling water are steps, also fashioned to look like stone, that lead up to the water slide. Because they live in a mild, subtropical climate, the Tudors have surrounded the pool area and the stone grotto with palm trees and other tropical plants, adding to the illusion of a South Sea paradise.

Washington, D.C., landscape architect Richard Arentz took a similar approach to a water slide he designed for a Virginia client. The slide is made of a fiberglass material that looks like stone. To further disguise it and integrate it with the rest of the pool landscape, he surrounded the slide with rocks and boulders blasted out of the bedrock on the building site. He admits that it's a challenge to make a slide fun and interesting for children as well as aesthetically pleasing for adults, but with some imagination, it can be done.

If your swimming pool is at the bottom of a steep slope, you have a golden opportunity to build a slide right into the hill. Many landscape architects, however, are reluctant to design water slides down a hillside into a pool because of the high risk of failure. Unless the structure is very stable and the plaster is handled just right when it is laid, the slide is likely to crack. This type of construction requires careful engineering and experienced workers. "The secret," said Ned Bosworth, a California-based landscape architect who successfully designed a water slide built into the steep hillside of a client's home, "is over-engineering." The slide he designed is laid on highly compacted soil. Built of concrete with plenty of steel reinforcement to prevent differential movement, it has a steel-trowel plaster finish and is sealed with concrete wax.

Working with the plaster is a tricky job. "It can graze [get cracks] if it is over-troweled, or if it is done on too hot a day," said Bosworth. "A cool day is crucial. You also must have experienced workers who can finish fast, or the over-worked plaster will get hairline fractures." Because of the technical challenge of putting a water slide on a slope, many designers build a simple concrete chute instead. Some are blended into the setting

with careful landscaping and colored-plaster finishes that are less stark than pure white.

Another idea is to swath the chute in tile. Using a pleasing blend of colors and an interesting pattern can give it a sense of bright, unadulterated energy. The slide then becomes like a magic carpet, there to transport you to a world of pure fun; it is a work of art, meant to be celebrated rather than disguised.

Whatever approach you take in creating a water slide to enhance your swimming pool fun, make sure the water is deep enough where people

"When I slip down the water slide, I feel like I'm being shot out of an elephant's trunk."

Reid Tudor, age 10, Encinitas, California

shoot off the slide into the pool. Check with a pool builder for recommended depths, which may vary depending on how long and steep the slide is (people will be propelled down faster on a steep, extended incline).

Fountains

Swimming pools and fountains are a natural combination. You already have pumps and access to electricity for the pool equipment, so adding a fountain is relatively easy. Just as important, the play of water on water is endlessly fascinating, and the sound of falling water is a delight.

The four main possibilities for fountains with swimming pools are fixtures that sit on the pool's edge and spout into the pool, wall fountains that spill either into the pool or into a separate basin, fountain heads mounted inside the pool, and self-contained fountains placed near the pool.

POOLSIDE SCULPTURES

The possibilities for sculptures that spout water are as endless as the human artistic imagination. In addition to custom-made sculptures created by fine artists, there is a wealth of commercially made fountain sculptures available through garden centers, mail-order catalogs, and the Internet.

When selecting one for your pool landscape, keep in mind the style of your house, garden, and pool. You want the fountain to complement the other elements in your design, not stick out like a turnip in a floral bouquet. Also consider scale. A tiny fountain in a large setting runs the risk of looking dwarfed and silly. By the same token, a monumental piece squeezed into a tiny pool area may be overbearingly dominant.

WALL FOUNTAINS

Fountains that mount on an outdoor wall are a great way to decorate an expanse of blank space. If the swimming pool is right up against the wall, the fountain can spout directly into the pool. If the pool is too far away, create a series of water

▼ Placed at the center far end of a pool in a flower bed planted with roses, pentas, and pin cushion flowers, this freestanding, two-tiered fountain, bottom left, is a beautiful focal point. A mounted fountain, bottom right, dresses up a niche in the wall backing this Washington, D.C., lap pool. The fountain spouts into a tiny pond filled with water plants.

basins, starting with a tall one set against the wall, then stair-step the basins until the last one is adjacent to the pool. Each basin should have a spillway dropping into the next lower reservoir so the water moves toward the pool and eventually spills into it. Depending on the style of your swimming pool and the hardscaping materials you have nearby, you can face the raised basins with tile, stone, brick, stucco, or a combination of materials.

Another idea is to build a wall fountain that, instead of spouting into the pool, feeds a tiny pond built in the space between the pool and the wall. A couple of bog plants and dwarf water lotus can accent the water feature and create a naturalistic setting.

Although fish and swimming pools do not mix (you wouldn't want fish waste in your swimming water, and chlorine kills fish), you can have a separate fishpond or a lily pond near the pool and install a fountain in that. Bear in mind that water lilies do not thrive when the water is constantly disturbed. If you combine a fountain and water lilies, plant the water lilies as far as possible from the fountain.

IN THE POOL

The main problem with fountain heads mounted in the pool is that they stick out, thus causing a hazard to swimmers. Fortunately, there are several ways to enjoy in-pool fountains while avoiding their potential to cause accidents.

For example, J. Liddon Pennock got around the problem by placing fountain heads in the pool's corners, where they are much less likely to be a hazard. When the fountains are turned on, his classically styled swimming pool in Meadowbrook, Pennsylvania, looks like a beautiful, decorative

▲ **With different fountain heads you can create a wide variety of spray patterns. In addition to the ones shown here, other possibilities include single jets of water shooting straight up, mushroomlike bubbles, and fluted columns.**

◄ **A recessed fountain head sprays an arc of water into the pool from outside without creating a toe-stubbing hazard.**

ton and the spray nozzles will rise up, ready to run. When people are in the pool and the nozzles could be hazardous, the push of a button makes them retract out of sight.

With the easy availability of relatively inexpensive computer chips that control sophisticated electronic equipment, it's possible for a homeowner to have a full-fledged water show in the swimming pool by installing a series of fountains and colored lights programmed to turn on and off as a choreographed dance to music. Combine different spray patterns for interesting effects. For example, a rotating fishtail fountain can sway in time to a Hawaiian hula, then a series of geysers can stand at attention during a military march. When the show is over, push the button that retracts the fountain heads so the pool will once again be ready to receive swimmers.

SELF-CONTAINED FOUNTAINS

A lovely accessory for any pool is a self-contained fountain, such as a tiered fountain that circulates water from a small upper basin into lower basins of increasing size. A tall fountain adds a pleasing vertical element in a setting dominated by horizontal lines. There are also a host of commercially made, self-contained fountains available. Visit local nurseries and page through mail-order catalogs to find one that suits your taste, budget, and style.

Another possibility is to make your own fountain. Two easy, do-it-yourself projects that are relatively inexpensive are a pot fountain, where water bubbles or sprays out of a large pot or urn, then falls back inside to be recirculated, and an in-ground cobblestone fountain, which can be built into the paving around the pool or set in a nearby garden bed or lawn. A pot fountain is easy to assemble with a water-pump kit and decorative accessories sold at garden and craft supply stores.

▲ **This self-contained pot fountain is fed by a reservoir buried in the ground. A tiny submersible pump inside the container circulates the water.**

▶ **An in-ground cobblestone fountain is easy and inexpensive to build. Place one in a lawn, as shown here, or incorporate it into your pool decking.**

pond, with water arching in graceful curves from the corners to the center. Traditional urns set on tall, fluted pillars stand on the decking at each corner of the pool and add to the ambience of this classic water feature.

Similarly, many swimming pools have small alcoves that add interest to a pool's design but are placed where swimmers are less likely to go because of the small space. Such alcoves are a safe location for a pretty fountain. For added security, add a barrier, such as a pool rope or a built-in wall, to discourage swimmers from entering that area. A high-tech approach is to install retractable fixtures. When you are entertaining poolside and want the sound of water music, you can simply push a but-

CHAPTER EIGHT

STRUCTURES AND FURNITURE

Architectural elements in a poolscape contribute enormously to creating a unique style that sets apart your design. In addition to being decorative and establishing the tone for the area, structures such as a pool house, cabana, gazebo, arbor, and pergola are practical. Pool houses provide the luxury of extra storage space for pool toys and equipment as well as a changing area and perhaps a bathroom and shower. Cabanas, gazebos, arbors, and pergolas are delightful garden focal points and shady retreats from the hot sun. Bridges are another architectural feature that can visually enhance the pool setting. Poolside furniture also is very important, both for comfort and to add to the look of the space. They serve practical functions as well — for lounging, dining, entertaining and more. Sculptures — from the classical to the whimsical — add character and beauty to any outdoor setting.

Poolside Structures

or many homeowners, the cost of putting in a pool eats up the budget, with nothing left over for other landscape structures. That's all right; it's not necessary to have everything at once. If you plan ahead for features you'd eventually like to have, however, you can add them as your budget allows.

POOL HOUSES AND CABANAS

Any pool owner who has had to cope with people in dripping bathing suits traipsing through the house to change, then had to pick up wet towels and suits left carelessly on carpets and wooden floors, can appreciate the benefit of a pool house or cabana.

A dream pool house would be one with wet bar and kitchen facilities for poolside drinks and dining; a recreation room (maybe even a room for fitness equipment); and storage space for pool toys, equipment, furniture, and cushions that you may want to bring indoors during inclement weather.

Of course, most people cannot afford their dream pool house, but there are compromises you can make to have at least some of the benefits of one. An inexpensive way of making storage space is to install a premade garden shed. Available at home improvement stores, large nurseries, and discount warehouses, premade sheds come in a wide range of styles and sizes. If there isn't one that suits your style, choose one that comes close, then modify it.

You can dress up a basic shed by putting shutters on the windows. If there isn't already a window, mount a mirror on the outside wall and put shutters on each side to frame it. A piece of screening over the mirror will reduce glare and create a more natural look. Add to the illusion by gluing strips of wood on the glass to represent the mullions dividing the panes. Attach a window box underneath the "window" and fill it with perpetually flowering tender perennials, such as scaevola, pelargoniums, and trailing petunias. This trompe l'oeil (fool-the-eye) "window" will reflect the surrounding scene, particularly the flowers in the window box, doubling the floral display. For extra pizzazz, paint the shutters, window box, and mullions a color that ties in with the flowers, or pick up a color from the cushions on the pool furniture or from some other feature in the area.

◄ **This arched wooden arbor is a shady shelter for sitting and dining near the pool and a striking focal point.**

▼ **With its shingled roof, rough clapboard sides, scalloped eaves, and arched doorway, this poolside storage hut is an attractive feature as well as very useful.**

Hiding Pool Equipment

The last thing you want spoiling your pool setting is a view of all the pumps and other machinery that make it work. If you don't have a storage room or pool house where they can be installed, then choose an out-of-the-way spot for the equipment and screen it with a small fence or some shrubbery. If there is a slope behind the pool, terrace out a level spot and put the equipment there so it will be out of sight. Be sure to leave access to the equipment for regular maintenance.

▶ **Lattice walls painted to match the shingle roof, and sheer curtains matching the comfortable cushions inside, make this cabana a distinctive poolside feature.**

Another trick is to mount a trellis on the side. Select an inexpensive prefabricated one with a square or diamond pattern, or create one with a motif that enhances the style of your pool or echoes nearby garden accents. Paint the trellis so it stands out as a feature against the wooden shed, then grow vines on it. If the shed is surrounded by paving, place containers next to the walls and

grow the vines — as well as trailing and upright plants — in the pots.

If a garage is adjacent to the swimming pool, you have a ready-made structure that can be converted into a pool house. With luck, your garage will be a generous one with extra space not needed for cars. Section off that spare space with framing and drywall, add a door that opens onto the pool area, and *voilà* — you have a pool house. You may want to dress up the wall facing the pool by adding architectural details to make it a special asset to the scene.

Cabanas can be a feature of their own or incorporated into a pool house design. Derived from the Spanish word for *hut*, a cabana is typically defined as a lightweight, three-sided structure with the open side facing the sea or swimming pool. It is a sheltered place to sit, and because it has a weatherproof roof, it is useful for storing furniture or cushions made of materials that are not resistant to the elements.

GAZEBOS

The term *gazebo* was created by combining the words *gaze* and *about*. The name describes its function: A gazebo is a structure designed as a sheltered place to sit and gaze about the garden. For centuries, garden owners have wanted to do just that. Based on ancient paintings, it is believed that the first gazebos date back 5,000 years to the ancient Egyptians, who built them in their royal gardens. They were placed at the intersection of waterways or under shady trees and valued as a quiet, beautiful place to mediate.

In fifteenth-century England, when the most up-to-date gardens were designed with intricate parterre patterns, wealthy landowners built gazebos on top of walls. From the high vantage point, they could get a clear view of the ingeniously planted designs.

Once the colonies in North America started to prosper in the early 1700s, a few landed gentlemen adopted the idea of gazebos as shelter from the hot summer sun. By the end of that century, they were common features on the estates of well-to-do Americans. Perhaps best known today is Thomas Jefferson's summerhouse perched on the south-facing edge of his terraced vegetable garden. Just large enough for two chairs, it had a commanding view of his 1,000-foot-long vegetable plot as well as a panoramic view of the tree-covered mountains around his property. The windows were paned so Jefferson could sit in comfort year-round to supervise the cultivation of his garden and enjoy what one contemporary visitor referred to as his "sea view."

Whether perched overlooking the pool or placed near the water, a gazebo is a great structure for a pool area, providing shelter from the sun and a vantage point from which to enjoy the scene. Make your gazebo a comfortable place so people will want to use it. If flying, biting insects are a nuisance, consider installing screens to keep them out. Put comfortable chairs inside and, if there's room, a table.

Gazebos are available in a wide range of prices, styles, and sizes. Less-expensive models are offered in season at many discount warehouse stores; at the other end of the spectrum are companies that specialize in finely crafted and custom-designed structures. Most gazebos are built with Victorian architectural flourishes, but there is no reason that the style of the structure can't be classic, art nouveau, Mission, Oriental, or any other historical period or national style that suits your pool and garden design. A gazebo, which at first might seem like an extravagant splurge, may well become your favorite poolside place for enjoying drinks and meals al fresco — or for just gazing about.

ARBORS AND PERGOLAS

Much pleasure in life comes from contrast. It's lovely to bask in the sun, but it's also pleasant to have a shady retreat from the heat and glare of midday. Arbors and pergolas are ideal for providing sheltered, filtered shade. In an environment that tends to be dominantly horizontal, arbors and pergolas also provide some architectural interest and a break from the monotony of level space, adding a third dimension to the garden prospect.

Often referred to by the more prosaic name "covered patio," an arbor is an open structure with posts supporting an open beam or lattice roof. The posts can be made of stone, wood, brick, metal (most likely iron or aluminum), or even living tree trunks. In the case of a living arbor, the tree branches are woven together to form the ceiling. This training technique, called pleaching, is done by bending and tying young branches into the desired pattern or form. In the case of a wood or metal arbor, the roof can consist of decorative beams evenly spaced across the structure or, for more shade, a lath or trelliswork covering. An arbor is frequently attached to the house, with the house wall serving as a backdrop to the three open sides.

A pergola is generally a tunnel-like walkway or seating area, with columns or posts supporting an open roof of beams or trelliswork. Also known as a colonnade, gallery, piazza, or portico, a pergola — by any name, and in any language — is a charming addition to a poolside design.

Just because a pool area is small doesn't necessarily mean there isn't room for a pergola. In many cases, it is simply a matter of placement and proportion. In a small pool area, consider putting a pergola along one edge of the property. In addition to creating an interesting architectural structure and providing a pleasant, shady place to sit, the semi-covered roof will give you some privacy.

◄ **Encircled by salmon-colored impatiens growing on top of a stone retaining wall and furnished with a large round table and comfortable wooden chairs, this arbor is a favorite place to dine.**

In terms of proportion, a pergola generally should be somewhat higher than it is wide, although there are exceptions. In a very large space you may opt for a pergola that's 8 feet tall and 15 feet wide. A medium-sized pergola might be 7½ feet tall and wide. For comfort, the minimum height should be about 7½ feet, tall enough for an adult to walk underneath without feeling cramped. If you want to sit under it, allow enough width for chairs and a small side table.

The uprights and beams that form the roof should also be in scale with the overall size of the pergola. If the supports are hefty, the overhead beams should be substantial. How far apart you space the roof beams depends on the effect you want. Wide spacing creates a skylight effect, with less support for a dense covering of plants and less shade underneath. Close spacing makes the pergola more tunnel-like.

Supporting columns can be made from tree trunks with the bark left on, stone, concrete, brick, wood, iron, or aluminum. Depending on the material and how it is used, a pergola may be formal or informal, contemporary or rustic. Whatever the style, make sure the roof and columns are sturdy enough to support the weight of heavy vines if you choose to go that route. A pergola that isn't clothed in climbing plants has a spare, clean look.

Because arbors and pergolas are structures, it is important that their style blend with and complement the other architectural elements on your property. If the swimming pool is close to the house, you probably want to reflect the house's architecture in an arbor's or pergola's design. For a traditional-style house, you may want to support the structure with classical columns made of concrete, fiberglass, or stone. To complement a brick house, support an arbor or pergola with brick posts; for a stone house, use stone pillars. Cast-iron or aluminum posts can be used to echo a property's wrought-iron features, such as a balcony railing and gates. If your pool is removed from the house — for example, in the middle of a meadow or in a clearing in the woods — a rustic structure would be in keeping with the setting. Don't forget, however, that the pool itself makes a dominant architectural statement. If the shape of the pool and the materials around it convey a formal sense, the arbor or pergola should reflect that formality as well.

Finally, remember that arbors and pergolas covered in vines must bear a lot of weight. The upright posts should be strong and properly rooted in a solid foundation, and the roof structure should be well constructed.

▶ **In a predominantly horizontal landscape of water and lawn, this pergola adds welcome vertical interest and a delightful, sheltered spot to sit near the swimming pool.**

▼ **Painted to match the foliage near the swimming pool, this pergola is connected to the house but stands out as an interesting contrasting element.**

Vines to Train on Arbors and Pergolas

The vines listed here will also grow on fences and trellises, softening the bareness of those structures with living greenery.

Actinidia deliciosa (kiwi or Chinese gooseberry vine); creamy white flowers in May; Zones 7–9

Antigonon leptopus (coral vine); likes heat; masses of tiny, rose-pink flowers from midsummer to fall; Zones 9–11

Aristolochia elegans (calico flower); needs rich soil, moisture, and partial shade; frost-free

Beaumontia grandiflora (Easter lily vine); fragrant, white, funnel-shaped flowers 4 inches across from April until September; frost-tender

Bignonia capreolata (cross vine); clusters of 2-inch-long tubular, funnel-shaped, orange flowers in early summer; Zones 6–10

Bougainvillea cultivars; papery pink, crimson, coral, and white flowers; Zones 9–11

Campsis radicans (trumpet creeper); bright orange or yellow trumpetlike flowers from July through September; Zones 5–9

Clematis spp.; combine species for bloom from spring through autumn; Zones vary with species

Clytostoma callistegioides (violet trumpet vine); violet, lavender, or pale purple trumpet-shaped flowers from late spring through fall; frost-tender

Distictis buccinatoria (red trumpet vine); copious clusters of funnel-shaped blossoms that open orange- red with yellow throats from mid-spring through summer; Zones 10–11

Distictis 'Rivers' (royal trumpet vine); 4- to 5-inch-diameter purple trumpet-shaped flowers with yellow throats; Zones 10–11

Gelsemium sempervirens (Carolina jessamine); fragrant, tubular yellow flowers in late winter and early spring; Zones 7–9. 'Plena' is a double-flowered form.

Hardenbergia comptoniana (lilac vine); clusters of violet-blue, pealike flowers cascade in late winter and spring; frost-tender

Hibbertia scandens (Guinea gold vine); bright yellow flowers start in May and continue until October; frost-tender

Humulus lupulus 'Aureus' (golden hops); beautiful, golden, lobed leaves; Zones 4–8

Hydrangea petiolaris (climbing hydrangea); large, lace-cap-type heads of white flowers in early summer; Zones 5–9

Jasminum polyanthum (jasmine); clusters of fragrant white flowers tinged inside with rose; February to July; Zones 9–10

Lonicera spp. (honeysuckle); sweetly scented tubular or bell-shaped flowers; Zones vary with species, generally 5–9

Macfadyena unguis-cati (cat's-claw vine); yellow, trumpet-shaped flowers in early spring; frost-tender

Mandevilla x amabilis 'Alice du Pont'; pink flowers; April to November; frost-free

Passiflora caerulea (passionflower); flowers up to 4 inches across in a mixture of blue, purple, and white; June to September; Zones 7–10

Podranea ricasoliana (Port St. Johns creeper); clusters of pink trumpet-shaped flowers with crimson stripes in summer; likes heat; frost-tender

Rosa cultivars (climbing rose)
  'Alberic Barbier'; Zones 5–10
  'Albertine'; Zones 5–10
  'American Pillar'; Zones 5–10
  R. banksiae (banksian rose); Zones 7–10
  'Blaze'; Zones 5–10
  'Cécile Brunner' (climbing form); Zones 5–10
  'Felicite Perpetue'; Zones 6–10
  R. filipes 'Kiftsgate'; Zones 6–10

  'New Dawn'; Zones 5–10
  'Seagull'; Zones 5–10
  'Veilchenblau'; Zones 5–10

Solandra maxima (cup of gold); golden yellow, bowl-shaped flowers with brownish purple stripes; frost-tender

Solanum crispum (Chilean potato vine); clusters of star-shaped, fragrant blue flowers with yellow centers; Zones 9–10

S. jasminoides (potato vine); clusters of small, pure white flowers; blooms year-round but most heavily in spring; Zones 8–10

Stephanotis floribunda (Madagascar jasmine); very fragrant, white, waxy tubular flower clusters in late summer; frost-free

Stigmaphyllon ciliatum (orchid vine, golden vine); lemon yellow flower clusters from July to September; frost-free

Tecomaria capensis (cape honeysuckle); clusters of bright, orange-red, tubular flowers October through winter; Zones 10–11

Thunbergia gregorii (orange clock vine); bright orange, tubular flowers year-round in warm areas, in summer where winters are cool; frost-free

Trachelospermum jasminoides (star jasmine); fragrant, white, starlike flowers in spring and summer; Zones 9–10

Tropaeolum peregrinum (canary bird vine); 1-inch-long lemon-yellow flowers from July through September; Zones 9–10

Wisteria floribunda (Japanese wisteria); large flower panicles open slowly from top to bottom; less dramatic than Chinese wisteria display but longer lasting; Zones 4–10

W. sinensis (Chinese wisteria); blooms all at once on bare wood; Zones 4–10

BRIDGES

A bridge can serve many functions in a pool and garden design. Most obvious is a pathway over water, but a bridge also can cross a dry, gravel stream in a Japanese garden or span a chasm or drainage swale. Bridges mark transitions, whether from one side of a body of water to the other or from one part of the garden to another.

A bridge that arches over water is a major focal point. When you're on a bridge, especially over water, you get a new perspective on the view. When the angle of light is right, the bridge's reflection in the water is another pleasing aspect. Swimming under a bridge is yet another experience, and it opens up possibilities for all sorts of variations on pool games such as Marco Polo and trolls under the bridge.

Such a bridge can take many forms and shapes. Most distinctive are the highly arched "moon" bridges associated with Japanese gardens. Designed so that the bridge plus its reflection in the water creates a complete circle, moon bridges symbolize the full moon and a state of perfection. Western-style bridges tend to have a less extreme arch but are still quite attractive. At the other extreme in Japanese gardens are flat bridges made from wood or huge slabs of granite or other stone. Depending on the width of the water these bridges cross, they may arrive at the opposite side in a straight, unbroken span or zigzag across in spliced-together sections. Zigzag bridges are often features of Zen gardens and are designed to foil evil spirits that may want to cross the water.

Whether Oriental or Occidental in style, bridges come in many styles, ranging from formal and elegant to informal and rustic, perhaps built from unmilled logs. In any case, the individuality of a bridge is often expressed in an unusual design for the railings or banisters. When you look at designs for railings and finials, keep in mind the style of your house and the features in your garden. You'll want the bridge to be in harmony with other elements.

In addition to its design, a wooden bridge adds an individual touch to your pool setting if you paint it a distinctive color. This is an opportunity to try out a color you might be uncomfortable using indoors. If you're feeling less adventurous, a safe bet is to match the bridge to the trim color of your house, thus linking the two architectural features. Claude Monet used this device in his famous garden in Giverny, France. He painted his garden benches and the bridge that spans his water lily

▼ **This unadorned glass bridge designed by Ron Gibbons for the "starry night" pool (see page 121) echoes the straight, clean lines of the house. It links the Misty Rose stone paving near the house with the teak decks on the opposite side.**

Sculptures

Sculptures and gardens go together like soup and sandwiches. The famous California-based landscape architect Thomas Church endorsed this view, writing, "After greenery, nothing, I believe, enhances a garden more than sculpture." Indeed, around a pool, a sculpture or two can add greatly to the scene, providing a focal point, adding a touch of whimsy, or marking the division between a pool and a spa. In the horizontal environment of a swimming pool with an expanse of decking, a tall sculpture can add important vertical interest to the scene.

Sculpture also is useful to distract from a less attractive aspect of the garden. For example, if a fence or wall is a visual stopper, place a sculpture against it so the eye has somewhere pleasing to linger. The rest of the wall or fence will be much less visually important. Another great place for sculpture is in a wall niche. If you are building a pool house, think about including one or two built-in niches or shelves for displaying sculpture.

Choosing the right sculpture for the right place around a pool is key. First, the sculpture should be in scale with its surroundings. A large sculpture needs a place of importance. Use

one as a focal point at the end of the pool or to draw the eye to a dramatic view beyond. On the other hand, you don't want to plunk a small ornament by itself in the middle of a large open space. It will look dwarfed and insignificant. Adding several little pieces will only increase the sense of clutter and lack of focus. Instead, tuck a small sculpture beside a decorative stone in a flower bed, or position it so it is sheltered and highlighted by arching foliage.

There are tricks you can employ to add importance to a relatively small sculpture. Elevate a bust or small figure on a pedestal. It addition to bringing the sculpture closer to eye level, the added bulk of the plinth or pedestal makes the statue more visually dominant. The plinth does not have to be an expensive piece of carved stone or molded cement. In an informal setting, a tree stump cut well above the ground serves as a whimsical pedestal.

Creating a backdrop for a sculpture will also increase its visual importance. For example, center a sculpture on a trellis arch against a wall or fence. Add a sense of depth with trompe l'oeil perspective so the trellis appears to be part of a tunnel receding into the distance. Pale-colored or white statues look especially striking when set against a dark green background, such as a yew hedge.

Don't overlook the possibility of displaying sculpture underwater. Skip Phillips, an award-winning pool designer in Escondido, California, suggests a below-water shelf designed to accommodate sculpture. Imagine the fun of seeing, for example, various sea creatures nestled on little underwater shelves inside the pool. Another innovative idea is to install a clear acrylic stand in the pool with a platform or shelf at the exact level of the water. Because the submerged acrylic is almost invisible to the casual observer, anything placed on that platform will appear to be floating on the water's surface. Of course, this display would be best in a shallow, out-of-the-way corner of the pool, where it won't interfere with swimming and other activities.

When considering garden sculptures, don't forget the possibility of natural items that have a sculptural quality to them. A hallmark of Chinese gardens is rocks weathered into appealing abstract forms or fascinating shapes resembling animals or craggy peaks. Large seashells, such as conches and others with spiraling shapes, make pretty poolside ornaments, reinforcing the water theme of the setting, and a significant piece of driftwood, twisted and smoothed by waves and sand, can be as arresting as a finely wrought abstract sculpture.

pond a deep green to match the shutters on his house. Another idea is to paint the bridge a color that picks up the color of nearby foliage — the red of a Japanese maple or the yellow of a shrub with golden foliage, for example.

Frequently, a bridge is practical as well as ornamental. In the case where a pool is sited close to an entry door to the house, you can build a bridge across the pool. This presents an interesting design challenge, as it must be high enough to provide clearance for swimming but must not be too high. A possible solution is to depress the level of the pool by placing a few steps around its periphery, then raise the bridge over the pool by a few steps. In a situation where form follows function, the design criteria can dictate an exciting architectural feature.

Another modern approach is to build a bridge made of thick, sandblasted glass. Although a glass bridge is an innovative use of an unexpected material, its form can be highly traditional. For example, if it stretches out straight and flat over the water, it will echo the appearance of traditional Japanese stone or wooden plank bridges that span streams and creeks.

BUILT-IN BARBECUES

Although not generally a thing of beauty, a built-in barbecue is a nice asset if you plan to do a lot of poolside entertaining and dining. Built-in grills can be elaborate features, complete with under-counter storage space, a refrigerator, and even a sink, or fairly simple structures with just a grill and some counter space. Whether simple or elaborate, choose materials for the countertops and surrounding walls that complement the pavings, walls, and other features around the pool.

Choose a spot that's downwind from the pool and sitting area so smoke from the barbecue doesn't

become an irritant. Ideally, select an area that is set apart from the pool, so the barbecue is not a dominant visual feature, but not so removed that the person doing the barbecuing feels isolated from the rest of the gathering. If you have different levels around the pool, consider putting a built-in grill either a few steps up or a few steps down from the pool to increase the sense of separation.

For example, the barbecue area near Lyle Arnold's swimming pool in Poway, California, is in an alcove off to one side. The barbecue and surrounding counters are turned sideways to the pool so they cannot be seen unless you walk into the alcove. A low retaining wall opposite the barbecue completes the alcove and makes a convenient place to sit for those who want to hover around the grill with the chef while the food is cooking.

▲ **The less attractive, working side of this barbecue island is out of view from the pool area, but the person who's cooking can still feel a part of what's going on. Shrubbery screens the workspace.**

Furniture

Swimming pools are about having fun and feeling good. Whether you achieve these two goals by splashing and playing in the water or by swimming laps and doing water aerobics, the point is to set aside your cares and relax. Your poolside furniture plays a big part in how successfully these goals are achieved because after spending time in the water, you'll want somewhere to sit by the pool.

The four major considerations to keep in mind as you choose poolside furniture are comfort, style, size/quantity, and durability. Of course, cost is another factor, but once you've settled on the other issues, you can shop around, watch for sales, and negotiate with dealers until you find the price you want.

COMFORT

Like the three bears with their large, medium, and small porridge bowls, chairs, and beds, large and small people prefer furniture that is proportioned to their size. Short people settle comfortably into small-scale chairs where the seats aren't too high

▼ The color of the lounge chair cushions matches the color of the pool water, and the pattern echoes the slatted shutters and blinds. The aesthetics are pleasing and, equally important, the cushions are comfortable.

or too deep. In contrast, tall, long-legged people prefer chairs that sit higher off the ground and have a deep seat. It is a rare chair that is universally comfortable. Even the Adirondack chair, which was specifically designed with comfort in mind, is awkward for older people, who have trouble getting out of the deep, angled seats. In general, furniture with an ergonomic design accommodates issues such as the depth of the seat, the shape of the back, the angle at which the seat meets the back, and the height of the armrests.

When you purchase poolside furniture, it's important to try out different chairs to make sure you choose ones you'd like to spend long hours sitting in as you relax by the pool reading a good book, watching others play in the water, or enjoying conversation with friends. If the people in your family vary greatly in size, think about choosing matching chairs in different sizes from a line of furniture.

Cushions can add greatly to the comfort of chairs and loungers. In addition, they provide a splash of color and pattern, enlivening the space. However, not all cushions are created equal: Some are definitely more comfortable than others. Choose ones you like, but also try them out to make sure they aren't too flat or too solid with no give, or that their buttons don't dig into your skin.

STYLE

There is a vast array of outdoor furniture styles, with something to suit just about every setting. The boom in gardening has led manufacturers to develop a wide range of wooden furniture. Among the many possibilities in wooden furniture are Chinese Chippendale furniture, with fretwork backs and plain, straight legs; Adirondack chairs and benches, with deeply angled seats and wide, flat armrests; Lutyens benches, with scrolled arms

Outdoor Cushion Care

Many manufacturers make weatherproof fabrics so you can leave out cushions all season long, even in the rain. While these fabrics definitely hold up to the elements, they are not dirt-proof. It won't take long for a cushion left permanently outside to become soiled by pollen and plant debris, ambient dust in the air, and even mildew. You'll keep pillows looking new, clean, and fresh much longer if you take the trouble to stack them indoors when you're not using them. The hours you'll spend washing soiled cushions is much more than the extra time it takes to bring them inside after each use. If you don't have a pool house or another space in which to store them, put them on the floor in an out-of-the-way corner of the family room or by the door nearest the swimming pool.

Eventually, even cushions kept indoors most of the time will need washing. When that time comes, scrub them with a solution of mild detergent and water. If the cushions are small, they may fit in your washing machine. For larger ones, either wash them in the bathtub or outside with a hose, a scrub brush, and a bowl of soapy water. Rinse the cushions thoroughly, then set them on their sides to air-dry.

If you can't bring yourself (and your family) to tote cushions indoors and out, then at least set them on their sides, off the furniture, to dry after a rain. The quicker they dry, the less likely they will mildew. It is particularly important to take wet cushions off steel and wrought-iron furniture, both of which are prone to rust.

▲ Clean, simple lines and color that tones with the paving and stucco walls harmonize these metal tubular chairs and glass-topped table with their surroundings.

▶ With their gently angled seats; tall, fanned backs; and armrests wide enough to hold a cool drink and a good book, Adirondack chairs are designed with comfort in mind.

and a sinuous back design that rises to a peaked curve in the center; Giverny benches modeled after those Claude Monet designed for his garden; Mission-style chairs and tables, with clean, vertical lines; and Gothic-style furniture, with pointed arches set into the back.

Cast-iron furniture was a by-product of the industrial revolution, which opened up a whole new world of innovative technology and building materials. As a result, much of cast-iron furniture — and its modern, cast-aluminum counterpart — has

Victorian styling with intricate patterns. Designers have also begun developing contemporary styles and patterns for cast-aluminum chairs and tables.

Tubular furniture is generally very modern-looking, and there are a number of styles with various nuances that can set a definite tone to your poolside decor. Some chairs are designed in a sling style; others are meant to be used with cushions. No matter what style you prefer, look through catalogs and visit large outdoor furniture stores to see the vast array of designs, materials, and prices available.

SIZE AND QUANTITY

When picking out poolside furniture, keep in mind the amount of space you have and how cluttered — or uncluttered — you want the area to be. While it's useful to have plenty of lounge chairs so everyone can stretch out in comfort, too many may become a nuisance, creating tripping hazards or blocking thoroughfares around the pool.

Some garden furniture is quite bulky. An Adirondack chair takes up more space than does a conventional seat; substantial wooden chairs are bigger than compact metal-framed ones. In a pool setting with great expanses of decking, large, heavy wooden furniture will be in scale with the surroundings, while lots of small chairs and tables will look busy and cluttered. For a compact pool area, one or two large chairs may overwhelm the space. In that case, you're better off choosing small-scale pieces.

You may find it useful, particularly if the area around the pool is tight, to make a scale drawing of the space on graph paper. Cut out rectangles and circles representing tables and chairs that are sized to the same scale as your pool drawing. Using these bits of paper to represent furniture, you can experiment with various arrangements and combinations of tables and chairs without having to lift and carry bulky, heavy pieces. It also means you can work out how much furniture it makes sense to have in your particular setting. When you calculate the space for dining tables and chairs, don't forget to allow room behind the chairs so people can pull them away from the table to get in and out.

To find out the measurements of various chairs and tables, look through catalogs featuring outdoor furniture and note the dimensions of the pieces you like, or visit a shop that stocks garden furniture and take measurements. Some stores will let you take pieces home to try them out in the actual setting before you commit to buying them.

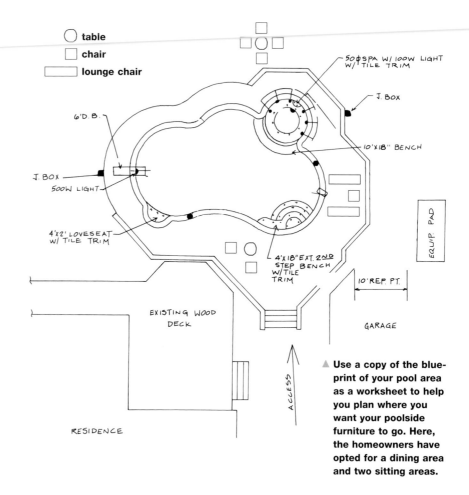

▲ **Use a copy of the blueprint of your pool area as a worksheet to help you plan where you want your poolside furniture to go. Here, the homeowners have opted for a dining area and two sitting areas.**

DURABILITY

In the world of furniture, you can find anything from cheaply made pieces in just about any of the mainstream styles to very expensive, handcrafted items. In some cases, such as the molded plastic chairs that cost just a few dollars each and last for years, you are getting good value — if not a thing of beauty — for your money. However, cheap pieces generally wear out more quickly than well-made ones do.

Depending on the materials used, the qualities to look for vary. For example, better-made tubular-aluminum furniture has extra reinforcements and a durable, baked-on, powder-coated finish. Wooden furniture put together with mortise-and-tenon joints tends to last longer than those screwed or bolted together. More expensive wrought-iron furniture comes with several coats of polyurethane paint of the type used on airplanes and yachts, as well as a hot-dipped, rust-inhibiting undercoating. Cheaper models are often merely painted.

The tempered-glass tops found on many tables are remarkably durable; however, they are still breakable. If strong winds that can blow over a fairly lightweight table are typical in your area, you would be wise to choose a design that does not feature glass. The replacement costs for a broken glass tabletop are extremely high, and normally you have to wait for one to be ordered from the manufacturer.

When buying poolside furniture, look for fine craftsmanship and good-quality materials. Also ask about guarantees. Many of the top garden furniture manufacturers offer a lifetime guarantee — a sure sign that they have confidence in the workmanship and durability of their products. Of course, if your budget is tight, you may have to make do with less expensive, less durable furniture. When your budget allows, you can replace the furniture with better-made models.

▲ With comfortably wide decking at the foot of a pool, there's plenty of room for three lounge chairs without blocking space to walk.

▶ Good-quality wooden furniture generally is built with mortise-and-tenon joints, meaning a tongue or wood projection (tenon) inserted into a slot or groove (mortise).

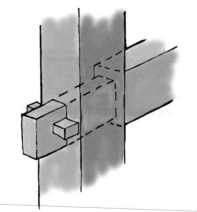

Caring for Outdoor Furniture

Your poolside furniture will look more inviting and last longer if you look after it properly and keep it clean. Here are some tips for taking care of different types of materials:

Aluminum. When dirty, wash aluminum furniture with a sponge or rag and soapy water. Do not use abrasive cleansers, such as scouring powders, or sharp-bristled brushes that can scratch the finish. If you notice nicks in the finish of cast-aluminum pieces, use a paintbrush — not an aerosol spray can — to touch them up with matching enamel paint. Repair scratches and nicks in tubular-aluminum furniture by sanding them with either wet, fine-grained steel wool or dry, fine-grained sandpaper. Once the area is smooth, apply several thin coats of matching touch-up paint. Check with a dealer or the manufacturer to find the right color. An annual coat of car wax on tubular-aluminum frames will help protect them from scratches. Do not wax textured aluminum finishes.

Plastic. When plastic gets dirty, use water and a nonscratch sponge to wash it off. If you want, you can add a mild detergent to the water, but do not scrub the furniture with abrasive soaps or powders, and do not use bleach.

Tubular steel and wrought iron. As necessary, wash wrought-iron and tubular-steel furniture with soapy water. Wrought-iron furniture is prone to rust wherever the paint wears off. Check it periodically, especially at the joints or welded areas. If you find rust, wash the spot with a household grease remover, then clean off the rust with an old toothbrush. Allow it to dry thoroughly, then apply several thin coats of rust-resistant paint. Wait for the paint to dry completely between coats. Some manufacturers recommend a coat of auto wax or spray furniture wax on wrought-iron furniture to give it an extra layer of protection. Follow the manufacturer's suggestions.

Wicker. The generic term for woven furniture, wicker is traditionally woven with natural materials, such as rattan, cane, reed, willow, raffia, and various dried grasses, all of which are unsuitable for outdoor use. However, there is now wicker made from a latex-coated fiber wrapped around stainless steel, making it possible to have beautiful woven furniture that can stand up to the rigors of life outdoors. When you purchase wicker furniture, make sure it is suitable for year-round outdoor use. As necessary, wash it with soapy water. Avoid silicone cleansers, abrasive powders, and scrub brushes that can scratch the finish. Chlorine bleach also can damage the finish.

Wood. Teak, redwood, and cedar are all rot-resistant woods that can be left in their natural state. If you want to preserve the wood's original color or want a particular finish, use a manufacturer-recommended oil or sealant, and reapply it as necessary. Do not seal wooden furniture with polyurethane. The sealed wood is likely to warp, and the finish may blister in the sun.

Over time wooden furniture may become soiled with mildew, particularly if it's kept in the shade. When that happens, scrub it with a soft-bristled brush and soapy water. If you want, you can add bleach (mix 4 parts detergent with 1 part bleach and then ¼ to ⅓ cup of that solution to 1 gallon of warm water) to kill any remaining mildew and lighten the color of the wood. For painted wooden furniture, reapply a new coat as necessary. Wash off painted wooden furniture as needed.

Furniture covers. Although furniture designed to remain outside throughout the year doesn't have to be covered, you'll minimize maintenance and cleaning tasks if you cover the pieces over the winter and any time you're not going to use the furniture for an extended period. Many manufacturers make covers specifically designed to fit their furniture, or you can buy generic covers made to fit different-sized chairs and tables.

CHAPTER NINE

SPAS AND HOT TUBS

The therapeutic benefits of warm water on tired muscles and tense minds has been recognized for centuries. The ancient Romans built state-of-the-art spas, or baths, wherever there was a natural hot spring, and they built under-floor central heating for their baths where there wasn't. The Japanese also have a centuries-long tradition of immersing themselves in tubs of hot water for health and relaxation purposes. In the 1960s, the idea caught on in Santa Barbara, California. Residents who enjoyed soaking in the nearby hot springs began adapting old wooden wine barrels into hot tubs. The enthusiasm for these makeshift hot tubs motivated manufacturers to create wooden hot tubs, and the hot-tub fad spread across the country. Today, homeowners can choose from a wide array of aboveground hot tubs, hot tubs built into decks or terraces, or in-ground spas connected to the swimming pool or set apart as a separate entity.

Materials and Features

In contrast to hot tubs, which are made of wood and are aboveground or built into decks, spas can be made of fiberglass, acrylic, thermoplastic, soft vinyl, concrete, tile, stainless steel, or other materials. They can be in-ground or aboveground, custom made or a prefabricated shell. As with swimming pools, aboveground spas are less expensive than those that are in-ground. They also can be moved to different locations as the need arises, because they are relatively light when empty and all the circulation equipment is contained under the frame.

Many people opt to have an in-ground spa included as part of their swimming pool package, built at the same time as the pool as an annex to the larger body of water. Not surprisingly, it is generally less costly to install a spa adjacent to the pool than to build one that is separate. Whether connected to the pool or not, however, in-ground spas cost approximately twice as much as aboveground ones.

The primary difference between a hot tub or spa and a swimming pool is water temperature.

Spa vs. Jacuzzi

In the same way that Kleenex is a brand name that has become synonymous in most people's mind with the generic facial tissue, and people talk about "Hoovering" when they vacuum the house, Jacuzzi is a brand name that has come to signify the spa. Technically, unless it is actually made by the Jacuzzi company, you have a spa. Another name for these therapeutic pools is a whirlpool, so called because of the bubbling air jets propelled into the water.

For swimming comfort, a pool should be maintained between 78 and 82°F. In contrast, hot tubs and spas need to be warmer. In order for the body to relax in water, the temperature needs to be between 99 and 104°F. Any cooler and you'll quickly feel chilled; any warmer can be dangerous, causing the blood pressure to rise and, in some cases, the heart to palpitate.

Most spas have two or more high-pressure water jets positioned about mid-back height around the seats. For milder bubbles throughout the water, rather than the hard pummeling provided by jets, look for models that have tiny water jets that fizz up from the bottom of the spa in addition to the major jets around the sides. Also, if you make your requests at the design stage, it is relatively inexpensive to add jets and have them located exactly where you want them. For example, Bob Spero, of Maryland Pools, Inc., in Columbia, Maryland, recalls one customer who wanted the jets to massage the calf area of his leg.

As buyers grow more demanding and sophisticated, spa manufacturers are offering a wider choice of water-jet types and locations. Among the jet types are whirlpool, synchronized massage, pressure-point therapy, and pulsating. The number of jets is less important than where they are placed. As writer Alan E. Sanderfoot put it, "One jet that provides you the lower back pain relief you are seeking is worth more than forty jets that hit you in the wrong places." Many spas include an adjustment so you can regulate the force of the air and bubbles to your needs. Before you make a purchase decision, make an appointment with the salesperson to try out various spas in your bathing suit.

In addition to testing the location and power of the water jets, think about the number of seats you want in your spa or hot tub. Will it usually be just one or two of you, or do you plan large gatherings of friends for a bubbly party? Some spas have seats set low so you are immersed to your shoulders and other seats higher up so you can cool off when you get too hot. That's a nice option. Check out how comfortable the seats are, how deep the water is, and how much room you have to stretch out and move around in the tub.

Whether in-ground or above, the medical benefits of spas and hot tubs are well substantiated. If you have an ailment, such as chronic back pain, that could justify a doctor's prescription for warm-water treatments, you can probably deduct the cost of the spa as a medical expense on your taxes. Check with your doctor and tax adviser.

SWIM SPAS

Another variation of the traditional bubbly spa is the swim spa. In addition to the water jets designed to massage the body and soothe the nerves, a swim spa has one major water jet that produces an adjustable current strong enough to swim against. With the current turned on, you can swim in one place, just as a treadmill allows you to clock miles without moving forward. Stronger swimmers, and those who want a more intense workout, can increase the water force.

Swim spas are economical on two counts: They are smaller than traditional full-size swimming pools and it costs less money to heat these smaller bodies of water to a comfortable swimming temperature. When it will be used as a traditional spa, you simply turn up the temperature.

These mini lap pools are ideal for people who want a lap pool but have too small a property. Swim spas are longer than a typical spa because

they need to be able to accommodate the length of a tall man, but they still take up significantly less space than even a small-scale swimming pool.

An example of successfully fitting a swim spa into a small space is the Krivec project in Burbank, California. With design ingenuity and the help of a crane, Larry Tison, a landscape architect in Glendale, managed to squeeze an 8- by 14-foot swim spa into a 15- by 20-foot property. Because the access to the backyard from the side of the house was only 5 feet wide, Tison used the crane to lift the prefabricated spa 128 feet up over the house. To create the illusion of space and increase the available length for the spa, Tison set the pool on a diagonal to the house and used a random flagstone pattern on the surrounding high desert flagstone. "Features placed on the diagonal throw off the eye and contribute to a sense of space," he said.

Along the back of the property, a waterfall fountain cascades over artificial river rock to create a visual and auditory treat. As space was at a

▲ **Perched several feet above the swimming pool, this in-ground spa is conveniently located near the house yet provides a comfortable vantage point from which to observe the activities below.**

▲ With its naturalistic waterfall and curving lines, the Haber's swim spa blends beautifully with the tropical land-scape — and takes up a lot less room in the garden than a regular swimming pool would.

premium, Tison used the wall of the neighbor's garage for the waterfall. "We got permission from the neighbor to put the artificial rock facia on the wall," he said. "It's great for him because we water-proofed his wall."

For the landscaping around the swim spa, Tison laced an existing Canary Island pine that was grossly overgrown, then added agapanthus, schef-flera, daylilies, azaleas, and a dwarf Japanese maple to the planters. At night, outdoor lighting accentu-ates the design features. The result of the entire

project is a clean, private, and easy-to-maintain garden and spa. As Tison put it, "I wanted to give a little serenity to my client's life."

When Joe Haber's old fiberglass spa in Del Mar, California, began to leak, he decided to replace it with a swim spa with a waterfall spilling into one end. The new freeform spa blended more naturally with the surrounding garden than the old round spa did, and without taking up as much garden space he obtained the benefits of a nearly full-size pool for his young grandchildren to play in when they visit.

Siting Spas and Hot Tubs

If a spa or hot tub will be separate from the swimming pool, consider carefully where you plan to put it. Many people prefer a private setting, such as a walled garden off the master bedroom. If you don't have a spot enclosed by a fence or wall, you can create a pleasing sense of enclosure by surrounding the spa or hot tub with shrubs or other plants. Trellises are attractive, and they provide a good way to section off a private space without erecting a solid, imposing barrier. However, a spa doesn't have to be surrounded to feel set apart and private. If it is physically removed from other activities in the garden and has even a partial screen of plants, you'll enjoy much the same psychological benefits as with one that's completely enclosed.

If your property has a view, consider positioning your spa or hot tub where you can sit cocooned in the warm water and look out over the prospect. A raised position overlooking the swimming pool is also a pleasing spot for a spa, especially

▼ **Located off the master bedroom in a walled garden, this spa is a personal, private retreat.**

if you have small children. It gives you a good view of their antics in the water, while at the same time keeping you removed from the immediacy of splashing and loud chatter. If the spa is above and near the swimming pool, you may want to install a waterfall feature where the falling water circulates from the pool back to the spa. (For more on waterfall features, see chapter 7.)

For frequent daytime use in a hot climate, think about locating a spa where it will be sheltered from direct sun. It can be overwhelmingly hot to sit in heated water under the baking sun. At night, however, an area open to the sky increases the possibilities for stargazing in the comfort of the warm, bubbly water.

Although the filtered shade from a tree may be welcome, and the moving pattern of shadows a pretty picture to look at while soaking away your cares, placing a spa under a tree may actually add to your cares. Avoid putting a spa under any tree that sheds continuously or drops fruit or berries, resin, or other debris.

In addition, consider access from the house to the spa. If you plan for nighttime use, the paths or paved areas between the house and the spa should be properly lit for safety (see chapter 6 for information on garden lighting). You probably don't want the spa to be too far from the house. On a cold night, you won't want a long, wet walk through the brisk air from the spa back indoors.

Also keep in mind that an aboveground spa or hot tub is extremely heavy when filled with water. If you plan to incorporate one into your deck, make sure the deck is structurally able to tolerate the weight. One gallon of water weighs 8 pounds. A typical portable spa holds anywhere from 100 to 500 gallons of water. Multiply those gallons by 8 and add a few people, and that's a lot of extra weight for a deck to bear. Other practical considerations include access to a dedicated electrical outlet (110 or 220 volts) and a garden hose for filling the spa.

Even when a spa will be connected to the swimming pool, you still have a choice of where to put it. Do you want it tucked in a corner or taking center stage? Working with architect Norm Applebaum, in Rancho Santa Fe, California, Linda Bateman had her spa set in a corner of the pool and raised slightly above water level. She specified that she wanted the warm water to spill over two sides of the spa so people could sit on benches in the pool below the spa and enjoy the warm water washing over their backs. As a bonus, the spa echoes the shape of the raised flower beds on the opposite side of the pool (see page 90). In contrast, Tammy Valley's spa in Olivenhain, California, is a circle set in the center of one side of her pool. From the spa she has a wonderful vista over the pool and its "vanishing edge" to the horse paddocks beyond.

▼ Linda Bateman planned her tiled spa so that people could sit on the underwater bench next to the spa and enjoy the warm water spilling over their backs.

DESIGNING AN IN-GROUND SPA

The design possibilities for an in-ground spa are as limitless as the human imagination and a budget to pay for it. Variations in style run from minimalist designs that blend with the decking to naturalistic ponds with grottoes and waterfalls, from spas that resemble Moorish reflecting pools to tiled affairs that gleam with color.

Ideally, the pool and spa design should blend with both the style of the garden and the architectural style of the house. There are exceptions to every rule, but generally a modern house demands a more streamlined design for a pool and spa; a house with a distinct international style, such as French or Spanish, should have a water feature that echoes those elements. If your pool and spa area is well removed from the house, then the connection between the two needn't be as strong, but don't forget that visual memory plays a part in our enjoyment of aesthetic things.

A good example of a spa designed to complement the architecture of the house is the one belonging to Dr. Roger Cornell of La Jolla, California. When he first purchased his Spanish-style

▲ Taking center stage at Tammy Valley's swimming pool, this spa has a view past the pool's "vanishing edge" to the horse paddocks and countryside.

▲ Although open to the rest of the garden, this spa is visually set apart by the border of gray pebbles and the tile surround. The ligularia plants in opposing corners produce bright yellow flower spikes in late summer that echo the yellow Spanish tile.

make the 6- by 8-foot rectangular shape more interesting, and matching blue tiles set into the terra-cotta paving that surrounds the spa accent the appealing shape by tracing the outline. A backdrop of arches adds drama to the setting and echoes arches that are a feature of the house and of an adjoining part of the garden.

Located conveniently near the master bedroom, the spa was originally in an area set apart from the rest of the garden by a low hedge of Yeddo hawthorn (*Rhaphiolepis umbellata* 'Minor'). (See photo on page 61.) The feeling was of a garden room, enclosed but not cut off. Recently, Cornell decided to remove the raphiolepsis hedge to create a more open space. The spa area is still visually set apart from the rest of the garden because of the terra-cotta and Spanish tiles around it, but now gray stones abut the terra-cotta paving around the spa, and bold-leaved ligularias, which are Portuguese good luck plants, mark each corner of the area. A pair of Howea palm trees stand as sentries on each side. The look is tidier and brighter.

In Bethesda, Maryland, the Walsh family wanted a swimming pool and spa that resembled a mountain pool and stream. To create the effect, designer Charlie Bowers of Garden Gate Landscaping Inc. in Bethesda, Maryland, designed two waterfalls that cascade over a natural stone spillway and into the swimming pool. The spa is set 2 feet above the pool between the two waterfalls. The water from the upper fall drops 2 feet into the spa, which looks for all the world like a natural mountain pool encircled with stone, then overflows down the next stone spillway into the swimming pool. From there it is recirculated to the upper fall. The spa is accessed from a deck off the family room of the house. Both overlook the pool, giving a delightful vantage point from which to enjoy the reflections on the deep blue water or the activities of swimmers.

house in 1980, Cornell called in landscape architect Jeff Stone to come up with a plan for the dilapidated garden. Their goal was to design a garden that blended with the old-world romance of the house, particularly the Moorish features of the architecture.

"I wanted to show how a landscape treatment can enhance the architectural features of a house," explained Stone, "while at the same time the garden can give the house more character than it had at first." The project has been a resounding success, affirmed by the American Society of Landscape Architects, who gave it the Merit Award for Design Excellence in December 1993.

Part of the design included a spa, which replaced the old redwood hot tub. In keeping with the Moorish motif, Stone created a raised, tiled spa that resembles a Spanish courtyard pool. Square notches cut out of each corner of the spa

DESIGNING AN ABOVEGROUND SPA

Although you don't have the limitless design options for an aboveground spa that a custom-made, in-ground one affords, aboveground models also offer a wide scope for various looks and treatments. Liner finishes range from a large selection of solid colors to faux granite for that mountain-pool look.

When a spa is set into a deck, the opportunity for an attractive, one-of-a-kind presentation is as varied as creative deck design. An aboveground spa also can be set into a stone terrace. Even if it isn't put into a raised structure, you can choose from a variety of cabinets or skirts that surround the spa shell to hide the plumbing and equipment. Manufacturers sell a selection of natural rot-resistant woods, such as mahogany, redwood, and cedar, as well as simulated wood made of polymers. The synthetic wood skirts are designed to pass for the real thing and do not require the periodic staining and treating needed to protect true wood. Many of the synthetic materials come with a manufacturer's warranty.

In addition to all the aesthetic design choices, you can equip an aboveground spa with all sorts of exciting, sybaritic options, such as underwater light-emitting diodes (LED), fiber-optic lighting, waterproof speakers for a CD or stereo system, a built-in television screen, cup holders, an ice bucket, and an aromatherapy system.

▼ Accessible from the deck off the house, this raised spa provided an excellent opportunity for the Walshes to incorporate waterfalls into the swimming pool design. The clever use of stone gives the effect of a rocky mountain pool.

CHAPTER TEN

FAVORITE POOLSIDE PLANTS

The plant kingdom is enormous, with hundreds of thousands of genera, species, and named hybrids that provide an overwhelming choice for poolside landscapes. No list of this scope can cover all the suitable possibilities, and of course plants that flourish in one part of the United States are unable to grow successfully in another. So don't discount a plant you like just because it's not described here. This chapter represents a selection of plants that have been useful in poolside settings and that do well in different climates of North America. Before you make your final plant choices, talk to experienced pool landscapers and experts at local garden centers to find out about plants in your region that do well near a pool. Also, visit as many pools as you can to get ideas, as well as botanic gardens and nurseries with display gardens.

The climate zones gardeners are familiar with were developed by the U.S. Department of Agriculture to rate the cold-hardiness of plants available in this country. These ratings, however, do not include a plant's tolerance to heat. To fill that information gap, the American Horticulture Society recently began a second climate rating system it calls AHS Heat Zones. The heat-zone ratings are included for the plants in this chapter whenever that information is available. See the climate zone maps on pages 196–197 to determine which heat- and cold-climate zone you live in.

Perennials

Perennials — generally flowering plants with soft stems that die down for underground dormancy each autumn and regrow each spring — are enjoying a renaissance in gardens. Every year new hybrids are introduced, and many genera that once were difficult or impossible to find are now readily available in nurseries and plant catalogs. Perennials offer a vast choice of heights and bloom times, as well as leaf and flower colors, forms, and textures. Try out different perennials in your garden — in beds or containers — and enjoy the wide diversity in this large family of plants.

Achillea spp. (yarrow)
Plant Description: The garden border yarrows (*A. filipendulina, A. millefolium,* and named hybrids such as 'Coronation Gold' and 'Moonshine') grow between 2 and 5 feet tall and sport aromatic, gray-green, toothed or finely divided foliage that has a ferny appearance. The flower heads bloom in flat-topped clusters of bold yellow and shades of pink, terra-cotta, red, and white.

Preferred Growing Conditions: Grow in full sun. They prefer poor but well-drained soil (rich soil and excess fertilization reduce growth and flower production) and thrive on little water.

Maintenance Tips: The plants form vigorous, spreading clumps. Divide every few years for best performance. They are sun-loving and drought tolerant but prone to powdery mildew if grown in moist, shady conditions. To minimize mildew problems, avoid watering late in the day and try to keep the leaves dry when watering. Cut back plants after flowering.

Zones: USDA Hardiness Zones 3–11, AHS Heat Zones 9–2

Alstroemeria spp. (alstroemeria)
Plant Description: These tuberous perennials grow to 3 feet tall and produce abundant clusters of azalea-like flowers in shades of pink, lilac, orange, yellow, white, and red. Some flowers are streaked and speckled with dark brown. In the past, alstroemerias were difficult to grow except in the Pacific Northwest, and the *A. ligtu* species would go dormant with browning leaves in the summer months. Today, new strains have been developed that are adaptable to many growing conditions, from USDA climate Zones 6 through 10, and make superb garden plants as well as an excellent source for cut flowers. One, named 'Sweet Laura' because of its spicy, carnation scent, is hardy to Zone 4.

The bloom cycle for these new alstroemerias varies depending on where you live. In southern regions of the United States, from southern Maryland to Georgia, established plants will flower in the fall until deep freezes send them into underground dormancy. They'll begin growing again in early spring, with blossoms appearing in March and continuing until the summer heat slows them down. Even during this summer dormancy they make an attractive clump of rich green foliage in the garden. In northern regions, where winters are longer and summers are cooler, they'll begin flowering in June and continue blooming throughout the summer. In frost-free climates, alstroemerias remain evergreen through the winter but stop blooming during the hot summer months.

Preferred Growing Conditions: Alstroemerias grow in full sun or partial shade and do best in fertile, well-drained soil.

Maintenance Tips: Give young plants a good dose of slow-release fertilizer to stimulate vigorous, floriferous growth. To encourage new bud growth and flower production, yank off the stem right down to the rhizome when you pick the flowers. Cutting in the traditional manner slows growth. During winters in Zone 6, protect the rhizomes from extreme cold with mulch.

Zones: USDA Hardiness Zones 6– or 7–10, depending on hybrid

Astilbe spp. (false spirea)
Plant Description: Plumelike flower clusters stand tall above clumps of handsome, fernlike foliage, with leaves that are either lobed or divided and toothed. The feathery flowers range in color from pure white to deep scarlet, bold magenta, and shades of pink. By combining hybrids that flower at different times, you can have astilbes blooming in the garden for much of the summer. Depending on the hybrid, the plants grow from 1 to 3 feet tall with a similar spread.

Preferred Growing Conditions: Astilbes do best in moist conditions in sun or partial shade, though they will tolerate dry conditions in shady spots. In USDA hardiness climate Zones 9 and 10, grow the plants in shade.

Maintenance Tips: To maintain plant vigor and flower production, fertilize them in spring, then feed them lightly during the growing season.

Water the plants when the soil becomes dry. Divide and replant every 3 to 5 years, discarding old, woody rhizomes.

Zones: USDA Hardiness Zones 3–10, AHS Heat Zones 8–2

Coreopsis spp. (tickseed)

Plant Description: Natives of North America, coreopsis belong to an easy-to-grow plant family with great garden potential. The plants are heat and drought tolerant. Daisylike flowers in yellow, orange, red, or mahogany envelope the plants. Some blossoms are even two-toned in yellow and orange. *C. verticillata,* which has fine, threadlike foliage, grows 18 to 24 inches tall and stays in flower for most of the summer. *C. grandiflora* is a little taller at 18 to 36 inches and produces 2½- to 3-inch-wide flowers all summer long. It self-sows readily and will bloom the first year from seed. *C. lanceolata* grows to 24 inches. The 1½- to 2-inch-wide yellow flowers are excellent for cutting.

Preferred Growing Conditions: Grow in full sun. These tough plants tolerate a wide range of soils.

Maintenance Tips: To encourage coreopsis to stay in bloom, deadhead as the spent flowers fade. When the number of dead flowers is overwhelming, shear back the plants. Although that may seem draconian, you'll be rewarded with a new flush of flowers in a few weeks. Do not fertilize heavily; too much food promotes spindly growth. Plants may get aphids (sticky leaves, stems and buds), four-lined plant bugs (deformed leaves), or aster leafhoppers (stippled, distorted leaves). Dislodge offending pests with a strong spray of water, try spraying insecticidal soap, or, as a last resort, use rotenone.

Zones: USDA Hardiness Zones 4–10, AHS Heat Zones 12–1

Delphinium spp. (delphinium)

Plant Description: A great source for true blue in the garden, delphiniums produce tall flower spikes in the familiar shades of blue as well as pink, lavender, purple, white, and even yellow. Depending on the cultivar, the flower stalks may reach anywhere from 1½ to 8 feet tall. These stalks are brittle and hollow, so they require

Delphinium grandiflorum 'Dwarf Blue Butterfly'

staking. Avoid growing them where strong winds may batter the tall flower spires. Because delphiniums languish in hot weather, many gardeners treat them as annuals.

Preferred Growing Conditions:
They grow best in fertile, moist, well-drained soil in full sun, though they are heat sensitive and welcome afternoon shade where summers are particularly hot. Even in shade, the plants will die if it gets too hot for them.

Maintenance Tips: Protect plants from snails and slugs, and feed regularly to keep them vigorous. Promote a second flowering in late summer by cutting back the spent flower spikes to the small flowering side shoots. Fertilize to provide the necessary energy for this second bloom effort. At the end of the growing season, cut back all growth to the ground.

Zones: most cultivars are USDA hardy in zones 3–10, AHS Heat Zones 6–1

Dianthus spp. (pinks)

Plant Description: Fringed flowers, either double or single, in shades of red, pink, white, and bicolor combinations, grace these plants in late spring and early summer. Many, including *D. deltoides, D. gratianopolitanus, D. plumarius,* and *D.* 'Rose Bowl', have a delightfully spicy scent. Most form attractive tufts

or mounds with gray-green, blue-green, or blue-gray foliage. Depending on the species, the height ranges from 4 to 10 inches for dwarf varieties and up to 2 feet tall for larger species. Experiment with different species and hybrids to find your favorites. The plants are generally inexpensive, and there is a delightful world of choices for you to discover.

Preferred Growing Conditions: Dianthus thrive in fast-draining soil in full sun or partial shade.

Maintenance Tips: Although drought tolerant, dianthus should not be allowed to wilt. Opportunistic spider mites (look for fine webbing) tend to attack water-stressed plants. Keep the plants properly watered to prevent the problem. Control aphids, which suck the life out of leaves and transmit viruses, by knocking off the pests with a forceful water spray and/or with insecticidal soap. In poorly drained soils and hot, humid regions, dianthus may develop rust or crown rot. *D. gratianopolitanus* 'Bath's Pink' is particularly tolerant of heat and humidity. Shear off the spent blooms. In some cases, you'll get a lesser flush of flowers later in the season.

Zones: USDA Hardiness Zones 3–10, AHS Heat Zones 9–1

Echinacea purpurea (purple coneflower)

Plant Description: Depending on the hybrid, purple coneflower produces white, pink, or purple daisylike flowers beginning in early summer and continuing until autumn. The cone-shaped flower centers, which are the seed heads, persist into winter, prolonging the interest. Purple coneflower grows 3 or 4 feet tall and self-sows readily.

Preferred Growing Conditions: A prairie native, purple coneflower can take poor soil and drought once established, though the plant will be healthier in better conditions. Excess fertilization — or deep shade — will cause leggy growth.

Maintenance Tips: To rejuvenate these short-lived perennials, divide plants every 3 or 4 years, spacing the divisions about 20 inches apart. Pinch back the plants in spring to encourage more branching and hence more flowers.

Zones: USDA Hardiness Zones 3–10, AHS Heat Zones 12–1

Geranium spp. (hardy geraniums)

Plant Description: This large, handsome family of plants generally has attractive foliage that is either lobed, kidney-shaped, or roundish, depending on the species. Five-petaled flowers, produced singly or in clusters of two or three, come in pink, blue, shades of purple, and white. They bloom from late spring to fall, depending on the species. Popular species include *G.* x *cantabrigiense* (USDA Zones 4–10), a rapid spreader with fragrant foliage that grows about 18 inches tall and is covered in pink flowers ('Biokovo' has pink-tinged white blossoms) in late spring; pink-tinged *G. cinereum* (USDA Zones 4–10), a 6-inch-tall, wide-spreading plant that sports 1-inch-wide pink flowers through summer ('Ballerina' produces lilac-pink flowers); and *G. endressii* (USDA Zones 5–10), a rhizomatous, evergreen plant that grows about 18 inches tall and 24 inches wide and features trumpet-shaped pink flowers 1¼ to 1½ inches wide from early summer to early autumn.

Other popular choices are *G. himalayense* (USDA Zones 5–10), which grows in a mound 12 to 18 inches tall and 24 inches wide and produces cymes of 1½- to 2½-inch-wide veined, violet-blue flowers in early summer and then on and off through the growing season; *G. incanum* (USDA Zones 8–10), a fast-spreading, trailing ground cover plant 6 to 10 inches high, with 1-inch-wide magenta flowers from spring through fall; *G. macrorrhizum* (USDA Zones 4–10), which grows about 20 inches tall and spreads by underground roots that can overwhelm small, less aggressive plants, but charms with its clusters of flat pink or white flowers and their protruding stamens in early summer; and *G. sanguineum* (USDA Zones 4–10), which grows about 18 inches tall and bears 1-inch-wide magenta flowers ('Album' blooms pure white) on and off from May through August.

Geranium species are often available at nurseries in 1-quart or smaller containers, so it is a small investment to try several varieties as a way of getting to know this diverse and appealing genus.

Preferred Growing Conditions: Most hardy geraniums flower well in full sun, though some will take partial shade. They perform best in moist, well-drained soil of moderate fertility but will tolerate periods of drought. Some can become invasive if the soil is too rich.

Maintenance Tips: Most species are easy to grow and require very little maintenance. Divide plants every 3 to 5 years.

Zones: USDA Hardiness Zones vary with species

Gypsophila paniculata (baby's breath)

Plant Description: This multibranched plant grows to 3 feet tall with slender, sharp, pointed leaves 2½ to 4 inches long. In midsummer, baby's breath produces a cloud of white, many-flowered panicles, each ⅜ inch across. Each flower spray can contain as many as 1,000 single or double flowers, depending on the hybrid.

Preferred Growing Conditions: Because it has a long taproot, baby's breath grows best in deep, alkaline soil with a light, free-draining texture. Grow it in full sun.

Maintenance Tips: Choose a permanent place for baby's breath, because the large, fleshy root means it does not take well to transplanting.

Prolong the floral display by removing spent blooms. In cold climates, spread mulch in winter, but to prevent rot, avoid covering the crowns until after the ground has frozen.

Zones: USDA Hardiness Zones 4–9, AHS Heat Zones 9–3

Hemerocallis spp. (daylily)

Plant Description: As the common name suggests, most daylily flowers last for only one day; however, during its blooming season, one plant will produce new flowers day after day, keeping an active display. There are thousands of hybrids available in just about any color except pure white and blue. Many of the hybrids are remontant, meaning they have a second bloom later in the season, and a few, such as 'Fragrant Treasure', have sweetly scented flowers. The trumpet-shaped flowers have different forms, including doubles, spider- and star-shaped blossoms, and triangular and circular contours. Plant sizes range from dwarf varieties suitable for edging beds and borders to tall versions reaching up to 3 feet.

Hemerocallis 'Bess Ross'

Preferred Growing Conditions: Tough, adaptive plants, daylilies will accept good or poor soil, full sun or partial shade, drought conditions once they are established, and minimum feeding (too much fertilizer pushes the plants to produce more foliage and fewer flowers).

Maintenance Tips: Divide clumps every 3 to 5 years to keep them in bounds and to refresh the plants (share extras with your friends). Prolong bloom by removing spent flower stalks. Protect daylilies from deer. If flower thrips attack the plants, causing flower buds to die and creating lesions on the stems, prune away the infested plant parts and destroy them. Encourage natural predators, including pirate bugs, ladybugs, and lacewings, by growing small, flat-headed flowers, such as yarrow, angelica, and tansy. Spider mites will seek out drought-stressed plants.

Zones: USDA Hardiness Zones 3–10, AHS Heat Zones 12–1

Heuchera spp. (coralbells, alumroot)

Plant Description: Excellent as a ground cover or as a highlight in front of a border, coralbells are tidy, low-growing, mounding plants. The leaves may be rounded or heart-shaped and are often lobed or toothed. Sprays of tiny, bell-like flowers (1⁄16 to 1⁄4 inch across) are produced on 15- to 30-inch-tall stems and are attractive to bees and hummingbirds. Many of the hybrids are grown for their fantastic foliage, rather than their flowers. An old standby is 'Palace Purple', which has rich brown or purple, maplelike leaves. Other popular hybrids include 'Garnet', which has green leaves veined with dark purple; 'Pewter Veil', which has purplish silver leaves and charcoal gray veins; and 'Plum Puddin'', with bright purple leaves and silver highlights.

Preferred Growing Conditions: Coralbells grow best in rich, organic, well-drained soil in full or partial shade. The foliage holds its color better if given some shade, especially in the South.

Maintenance Tips: Coralbells do best when watered regularly. To prevent powdery mildew, water early in the day and avoid wetting leaves; keep the ground clean of any debris that may collect around the plants. Destroy infected plants

to prevent fungal spread. Thin overgrown clumps every 3 or 4 years in fall (spring in cold climates).

Zones: USDA Hardiness Zones 3–8, AHS Heat Zones 8–2

Hosta spp. (hosta)

Plant Description: Hostas are grown primarily for their foliage, though several named varieties boast attractive — and, in some cases, scented — flowers. They come in a wide range of sizes from petite cultivars just a few inches tall ('Ginkgo Craig', 'Gold Edger', and 'Kabitan') to large specimens that grow 3 or 4 feet tall and wide ('Big Daddy', 'Sum and Substance'), and all sizes in between. Depending on the hybrid, the leaves may be long and slender, round or heart-shaped. Textures vary from smooth to crinkled to heavily veined. Leaf colors include many shades of green, yellows, golds, and even blue. A number of varieties are variegated with gold, cream, or white markings. With the enormous choices of size, leaf shape and texture, and color, there is a hosta to suit almost any landscape situation.

Preferred Growing Conditions: Versatile plants, hostas will grow in conditions ranging from boggy to dry. They flourish with ample water in shade to part sun.

Maintenance Tips: Hostas are a favorite of snails and slugs, so protect the area around them with barriers of scratchy materials, such as diatomaceous earth and wood ashes, that will irritate the soft bodies of pests and keep them away. Some people surround hosta roots with wire mesh to stop moles and voles from eating the plants.

Zones: USDA Hardiness Zones 3–9, AHS Heat Zones 9–2

Iberis sempervirens (edging candytuft)

Plant Description: An evergreen, front-of-the-border plant that produces white flower clusters from spring to early summer, candytuft grows anywhere from 8 to 18 inches tall and spreads up to 18 inches wide. The short, narrow leaves are dark green. Some hybrids, such as 'Snowflake', bloom sporadically throughout the year in mild climates.

Preferred Growing Conditions: Candytuft prefers full sun in well-drained soil. Although it will grow in part shade, the flowers will not be as profuse. Drought also reduces flower production.

Maintenance Tips: To maintain compact growth, cut back candytuft after it flowers. In exposed, windy locations where temperatures are very cold, mulch lightly to protect foliage.

Zones: USDA Hardiness Zones 5–10, AHS Heat Zones 9–1

Iris spp. (iris)

Plant Description: Named after the Greek goddess of the rainbow, iris plants flower in a wide range of colors and color combinations. This large family includes bog-loving species, such as *I. laevigata* and *I. pseudacorus,* as well as drought-tolerant bearded iris, so you can find an iris for just about any garden situation. Characterized by leaves that resemble swords or grass (depending on the species), iris can grow anywhere from a few inches tall (*I. cristata, I. reticulata*) to 3 or 4 feet high. Most bloom in spring or early summer, but some bearded iris hybrids flower again in fall.

Preferred Growing Conditions: Bearded iris, Siberian iris, and Japanese iris grow best in full sun or very light shade in moderate to fertile, well-drained soil. In clay conditions, plant in raised beds to ensure adequate drainage. Japanese iris thrive in acidic soil and appreciate an inch or two of mulch in summer.

Maintenance Tips: Divide bearded iris every 3 or 4 years in early fall. Each division needs a small fan of leaves and a section of rhizome. You can break or cut apart the rhizomes, discarding the old, leafless sections in the center. To compensate for root loss, trim back the leaves to about 6 inches, and when you plant, point the leaves in the direction you want them to grow. To prevent rotting, leave the top of the rhizome uncovered. The roots will burrow deep into the soil. Keep bearded iris well watered until about 6 weeks after flowering. After that, they go dormant, and then they can tolerate drought conditions.

Zones: USDA Hardiness Zones 4–11, AHS Heat Zones 8–4

Lavandula angustifolia (English lavender)

Plant Description: Lavender grows in a dense clump, making it ideal to create floral pools of blue in a border. Set in close together in a row, plants form a fine dwarf hedge. The 2-inch-long, silver-gray foliage makes a handsome display, and during the July and August bloom season, the flower spikes dominate in shades of blue to purple or even white, depending on the hybrid. Famous for its scented leaves and flowers, lavender in ancient times was burned as incense to cleanse hospitals and was used to perfume baths.

Preferred Growing Conditions: Lavender thrives best in a slightly dry, sunny spot with good drainage.

Maintenance Tips: Flowers appear on its current-year growth. Trim back plants in early or mid-spring to encourage new flower-producing growth. After flowering is finished in late summer, cut back the shoots to within 1 inch of the previous year's growth.

Zones: USDA Hardiness Zones 5–10, AHS Heat Zones 12–3

Liriope spp. (lilyturf)

Plant Description: Evergreen, clumping, grasslike perennials, liriope, and their close relative *Ophiopogon,* produce spikes of white or lavender flowers in autumn. Some cultivars have variegated leaves. Use them to edge paths, mass plant them as a ground cover, tuck a few into a rock garden, or use them as an accent in the front of a border.

Preferred Growing Conditions: Liriope prefer full sun in cooler climates, such as coastal areas, but appreciate shade in hot regions. Plants are tolerant of drought and poor soil, though they do best in well-drained, slightly acidic conditions.

Maintenance Tips: Cut back unattractive, old foliage in spring when new leaves begin to appear. Protect plants from snails and slugs. If a clump grows larger than you like, or if you want additional plants, divide in early spring before it begins actively growing.

Zones: USDA Hardiness Zones 5–11, AHS Heat Zones 8–3

Phlox paniculata (summer phlox)

Plant Description: This 3- to 5-foot-tall, deciduous perennial produces beautiful, dome-shaped clusters of fragrant flowers in mid- to late summer. Flowers range in color from pure white to shades of pink, lavender, rose, and red. Many hybrids have a contrasting eye.

Preferred Growing Conditions: Summer phlox loves the sun and rich, moist, organic soil. Good air circulation will help control mildew.

Maintenance Tips: Mulch plants to retain moisture and keep roots cool. Divide clumps every few years, replanting the younger roots and shoots on the outside of the clump. Deadhead to extend the blooming season and to prevent self-sowing. Seed-grown phlox will not grow true to the parent.

Zones: USDA Hardiness Zones 3–9, AHS Heat Zones 9–4

Rudbeckia fulgida (black-eyed Susan)

Plant Description: This tough perennial produces bright golden yellow, daisylike flowers from late summer to mid-fall. Each flower center has a blackish brown disk, earning the plant its common name: black-eyed Susan. Depending on the hybrid, the plant will grow anywhere from 1½ to 3 feet tall. It self-sows with gusto and is a great magnet for birds and butterflies.

Preferred Growing Conditions: An easy-to-grow sun-lover native to the eastern United States, black-eyed Susan will grow in just about any soil except wet.

Maintenance Tip: Deadhead rudbeckia to keep it looking tidy.

Zones: USDA Hardiness Zones 4–10, AHS Heat Zones 12–2

Santolina chamaecyparissus (lavender cotton)

Plant Description: Grown primarily for its finely toothed, aromatic foliage and mounding growth habit, lavender cotton also produces yellow, buttonlike flowers in summer if the plant isn't sheared. Hybrids include 'Lemon Queen', with green foliage, and 'Lambrook Silver' and 'Pretty Carol', both with silvery gray foliage. The plants make an attractive clipped hedge, ground cover, or foreground planting in a border.

Preferred Growing Conditions: A tough plant, lavender cotton does best in a sunny location in dry, infertile soil. In good soil, the plant loses its attractive, compact form. It also tolerates difficult conditions, such as salt spray.

Maintenance Tips: Lavender cotton looks most full and tidy when it is pruned back to about 12 inches tall in early spring. Also, shear off spent flowers. As the plant ages, it'll grow more woody, at which point you may want to replace it. In cold climates, it will die down to the ground in winter, but the roots should survive and sprout again in spring.

Zones: USDA Hardiness Zones 6–10, AHS Heat Zones 12–1

Sedum spectabile (showy stonecrop)

Plant Description: This clump-forming perennial has fleshy, succulent, gray-green leaves and grows about 18 inches tall. It is particularly valued for its flower heads, which begin to form in summer and finally mature and open in early fall to reveal tiny, star-shaped blossoms borne on dense flat cymes. The dried flower heads remain long after the deciduous plant has retreated underground, thus adding winter interest.

Preferred Growing Conditions: Tolerant of poor soil and drought, showy stonecrop will perform better if given good drainage. It flowers best in full sun but will put up with some shade.

Maintenance Tips: This plant is generally pest- and maintenance-free, though deer may munch on the maturing flowers. The plant roots easily from cuttings (just stick a broken stem into the ground and wait), and also takes well to being divided.

Zones: USDA Hardiness Zones 3–10, AHS Heat Zones 8–3

Ground Covers

The world of ground covers is a lot larger than just the low-growing, stoloniferous plants that creep along the ground, rooting wherever their stems touch earth. Just about any plant that can be massed together to blanket the ground is suitable for a ground cover. For example, small- and medium-sized hostas and clump-forming daylilies make excellent ground covers when they are planted close together. Low-growing, spreading shrubs, such as creeping juniper, creeping St. John's wort, and the horizontal forms of cotoneaster, are also candidates for low-maintenance ground covers.

Alyssum montanum (madwort)

Plant Description: A mat-forming, evergreen ground cover with gray, hairy leaves and fragrant, yellow flowers that blossom in early summer, alyssum grows 4 to 6 inches tall. It is great in rock gardens, cascading over retaining walls, and spreading out in front of a border.

Preferred Growing Conditions: Native to the Mediterranean, it thrives in full sun in infertile, rocky soil with good drainage.

Maintenance Tips: Gritty soil with good drainage will help prevent basal stem and root rot, two problems to which it is prone. To propagate, take root cuttings in early summer.

Zones: USDA Hardiness Zones 4–11

Arabis caucasica (wall rock cress)

Plant Description: This mat-forming evergreen perennial grows about 6 inches tall and spreads vigorously to 20 inches. The hairy, gray-green leaves are serrated for a pleasing texture. 'Variegata' has green leaves with pale yellow margins. In late spring, the plant is nearly covered in fragrant white flowers, each about ½ inch in diameter with a small, pale yellow eye.

Preferred Growing Conditions: Although arabis requires a well-drained situation to prevent rot, it will tolerate infertile soil. It thrives in hot, dry, sunny areas but does not respond well to high humidity. If the plant dies out in the center, that is an indication of stress due to humidity.

Maintenance Tips: Cut back after flowering to promote dense growth. If you see signs of arabis midge, indicated by deformed flower shoots, remove and destroy the affected shoots. In cold climates, protect with mulch in winter.

Zones: USDA Hardiness Zones 4–10, AHS Heat Zones 8–1

Armeria maritima (sea pink)

Plant Description: A tufted, grasslike perennial about 6 inches tall that spreads up to 12 inches, armeria bears round clusters of white, red, or pink flowers atop 6- to 10-inch-tall stalks in late spring. In temperate coastal climates, the plant will flower sporadically throughout the year; in hotter regions, it blooms profusely in spring, finishing its floral display in early summer.

Preferred Growing Conditions: Armeria does best in full sun in fast-draining soil.

Maintenance Tips: Feed once annually in spring with a slow-release fertilizer, and dead-head the spent flowers at the end of the bloom season. To increase your collection, divide sea pink in spring or fall.

Zones: USDA Hardiness Zones 3–10, AHS Heat Zones 9–4

Asarum europaeum (European wild ginger)

Plant Description: An evergreen, low-growing ground cover, European wild ginger grows 3 or 4 inches tall and spreads to 12 inches. The dark green, heart-shaped leaves are glossy and form tidy, attractive clumps. Small, greenish purple flowers are borne in spring but are hidden by the 3-inch leaves. That is an insignificant loss compared to the handsome landscape benefits of the foliage. European wild ginger is preferable to *A. canadense,* a deciduous ground cover with dull, matte foliage.

Preferred Growing Conditions: A great shade ground cover, European wild ginger does best in moist, moderately fertile soil that is neutral to slightly acidic.

Maintenance Tip: Ample water will encourage healthy spread.

Zones: USDA Hardiness Zones 4–9, AHS Heat Zones 9–3

Armeria maritima

Cerastium tomentosum (snow-in-summer)

Plant Description: An aggressive, spreading ground cover, snow-in-summer earns its name because the silvery gray foliage is completely hidden by a profusion of pure white, ½-inch flowers in early summer. The plant grows 6 to 8 inches high and spreads as much as 3 feet in just a year. Although it is not long-lived, you can acquire new plants by division and quickly renew a tired patch. Snow-in-summer is ideal on hillsides, in rock gardens, cascading over walls, growing between stepping-stones, or as edging along paths or paving.

Preferred Growing Conditions: Snow-in-summer is flexible about soil quality as long as drainage is good; too much moisture promotes rot. It generally wants to grow in full sun, though it appreciates a little shade in very hot climates.

Maintenance Tips: Shear off spent flowers. Fertilize if you want to encourage more rapid growth, and divide in fall or early spring for additional plants.

Zones: USDA Hardiness Zones 3–10

Convallaria majalis (lily of the valley)

Plant Description: Famous for its fragrant white or pink, bell-shaped flowers that rise on 6- to 8-inch stems above two pointed, broad basal leaves in spring, lily of the valley spreads with creeping rhizomes to carpet woodland floors. 'Albostriata' leaves have creamy white stripes; 'Aureo Variegata' is variegated with narrow yellow stripes.

Preferred Growing Conditions: Lily of the valley thrives in rich, moist soil in light to full shade.

Maintenance Tips: Fertilize in fall, and divide crowded beds in late fall to encourage more bloom. Lily of the valley can be invasive.

Zones: USDA Hardiness Zones 2–9, AHS Heat Zones 9–1

Cotoneaster adpressus (creeping rockspray)

Plant Description: A deciduous, prostrate shrub (12 inches tall, spreading to 6 feet), cotoneaster bears small white flowers tinged with red in summer. The flowers are followed by

Cerastium tomentosum 'Silver Carpet'

bright red berries, about ¼ inch in diameter, that stand out against the maroon-red fall foliage.

Preferred Growing Conditions: Creeping rockspray is easygoing about soil type (dry, infertile soil promotes flower and berry production), but it does need good drainage. It prefers full sun, though it will take light shade. Tolerant of wind, drought, and salt spray, this is a good ground cover for rigorous growing conditions.

Maintenance Tips: Blackened leaves, flowers, and branches indicate fire blight, a bacterial disease. Prune out and discard infected tissue, sterilizing the pruners between cuts by dipping them into a solution of 1 part bleach to 9 parts water. In spring, when the plant is in flower, spray copper or bordeaux mix to control disease spread.

Zones: USDA Hardiness Zones 5–10, AHS Heat Zones 8–3

Euonymus fortunei (wintercreeper)

Plant Description: This evergreen trailing shrub will either spread out horizontally or climb and cling with rootlets. When used as a ground cover, it reaches only about 24 inches tall, but it will spread to 20 feet. A smaller named variety is 'Emerald Cushion', which has deep green leaves

and stays a compact 12 inches by 18 inches. For winter color, look for 'Coloratus' (purple-leaf wintercreeper), which has dark green leaves that turn deep burgundy-red in cold weather. 'Emerald 'n Gold' has bright green leaves with broad buttercup yellow margins that tinge pink in winter. It spreads to 3 feet.

Preferred Growing Conditions: Wintercreeper will do well in moderately fertile soil in full sun or partial shade.

Maintenance Tip: Subject to winter burn, wintercreeper is best used as a ground cover, rather than a climber, in harsh winter areas. As a climber, it is more exposed to burning winds.

Zones: USDA Hardiness Zones 5–9, AHS Heat Zones 9–5

Fern spp.

(common names vary with genera and species)

Plant Description: A large and diverse group of perennials prized for their foliage, ferns range in height from a few inches to 50-foot tree ferns. Many that are native to the eastern United States are hardy in extreme cold. Among the natives that are excellent in gardens are *Adiantum pedatum* (American maidenhair fern, Zones 3–8, 12 to 16 inches tall and wide); *Asplenium scolopendrium* (hart's tongue fern, Zones 6–8, 18 to 24 inches tall); *Dryopteris filix-mas* (male fern, zones 4–8, 3 feet tall and wide); *Onoclea sensibilis* (sensitive fern, Zones 4–9, 24 inches tall); *Osmunda regalis* (royal fern, zones 4–9, up to 6 feet tall); *Polypodium virginianum* (American wall fern, Zones 5–8, 10 inches tall); *Polystichum munitum* (western sword fern, zones 3–8, 36 inches tall); and *Woodwardia areolata* (netted chain fern, Zones 2–6, 6 inches tall).

Preferred Growing Conditions: Most ferns grow in shade or partial sun. Some prefer damp conditions; others are drought tolerant. Read plant labels in the nursery or descriptions in catalogs to determine which genera and species best suit your specific situation.

Maintenance Tip: During the growing season, cut off dead fronds at the base to keep plants looking tidy.

Zones: Zones vary with genera and species

Gaultheria procumbens (wintergreen)

Plant Description: A native of the eastern United States, wintergreen creeps along the ground on 6-inch-tall stems. The shiny, 2-inch-long oval leaves are clustered toward the tips and smell of wintergreen when crushed. The fresh spring leaves are red. They mature to green in summer and turn bronze in fall. In summer, the plant is dotted with small white or pale pink flowers, which mature into edible scarlet berries that often persist until the next spring.

Preferred Growing Conditions: Wintergreen is a woodland plant that thrives in moist, acidic, peaty soil in partial shade.

Maintenance Tip: Mulch wintercreeper to keep it moist.

Zones: USDA Hardiness Zones 3–8, AHS Heat Zones 8–3

Gazania rigens var. leucolaena (trailing gazania)

Plant Description: Brightly colored daisylike flowers cover the plant for most of the summer. The flowers close up at night, in cool weather, and on cloudy days, but they reopen when the sun shines. The foliage is silvery gray, and the flowers come in white, yellow, orange, or bronze. Among the new larger-flowered hybrids are 'Sunburst' (yellow with a black eye) and 'Sunglow' (pure yellow). In addition to being an excellent ground cover on a dry slope or level patch, gazania looks lovely sprawling over a wall or cascading out of a hanging basket.

Preferred Growing Conditions: A sun- and heat-lover from South Africa, gazania will grow happily in almost any soil.

Maintenance Tips: Feed trailing gazania in spring with a slow-release fertilizer. Divide every 3 or 4 years. In regions where it is not hardy, maintain your stock by taking cuttings in fall and overwintering them in a frost-free environment. Like pelargonium (tender geranium), gazania roots easily.

Zones: USDA Hardiness Zones 8–11, AHS Heat Zones 12–3

Hedera helix (English ivy)

Plant Description: A diverse family of vigorous-growing plants that either climb and cling with aerial rootlets or trail over the ground, English ivy has hundreds of named varieties. Leaf size can be as small as 1 inch or as large as more than 2½ inches. Leaf color ranges from gold to shades of green, blue, blue-gray, and variegated combinations. 'Gold Dust' is golden green sprinkled with dark green highlights and 'Glacier' is mid-green with silver variegations and white margins. Generally, the leaves have three or five lobes and range from oval to triangular in shape. English ivy is a great choice for an inexpensive, evergreen way to cover a chain-link fence.

Preferred Growing Conditions: Although it grows best in fertile, moist, well-drained soil, ivy is appreciated for its ability to tolerate deep shade, drought, and competition from other roots.

Maintenance Tips: Ivy is sturdy once established, but it needs care when first planted. Water well until it is established, and feed with a high-nitrogen fertilizer in spring and again in August. To keep an ivy ground cover looking tidy and to keep the plants in bounds, use a hedge shears or sharp spade to trim around the edges as needed — probably two or three times a year. If the plants grow too tall, use a sturdy power rotary mower or hedge shears to mow them to the desired height. If you do this job in spring, new growth will quickly fill in the bald spots. Ivy tends to harbor snails and slugs. Use bait to keep them under control.

Zones: USDA Hardiness Zones 5–10

Helianthemum nummularium (rock-rose, sun rose)

Plant Description: Growing about 6 inches high and spreading to 3 feet, helianthemum blooms for months in bright shades of yellow, orange, red, rose, pink, apricot, salmon, peach, white, or bicolors. Bloom time varies by region. In California and Arizona, flowering continues from April to June; in the Northwest, the floral display begins in May and finishes around July. Plant sun rose among paving stones, in a rock garden, or in a planter or pot next to the swimming pool.

Preferred Growing Conditions: Helianthemum adapts to poor, dry, alkaline soil, though it appreciates good drainage. As the name suggests, it loves the sun.

Maintenance Tips: Shear sun rose after flowering to encourage a second flush in fall. In cold regions, cover it with evergreen branches to minimize foliage dehydration.

Zones: USDA Hardiness Zones 6–10, AHS Heat Zones 10–3

Hypericum calycinum (creeping St. John's wort)

Plant Description: A 12-inch-tall evergreen or semievergreen shrub that spreads by vigorous underground stems, creeping St. John's wort has 4-inch-long oblong or elliptical leaves that have dark green tops and are pale green underneath. Bright yellow flowers, 3 or 4 inches across, grace the plant from midsummer until mid-fall.

Preferred Growing Conditions: Creeping St. John's wort is a tough plant that can compete with tree roots and will grow in sun or shade and even in poor soil.

Maintenance Tips: The plant's strength — that it can grow in difficult situations — is also its weakness: It can be invasive if not confined. Every 2 or 3 years, shear or mow the plants when they are dormant.

Zones: USDA Hardiness Zones 5–10, AHS Heat Zones 9–2

Gazania rigens var. leucolaena

Juniperus spp. (juniper)

Plant Description: Among the junipers suitable for ground covers are *J. horizontalis* (creeping juniper), *J. sargentii* (Sargent juniper), and *J. squamata* (singleseed juniper). A prostrate member of the large juniper family, creeping juniper has gray-green, needlelike foliage and produces round, dark blue fruit. It grows about 12 inches high and can sprawl up to 10 feet. Notable hybrids include 'Bar Harbor' (gray-green leaves that shade to purple in winter); 'Blue Chip' (pronounced blue foliage); and 'Emerald Spreader' (bright green foliage). Sargent juniper grows 12 inches tall with an indefinite spread. It has blue-green, camphor-scented foliage that resembles scales. 'Viridis' has bright green foliage. *J. squamata* 'Blue Carpet' is a slow-growing species that has a low, mounding habit and reaches 1 foot tall and 5 feet wide. It has bright blue-gray foliage. For a more silvery effect, look for *J. squamata* 'Blue Star', which has silvery blue leaves, grows about 16 inches tall, and spreads to 36 inches.

Preferred Growing Conditions: Junipers will grow in heavy or sandy soil that is either alkaline or acidic as long as they receive full sun. They are drought tolerant, requiring little or no summer water. In fact, the roots are likely to rot (indicated by yellow foliage and the ultimate demise of the plant) if they are overwatered.

Maintenance Tips: Because they prefer drought conditions, avoid planting juniper next to sprinklers that are used regularly in summer. Until the plants fill in as a ground cover, mulch to keep down weeds.

Zones: USDA Hardiness Zones 3–10, AHS Heat Zones 9–1

Pachysandra terminalis (spurge)

Plant Description: Spreading by underground runners, pachysandras, once established, grow into a tight mat that blocks out any other vegetation, including weeds and bulbs. The coarsely toothed leaves, which are a rich, dark green, grow in clusters on top of 4-inch-tall stems. 'Variegata' has white-edged leaves that brighten a dark, shady spot. Clusters of tiny, tubular white flowers appear in late spring. Evergreen perennials, pachysandras are an excellent choice in difficult shady locations, such as under trees and on slopes.

Preferred Growing Conditions: Pachysandras will grow in average soil in full or part shade. They are moderately drought tolerant.

Maintenance Tips: Bait for snails and slugs if they become a problem. To encourage compact growth, shear back about one fourth of the plant's height in spring. If you see signs of a fungal disease (leaf spot, dieback, or stem rot), remove infected plants and thin out the rest to improve air circulation.

Zones: USDA Hardiness Zones 5–9, AHS Heat Zones 8–3

Phlox divaricata (wild sweet William), P. stolonifera (creeping phlox), and P. subulata (moss phlox)

Plant Description: Woodland creepers, *P. divaricata* and *P. stolonifera* are both semi-evergreen and flower in spring. *P. divaricata* has narrow, ovate, hairy leaves and grows up to 14 inches tall. The five-petaled flowers bloom in lavender, pale violet, or white. *P. stolonifera* hugs the ground more closely than does *P. divaricata*, staying as low as 2 to 6 inches. It has rounded, dark green leaves up to 2 inches long and spreads by stolons. The salver-form flowers are 1¼ inches across and come in pale to deep purple, and named varieties flower in white or bright pink. Sun-loving *P. subulata* grows 2 to 6 inches tall and forms a dense cushion of linear, needlelike leaves about ¼ inch long. In spring, the entire plant is covered in flowers in shades of purple, lilac, pink, white, or two-tone combinations.

Preferred Growing Conditions: Wild sweet William and creeping phlox grow in partial shade in average soil. Moss phlox requires full sun in average soil. All three are fairly drought tolerant.

Maintenance Tips: These low-maintenance plants are rarely bothered by pests or disease and require no pruning.

Zones: USDA Hardiness Zones 4–8, AHS Heat Zones 9–4

Sedum spp. (stonecrop)

Plant Description: Tough, low-maintenance succulents, there are several species of sedum that make excellent ground covers. *S. acre* (goldmoss sedum) is evergreen with tiny, light green leaves. It grows 2 to 5 inches tall and

Phlox subulata 'Laurel Beth'

spreads indefinitely, forming a dense mat. It can become invasive, so keep it in bounds. In summer, it produces an abundance of clustered yellow flowers. *S. kamtschaticum* has slightly triangular, toothed leaves that grow 1 to 1½ inches long and produces clusters of ¼-inch-wide, star-shaped yellow flowers in late summer. It grows 4 inches tall. *S. spathulifolium* adds interesting color and texture to the garden floor with its silvery, spoon-shaped leaves that are gathered into rosettes. 'Cape Blanco' (also sold as 'Cappa Blanca') has a powdery white bloom on the fleshy foliage, which increases the silvery effect; 'Purpureum' has deep purple leaves. The plants, which will tolerate light shade, grow 4 inches tall and 24 inches wide. In summer, star-shaped yellow flowers bloom in clusters on stems that stand above the mat of foliage.

Preferred Growing Conditions: Although they will tolerate poor soil and drought conditions, sedum will grow better and flower more if grown in moderately fertile, well-drained soil in full sun. Too much water will encourage rot.

Maintenance Tip: Provide boundaries for the vigorous, invasive varieties.

Zones: USDA Hardiness Zones 4–10, AHS Heat Zones 8–3

Vinca minor (lesser periwinkle)

Plant Description: A mat-forming, evergreen ground cover that spreads by long, trailing shoots, lesser periwinkle has handsome, glossy, dark green leaves that are about 2 inches long. In spring and sporadically through the summer in sunnier settings, it bears violet-blue or white flowers about 1 inch across. *V. minor* 'Argenteovariegata' has leaves with creamy white edges and produces violet-blue blossoms. *V. minor* 'Aureavariegata' has pale yellow leaf margins and white flowers. Vinca grows 4 to 8 inches tall with an indefinite spread.

Preferred Growing Conditions: This is a drought-tolerant, shade-loving ground cover that adapts well to poor soil. It can be invasive in favorable conditions.

Maintenance Tip: Cut back hard in early spring if you want to restrict growth.

Zones: USDA Hardiness Zones 4–9

Ornamental Grasses

rnamental grasses are wonderful around a swimming pool. They are tidy, generally remain pest- and disease-free, require little maintenance except the annual spring shearing to the ground, and, when the wind catches the billowing blades of the taller specimens, they sway in the breeze and make lulling, susurrous sounds.

Arundo donax (giant reed)

Plant Description: Giant reed is a bamboolike grass that grows 10 to 25 feet tall on stout stems, creating a dense thicket. The gray-green leaves, which grow about 3 inches wide and 2 feet long, are evergreen in mild regions. In colder areas, they turn tan after the first hard frost. 'Variegata' is striped with creamy white that darkens to yellow in hot weather. In late summer, the plants produce feathery panicles of silvery pink flowers.

Preferred Growing Conditions: Although tolerant of any soil, giant reed performs best in full sun in rich, moist soil, such as a pond margin or a bog garden. Because it can be invasive, however, poorer soil will help slow its expansion.

Maintenance Tips: Cut back the dead stems to the ground in winter. Wear heavy gloves to protect your hands from the sharp leaf edges. The pruned stalks are useful as plant stakes.

Zones: USDA Hardiness Zones 6–10

Calamagrostis x acutiflora (feather reed grass)

Plant Description: A handsome, erect, clump-forming grass with narrow bright green leaves, feather reed grass is an excellent vertical accent in the garden. Height ranges from 1½ to 4 feet, with flowering stems that rise above the foliage in late spring or early summer.

The flowers begin life colored purplish green and mature to a golden yellow. By winter, they are tan. 'Karl Foerster' grows to 6 feet tall and 24 inches wide and flowers 2 or 3 weeks earlier than the ordinary species. 'Overdam' is variegated with pale yellow stripes, growing to 4 feet tall. Its flowers age to a grayish pink.

Preferred Growing Conditions: A sun-loving perennial, feather reed grass is adaptable to most soil conditions, including drought or wet.

Maintenance Tips: Cut back to within 6 inches of the ground in late winter before the new spring growth begins.

Zones: USDA Hardiness Zones 5–10, AHS Heat Zones 9–3

Festuca glauca (blue fescue)

Plant Description: A fine-leafed, tufted grass that grows just 4 to 10 inches tall, blue fescue is a useful ground cover (though it cannot tolerate foot traffic) or accent in a perennial garden. It also grows well in containers. In midsummer the soft, silvery blue foliage is accented with purple-tinged, blue-green flowers growing on 4-inch-long spikes.

Preferred Growing Conditions: Blue fescue will grow in poor soil as long as it is well drained. It prefers full sun and is drought tolerant.

Maintenance Tips: Trim back to the ground after flowering or to reinvigorate a shabby display. If you plant blue fescue as a ground cover, keep it well weeded. Divide the tufts every 2 or 3 years to maintain foliage color and renew the display.

Zones: USDA Hardiness Zones 4–10

Hakonechloa macra (Japanese forest grass)

Plant Description: Resembling a tiny bamboo, this clump-forming ornamental grass has long, slender leaves that droop from arching stems. At 14 inches tall and with a 16-inch spread, it makes a good ground cover as well as an accent plant in a border, in a rock garden, or on special display in a container. 'Aureola' has leaves striped with narrow bands of bright yellow and green. The foliage flushes red in autumn, often holding that blush through many of the winter months.

Preferred Growing Conditions: One of the few shade-tolerant ornamental grasses, Japanese forest grass needs moist, fertile soil that drains well. The variegated varieties hold their color best in shade. In sunny locations, keep the plants well watered.

Maintenance Tips: Divide in spring if you want to increase your plant supply. *Hakonechloa* is rarely bothered by pests or diseases.

Zones: USDA Hardiness Zones 5–10, AHS Heat Zones 9–2

Helictotrichon sempervirens (blue oat grass)

Plant Description: An evergreen grass, blue oat grass grows in dense tufts up to 4½ feet tall with a spread of about 24 inches. The narrow, blue-gray leaves form a tidy, fountainlike spray, making the grass a great texture and color feature in a perennial border or rock garden. In early and midsummer, loose panicles of buff-colored flowers blossom on stiff stems held above the foliage clump.

Preferred Growing Conditions: Tolerant of almost any soil, blue oat grass does require full sun and good drainage. It is drought tolerant.

Maintenance Tips: To keep the plants looking tidy, remove dead leaves and spent flowers. Cut back the clumps to within 3 inches of the ground in early spring.

Zones: USDA Hardiness Zones 4–10, AHS Heat Zones 9–1

Imperata cylindrica 'Rubra' (Japanese blood grass)

Plant Description: The blood red tops of the narrow, erect foliage inspire the common name of Japanese blood grass. Displays look especially striking when the sun is behind the clumps, shining through the bright red blades. This slow-spreading ornamental grass grows 16 to 24 inches tall and 12 inches wide. In regions where summers are long and hot, the clumps produce fluffy, silvery flowers.

Preferred Growing Conditions: Grow Japanese blood grass in full sun or partial shade in well-drained soil.

Maintenance Tips: If a portion of the foliage reverts to pure green, dig out and throw away that section. The green form is highly invasive and is listed as a noxious weed in the United States. To propagate plants, divide Japanese blood grass in spring or early summer.

Zones: USDA Hardiness Zones 4–10, AHS Heat Zones 9–4

Miscanthus sinensis (eulalia grass)

Plant Description: A dramatic, clump-forming ornamental grass that grows 6 to 12 feet tall, eulalia grass is ideal as a single focal point in the garden or as a screen. In late summer, the plant produces tall plumes of feathery, beige flowers that are suitable for dry or fresh flower arrangements. The flowers persist through winter. In fall the long, narrow, arching leaves turn tan. Notable hybrids include 'Morning Light' (white-edged foliage imparting a silvery appearance); 'Variegatus' (foliage has lengthwise white stripes); 'Yaku Jima' (a dwarf variety that grows just 3 to 4 feet tall); and 'Zebrinus' (horizontal yellow bands encircle each leaf).

Preferred Growing Conditions: Eulalia grass will grow in almost any soil in full sun or shade, though it grows best in full sun. If the soil is too rich, the stems may collapse.

Maintenance Tips: Cut back clumps to the ground in early spring before new growth commences. Because of the size of the clumps and the tough nature of the grass, you may need a bow saw to do the job.

Zones: USDA Hardiness Zones 4–10, AHS Heat Zones 8–1

Panicum virgatum (switchgrass)

Plant Description: An upright, clump-forming grass that stands about 3 feet tall and spreads to about 30 inches, switchgrass has green to gray-green leaves that turn yellow in fall. In early fall, flower panicles laden with tiny, tan-colored flowers arch over the plants. The seed heads persist through winter. Notable hybrids include 'Dallas Blues' (powder blue foliage that grows 4 feet tall); 'Haense Herms' (red summer foliage with a fountainlike habit and gray seed heads); and 'Heavy Metal' (stiff, metallic blue leaves that turn yellow in fall).

Preferred Growing Conditions: Switchgrass enjoys moist, well-drained soil and full sun. It also can tolerate dry spells.

Maintenance Tip: Cut back grass to the ground in early spring.

Zones: USDA Hardiness Zones 5–9, AHS Heat Zones 9–1

Pennisetum alopecuroides (fountain grass)

Plant Description: As its common name suggests, fountain grass forms arching, fountainlike sprays of foliage. It grows 3 to 6 feet tall and in 2- to 4-foot-wide clumps. In summer, pinkish flowers that resemble bottle brushes form long, slender, drooping cylinders above the foliage. The bright green leaves turn yellow in fall. *P. setaceum* is hardy only in Zones 9 and 10, but it is worth growing in those climates for the hybrids 'Burgundy Giant' and 'Purpureum', which have burgundy and buff-colored flower plumes and dark purple leaves, respectively. Where not hardy, *P. setaceum* is grown as an annual. Either species is excellent in containers, as an accent plant, as part of the team in a perennial or shrub border, or as a low-maintenance plant on a steep slope.

Preferred Growing Conditions: Fountain grass grows best in fertile, well-drained soil in full sun. It is tolerant of humidity and appreciates extra water in dry summer climates.

Maintenance Tips: Remove seed heads to prevent invasive self-sowing. Cut back leaves to the ground in early spring before new growth begins, and divide plants every 5 to 10 years to prevent individual clumps from falling open in the center.

Zones: USDA Hardiness Zones 5–10, AHS Heat Zones 9–2

Saccharum contortum, also *Erianthus contortus* (bent-awn plume grass)

Plant Description: An excellent grass for screens and boundaries or at the back of a perennial border, bent-awn plume grass has upright, then arching, bluish green foliage in summer, which turns purplish red in fall.

In early fall, purple-brown plumelike flowers stand tall on 6- to 8-foot stems.

Preferred Growing Conditions: Grow *S. contortum* in full sun in well-drained soil. It can tolerate moisture and drought.

Maintenance Tips: Mulch the plant crowns in winter to protect them. In spring, cut off any of the flowers remaining from the previous season's bloom.

Zones: USDA Hardiness Zones 6 or 7–9

Saccharum ravennae, also *Erianthus ravennae* (hardy pampas grass, Ravenna grass)

Plant Description: Similar in form to pampas grass, this plant is a good substitute in cold climates where pampas grass is not hardy. The clump-forming plant grows between 7 and 15 feet tall, making it a dramatic specimen as well as a useful screen or border plant. The long, narrow, gray-green leaves turn brown with orange and purple tinges in fall. From late September until late October, the clumps send up silvery white flower plumes that stand tall above the foliage. Early frost will nip flowers in the bud.

Preferred Growing Conditions: Hardy pampas grass grows best in full sun in moist, moderately fertile, well-drained soil. Protect the grass from strong winds.

Maintenance Tips: Mulch the plant crown in winter to protect it. In spring, cut off any of the flowers remaining from the previous season's bloom.

Zones: USDA Hardiness Zones 6–10

Sporobolus heterolepsis (prairie dropseed)

Plant Description: A native American prairie grass, dropseed forms clumps of finely textured, emerald green leaves that sprout from the center of the plant and then arch gracefully toward the ground. The clumps grow 18 to 24 inches tall and wide. Fragrant, pale pink flower panicles blossom in late summer on stems that stand above the grassy clumps. In fall, the foliage and remaining seed heads turn a blend of tan and bronze. The grass makes a nicely textured ground cover and is ideal for erosion control on

a difficult slope. It is equally at home in a perennial border, and the airy flowers and seed heads are valued for dried flower arrangements.

Preferred Growing Conditions: Prairie dropseed thrives in sandy, dry soil in full sun. It will tolerate a little shade, though it is most appreciated for its ability to withstand extreme heat and drought.

Maintenance Tips: Don't overwater the plants, as root rot and fungus diseases, such as rust and seed smut, can be a problem. Cut the grass to the ground in winter.

Zones: USDA Hardiness Zones 3–9, AHS Heat Zones 10–2

Stipa gigantea (giant feather grass)

Plant Description: Narrow, mid-green leaves grow in a fountainlike form, arching to form a lax, grassy clump that can grow as tall as 8 feet with a 4-foot spread. In summer, buff-colored, oatlike flowers bloom on long stiff stems that stand tall above the clumps of narrow leaves. These inflorescences wave in the slightest breeze, adding motion and an airy lightness to the garden. Use giant feather grass as a special garden accent or as a feature in a perennial or shrub border.

Preferred Growing Conditions: Giant feather grass enjoys full sun. Provide ample water the first year or two until the plant is established. After that, it can tolerate some drought.

Maintenance Tip: Remove dead leaves in early spring.

Zones: USDA Hardiness Zones 9–10

Saccharum ravennae

Vines

Under used in many American gardens, vines provide vital vertical interest, particularly around a swimming pool, where the horizontal plane is so dominant. In addition to growing vines up support posts of arbors and pergolas, consider adding a freestanding, decorative pyramid support in a perennial or shrub border, then growing a vine on it. You can also dress up a blank fence or wall with a vine-covered trellis. Living supports for vines include trees (a vigorous climbing rose scrambling through the branches of a tree gives new meaning to the idea of rose trees) and shrubs (enjoy the oohs and ahs when a yew or other shrub not grown for flowers suddenly bursts forth with clematis blossoms). A stout sunflower stalk is an excellent support for an annual vine, such as hyacinth bean, morning glory, or moonflower.

Akebia quinata (five-leaf akebia)

Plant Description: This is a semievergreen climber with dark green leaves, each composed of five ovate leaflets 2 to 3 inches long. In early spring, the vine bears spicy-smelling deep maroon flowers on 5-inch-long, hanging racemes. The flowers may be followed by an edible, purple fruit that resembles a thick, 2½- to 4-inch-long sausage, though fruiting does not always happen.

Preferred Growing Conditions: Akebia enjoys moist, well-drained, fertilized soil in full sun or partial shade.

Maintenance Tips: Trim back vines as necessary to keep them to the size you want. Akebia will recover quickly, even if cut to the ground. For a tracery effect, cut all but two or three basal stems.

Zones: USDA Hardiness Zones 5–10, AHS Heat Zones 8–3

Antigonon leptopus (Mexican creeper, coral vine, queen's wreath)

Plant Description: A fast-growing, heat- and sun-loving Mexican native, this vine climbs by tendrils to 40 feet. The dark green, 2- to 5½-inch-wide leaves are either arrow- or heart-shaped. Trailing 6-inch-long sprays of tiny pink or white flowers grace the vines for a long season, starting in summer and continuing into fall. Grow it over an arbor or a pergola, cultivate it through tree branches, or allow it to drape over fences and walls or along eaves.

Preferred Growing Conditions: Drought tolerant when established, Mexican creeper grows in full sun in moderately fertile, well-drained soil.

Maintenance Tips: Mulch the roots in the colder sections of Zone 9 where temperatures drop below 25°F. Most of the top will die back in colder climates, but the plant will regrow in spring.

Zones: USDA Hardiness Zones 9–11

Campsis radicans (trumpet creeper)

Plant Description: A native of the eastern United States, trumpet creeper is a vigorous-growing vine that can become invasive, spreading with suckering roots. Any piece of root left in the ground will produce a new plant. The vines use their aerial rootlets to cling to wood, brick, and other surfaces, quickly reaching 40 feet tall if not pruned back. Give them a sturdy support; they have been known to get top heavy, either pulling down their support or pulling away from it. The dark green, 2½-inch-long leaves are a restful background to the bright orange or red tubular flowers that bloom in clusters on 6- to 12-inch-long cymes from late summer to fall. Each flower is 2 to 3 inches long and about 2 inches wide at the mouth. They attract hummingbirds.

Preferred Growing Conditions: Although it will tolerate poor soil, trumpet creeper will flourish in moist, moderately fertile, well-drained soil. In colder climates, grow the vine against a warm wall in full sun. In warmer regions, it will accept partial shade.

Maintenance Tips: Thin out overcrowded shoots annually in winter. At the same time, head the previous-season's growth to two or three buds, leaving the replacement shoots. On the lower parts of the vine, pinch back the shoots to keep the plant full. Trumpet creeper flowers on the current year's growth.

Zones: USDA Hardiness Zones 5–9

Clematis spp. (clematis)

Plant Description: A large and diverse genus of vines, clematis has vigorous varieties, such as *C. montana,* that can stretch to 46 feet; compact varieties that top at 8 feet, such as 'Nelly Moser' and 'Niobe'; and just about everything in between. Bloom season varies widely as well. Some flower in spring, others in summer, and a few late-bloomers give their display in fall. A few will flower once in spring and again in the fall. The blossoms, which vary in size from ½ inch across for early-flowering species to 8 inches for some of the large-flowered hybrids, come in a wide range of colors and color combinations, including shades of pink, purple, yellow, red, and white.

Preferred Growing Conditions: Clematis require rich, loose, well-drained soil that is neutral or slightly alkaline. Although the tops like the sun, the roots and lower plant need to be shaded. You can achieve this sun/shade mix by planting a shallow-rooted ground cover at the base; mulching; placing a large, flat stone over the root

Campsis radicans 'Minnesota Red'

area; or planting where shrubs or other vegetation will shade the roots. Give clematis a support, such as a trellis, fence, or tree, that they can twine around.

Maintenance Tips: Mulch the plants with compost or well-rotted manure in late winter, being sure to keep the material from touching the crown. Pruning requirements depend on the type of clematis. Spring-flowering varieties bloom on the previous year's wood; they should be cut back a month after flowering, preserving main branches but reducing sprawl. The summer- and fall-blooming vines flower on new wood produced in spring. Two- and 3-year-old plants should be cut back to within 6 to 12 inches of the ground in late fall after they bloom, or in early spring just as the buds swell. Cut more-mature vines down to 2 feet.

Zones: USDA Hardiness Zones vary with species and hybrids, generally 5–9; AHS Heat Zones 9–1

Hydrangea petiolaris (climbing hydrangea)

Plant Description: Climbing hydrangea is a deciduous vine that climbs as high as 50 feet, clinging with aerial rootlets. Slow to get established (the old saying is "The first year it sleeps, the second it creeps, the third it leaps"), once it decides to grow, it does so with vigor. The heart-shaped leaves are 2 to 5 inches long and make a shiny, dense green cover over the support surface. In spring, the vines produce creamy white clusters of small, starlike fertile flowers surrounded by larger, showier infertile blossoms. Each flower cluster is up to 10 inches across.

Preferred Growing Conditions: Ordinary garden soil is adequate for climbing hydrangea, though it really thrives in cool, rich, well-drained, slightly acidic conditions. The plant flowers best in full sun but will also grow in partial shade.

Maintenance Tips: Water frequently to maintain soil moisture. If you decide to trim back the vine, do so immediately after it flowers, as it blooms on the previous year's branches.

Zones: USDA Hardiness Zones 4–9, AHS Heat Zones 9–3

Parthenocissus quinquefolia (Virginia creeper) and P. tricuspidata (Boston ivy)

Plant Description: A vigorous, deciduous vine that clings to supports with suckers on the tips of its tendrils, *Parthenocissus* is grown for its beautiful foliage. The leaves of *P. quinquefolia* are mid-green and divided into five oval "fingers," or leaflets, each about 4 inches long. In fall, the foliage turns brilliant red. *P. tricuspidata* has bright green leaves that are divided into three toothed lobes. They turn bright red or purple in fall. Either vine is excellent to cover an unattractive wall or fence. Virginia creeper will grow up to 50 feet; Boston ivy reaches an impressive 70 feet.

Preferred Growing Conditions: Any fertile, well-drained soil will suit both Virginia creeper and Boston ivy. They are equally happy in sun or shade.

Maintenance Tip: Prune the vines as needed to keep them in bounds.

Zones: (Virginia creeper), USDA Hardiness Zones 3–10; (Boston ivy), USDA Hardiness Zones 4–10

Passiflora spp. (passionflower)

Plant Description: These vines were nicknamed passionflower because the various parts of the complex flower represent the symbols of Christ's passion. The five red anthers suggest the five wounds inflicted on Christ, the fringed corona represents the crown of thorns, the 10 petals represent the faithful apostles who were present at the crucifixion, and the central column formed by the stamens resembles the cross. Depending on the species, the flowers can be white, cream, various shades of purple and lavender, red and coral, or mixtures of these colors. The flowers are borne in summer and are followed by edible fruit. These vigorous vines (to 30 feet) cling with tendrils and require stout support.

Preferred Growing Conditions: Passionflowers grow best in well-drained soil in full sun or part shade. They appreciate protection from drying wind.

Maintenance Tip: As soon as the vines have finished flowering, trim out weak shoots and cut the rest back to about one third their

Wisteria sinensis 'Alba'

length. Leave the thin, short growth, which will bear next year's flowers.

Zones: USDA Hardiness Zones 6–10, AHS Heat Zones 12–1

Wisteria floribunda (Japanese wisteria), and W. sinensis (Chinese wisteria)

Plant Description: Wisteria are vigorous, deciduous, twining climbers with 12- to 16-inch-long leaves divided into leaflets. Japanese wisteria flower colors include white, shades of blue, purple, lavender, and pink. Chinese wisteria, grown for its fragrant, pendulous flowers that display in spring, is available in white or violet-blue blossoms. Chinese wisteria flowers all at once in April or May, giving a spectacular show on bare wood before the leaves emerge. In contrast, from April to May the long, pendant racemes of Japanese wisteria open with the new foliage, beginning at the base of the cluster and gradually moving toward the bottom. The bloom season is longer than that of Chinese wisteria, but with a less spectacular burst of color.

For either species, to ensure you get the flower color you want — and a plant that will indeed bloom — purchase wisteria when it is in flower. The best plants are grafted or grown from

cuttings, rather than seeds, so be sure to ask about that when you make your purchase. It can take years for a seed-grown wisteria to flower.

Preferred Growing Conditions: Although they will grow in most soils, wisteria will perform best in a deep rich soil. They won't take well to transplanting, so don't plan to change your mind about their location. They enjoy full sun or partial shade.

Maintenance Tips: To give newly planted wisteria a good start, manure heavily the first year and water well when the plants are young. Mature, established vines are fairly drought tolerant and flower better if they are given less food.

To encourage profuse flowering and to control the vine's size and shape, prune twice annually, in late summer and again in late winter or early spring. The August pruning consists of cutting back to about 6 inches the newly grown long streamers you don't want and tying the ones you do to the support. In winter, cut back lateral branches by one third and sublateral branches to the second or third bud. The new flowers will grow from these points. Remove any suckers that sprout from the base. Wisteria vines are extremely heavy. Make sure the support is strong enough to bear their weight.

Zones: *W. floribunda,* USDA Hardiness Zones 4–10; *W. sinensis,* USDA Hardiness Zones 5–10; AHS Heat Zones 9–4

Shrubs

The backbone of most gardens, shrubs provide structure and framework to a design. Although they are invaluable as a backdrop for showy annuals, perennials, and bulbs, many shrubs also have a season or two of glory when they take center stage. For example, mountain laurel (*Kalmia*) produces bouquets of striking, cup-shaped flowers in late May, and the deciduous winterberry holly (*Ilex verticillata*) puts on a stunning display of shiny red berries in autumn. When selecting shrubs for your poolside garden, consider their size, shape, foliage color and texture, and any potential flower or berry display.

Abelia x grandiflora (glossy abelia)

Plant Description: A semievergreen, mounding shrub that grows 8 to 10 feet tall and 5 feet wide, glossy abelia sports pointed leaves that are bronze when young, then mature to a rich green. In fall, the leaves revert to their bronze tint. From June to October, the shrub is filled with small, fragrant, funnel-shaped flowers that are white with a pink tinge. A smaller variety, 'Francis Mason', grows to just 5 feet tall and has yellow leaves highlighted with dark green. This is a good shrub to attract butterflies.

Preferred Growing Conditions: Although abelia will grow in part shade, it blooms best in full sun. It tolerates poor soil as well as humidity.

Maintenance Tips: To maintain the shrub's graceful, fountainlike form, prune selectively, cutting back old stems close to the ground during the dormant season. In spring, trim back branches to keep the shrub to the size you want.

Zones: USDA Hardiness Zones 6–10, AHS Heat Zones 12–6

Cistus x purpureus

Camellia spp. (camellia)

Plant Description: Known as "The Queen of Winter" because of the spectacular flowers that blossom during the winter months in the South and in Southern California, camellias are evergreen shrubs or small trees. With their glossy foliage and eye-catching flowers, camellias are excellent as specimen plants, as part of a shrub border, or as a hedge. By selecting early-, mid-, and late-flowering varieties, you can stretch the camellia bloom season from November to about May in mild-winter climates. Although generally considered hardy only to USDA Zone 7, recent hybrid introductions from the U.S. National Arboretum, including 'Snow Flurry', 'Winter's Charm', 'Winter's Dream', 'Winter's Interlude', and 'Winter's Rose', are fall blooming and cold hardy to Zone 6.

Preferred Growing Conditions: Camellias thrive in partial shade in rich, moist, peaty, acidic soil.

Maintenance Tips: To prevent flower blight, a soilborne fungus that causes flowers to turn brown and drop, deadhead blossoms as they fade, and rake up any fallen petals around the plants. Provide a 3-inch layer of mulch to maintain moisture, protect the shallow roots, and prevent flower blight spores from splashing up onto the plants from the soil.

Zones: USDA Hardiness Zones 7–11, AHS Heat Zones 10–3

Chamaecyparis spp. (false cypress)

Plant Description: Coniferous evergreens with flattened sprays of leaves, the false cypress genus encompasses a wide range of plants, from *C. lawsoniana* (Lawson false cypress), which grows 50 feet tall, to slow-growing dwarf plants, such as *C. obtusa* 'Nana Gracilis', that are ideal for containers, rock gardens, and bonsai. Depending on the species and named variety, you'll find tall, columnar shapes; short rotund specimens; and weeping forms. Foliage color runs from the expected green to hybrids with gold or shades of blue; *C. thyoides* 'Heather Bun' (white cedar) turns intense plum purple in winter.

Preferred Growing Conditions: With the exception of *C. obtusa* (Hinoki cypress), which will take light shade, most false cypress do best in full sun in moist, not-too-heavy soil that is neutral to slightly acidic. Because the trees are prone to root rot, the soil must have good drainage.

Maintenance Tips: Dead foliage in the center of the plant can be due to natural aging or spruce mites. In either case, a forceful jet of water from the hose will dislodge both the mites and the unattractive dead leaves. Hedges may be trimmed from late spring to early fall, but do not cut into mature wood.

Zones: USDA Hardiness Zones 4–8, AHS Heat Zones 8–3

Cistus spp. (rock rose)

Plant Description: Mounding, evergreen shrubs that grow 3 to 5 feet tall, rock roses bear showy white to deep pink flowers with yellow eyes in summer. Each flower lasts just one day but is replaced with a new flower the next morning. Because the aromatic foliage is resistant to burning, rock roses are often planted in areas where wildfires are a concern. They also are ideal for dry slopes and shrub borders. Taller varieties are excellent for screens.

Preferred Growing Conditions: Natives of the dry, stony soils of the Mediterranean region, rock roses will grow in poor, alkaline soil in full sun. They will stand up to cold, salty coastal winds or dry desert heat. Make sure they have well-drained soil if they are in a spot where they'll be watered. To help root-bound plants spread their roots deep into the soil for drought tolerance, cut away the circling roots and spread out the remaining root mass when you plant.

Maintenance Tips: After flowering, pinch back the plants to encourage bushy growth, or give them a light, overall shearing. If a lot of old wood is allowed to remain, rock roses will eventually grow too woody. To prolong a plant's youthful stage, remove a few old branches each year. Once a shrub becomes woody, you probably need to replace it, as it is unlikely to survive a severe, rejuvenating pruning job.

Zones: USDA Hardiness Zones 8–10, AHS Heat Zones 12–1

Euonymus alatus (burning bush, winged euonymus)

Plant Description: This deciduous shrub features toothed, dark green leaves up to 3 inches long that turn fiery red in autumn, earning it its common name burning bush. The flowers in spring are inconspicuous, but they mature into small orange seeds that attract birds. Those that are left persist into winter. Eventually, the plants will grow 7 to 10 feet tall and 10 to 15 feet wide. A dwarf variety, 'Compactus', grows to about 5 feet tall and wide, and has pinker fall coloring. The plant self-sows readily.

Preferred Growing Conditions: For the best color display in autumn, grow *E. alatus* in full sun. It does best in any well-drained soil.

Maintenance Tip: In late winter or early spring, remove any inside branches that cross over others to maintain an attractive, healthy framework.

Zones: USDA Hardiness Zones 4–9, AHS Heat Zones 9–5

Fatsia japonica (Japanese fatsia)

Plant Description: An excellent poolside shrub that grows up to 8 feet tall, fatsia has large, tropical-looking leaves that are deeply lobed like the fingers on a hand. The dark green foliage stands out in dramatic contrast to the prominent yellow stems and the central vein that runs down each leaf section. In fall, clusters of creamy white flowers stand above the 16-inch-wide leaves on branching umbels. The flowers

ripen into spherical black fruits that persist through winter and may produce new plants.

Preferred Growing Conditions: Tolerant of both clay and sandy soil as long as it's not too wet, fatsia does best in shade except in cool-summer regions, where partial shade is acceptable.

Maintenance Tips: Because the leaves are easily burned, shelter plants from drying winds. Thin them to show off the attractive branch structure. Cut back leggy plants hard in early spring to rejuvenate them. Yellowing leaves indicate iron deficiency; add iron to the soil if indicated. Because the large leaves easily gather dust, wash them down with a hose to clean them and to remove potential pests, such as spider mites and whiteflies. Bait for snails and slugs, or hand-pick them in the evening when they are active.

Zones: USDA Hardiness Zones 8–10, AHS Heat Zones 12–2

Hibiscus rosa-sinensis (tropical hibiscus)

Plant Description: A large evergreen, tropical hibiscus is a very showy flowering shrub that will produce blossoms 12 months of the year if conditions are right. The flowers, which come in

Euonymus alatus 'Compactus'

shades of pink and red, oranges and yellows, white, or two-toned in single or double forms, can range from 4 inches to a dramatic 8 inches wide, depending on the hybrid. They have five petals and long anthered stamens. Shrub size varies with the hybrid. Compact varieties, such as 'Bride', grow slowly to an open-branched 4 feet tall; mid-sized hybrids, such as 'President', grow 6 to 7 feet tall and wide; and large specimens, such as 'All Aglow', reach 10 to 15 feet in height.

Preferred Growing Conditions: Tropical hibiscus will flower best in full sun, though in hot, inland areas it appreciates some shade protection from afternoon sun. Good drainage is very important to prevent root rot. In climates with freezing winters, grow the plants in containers and overwinter indoors.

Maintenance Tips: Fertilize in-ground plants monthly between April and September. Specimens growing in containers should be fed twice a month. Renew mature plants by pruning out about one third of the old wood each spring. For increased flower production, pinch back stem tips in spring.

Zones: USDA Hardiness Zones 9–11, AHS Heat Zones 12–1

Hibiscus syriacus (rose of Sharon)

Plant Description: An excellent deciduous shrub for late summer and autumn floral interest, rose of Sharon grows rapidly to about 10 feet tall and 6 feet wide. The medium-sized, dark green leaves are diamond-shaped, often with three lobes and coarse serration. The flowers, which can be single or double depending on the variety, are 2½ to 3 inches across. Floral color possibilities include white as well as shades of violet, blue, and pink. Some hybrids, such as 'Helene', have deep red eyes. Although generally multistemmed, the shrub is easily trained to a single trunk with a treelike canopy.

Preferred Growing Conditions: Grow rose of Sharon in full sun in well-drained, fertile soil.

Maintenance Tips: To encourage larger flowers, cut back the previous season's growth to two buds in winter. Remove wayward or crossing shoots to maintain an open, attractive framework.

Zones: USDA Hardiness Zones 5–9

Hydrangea macrophylla (bigleaf hydrangea)

Plant Description: A fast-growing shrub that reaches 3 feet to as much as 10 feet in height and spread (choose named varieties to predict mature size), bigleaf hydrangea is loved for its spectacular flowers that enliven the plant in summer. The two flower forms are pompom Hortensias (also known by the descriptive moniker mopheads) and lacecaps, which are flattened flower heads with small fertile flowers in the center surrounded by larger-petaled, sterile flowers around the rim. Blooms range in color from white to shades of pink, blue, magenta, and purple. Deciduous in colder climates (if the plant freezes to the ground each winter, it may never flower), bigleaf hydrangea remains evergreen in frost-free areas. It is excellent in a shrub border, as a specimen plant, and in containers.

Preferred Growing Conditions: As the Latin root *hydro* suggests, hydrangea prefers moist, well-drained soil in bright shade to full sun. In acidic soils, the shrub produces blue flowers. Alkaline soil promotes pink coloration. White-flowering varieties remain true to color regardless of the soil's chemistry.

Maintenance Tips: Cut back dried flower heads to a strong new bud in early or mid-spring, when new growth begins.

Zones: USDA Hardiness Zones 6–10, AHS Heat Zones 9–3

Nandina domestica (heavenly bamboo)

Plant Description: Although a member of the barberry family, nandina, with its delicate foliage and canelike stems, resembles bamboo. New leaves emerge pink or copper-colored, then mature to bluish green. In fall, the fine-textured foliage is reddish purple, though the shrub rarely drops its leaves. Loose, 6- to 12-inch-long panicles of creamy white flowers arch from the plant in spring or early summer. As long as there is another nandina nearby, the flowers develop into spectacular clusters of shiny red berries that persist until the following spring. A nandina growing by itself usually will not fruit well.

Preferred Growing Conditions: Tolerant of a wide range of soils (though it prefers an acidic loam), nandina is capable of competing with tree roots in dry shade. It is equally happy in full sun.

Maintenance Tips: Yellowing leaves are an indication of iron deficiency, a problem when nandina is grown in alkaline soil. Treat it with iron sulfate or chelates. To keep a mature plant small, prune the oldest canes to the ground.

Zones: USDA Hardiness Zones 6–10, AHS Heat Zones 9–3

Pittosporum tobira (Japanese mock orange)

Plant Description: A dependable shrub for gardens in the western United States and excellent near swimming pools, pittosporum grows as tall as 15 feet, but it can be kept to as small as 6 feet by heading back the tall stems. The dark green, leathery leaves are about 4 inches long with rounded ends. 'Variegatum' has smaller, gray-green leaves highlighted with white margins. In early summer, each branch tip frames a cluster of small, bell-shaped, creamy white flowers that have the sweet fragrance of orange blossoms. They ripen into fruits that turn brown in fall and then split open to reveal orange seeds. Useful as a windbreak or screen, pittosporum makes an intriguing accent when it is pruned to show off its crooked branching habit.

Preferred Growing Conditions: An adaptable, sturdy plant, pittosporum will grow in either dry sandy soil or moist clay, as long as it is well drained. It also isn't picky about light, accepting full sun or even full shade. In addition, the shrub is happy with salt spray and revels in hot, humid conditions.

Maintenance Tips: Feed plants with a complete, balanced fertilizer once in either spring or summer. Black, sooty mold growing on the leaves is an indication of scale, aphid, or mealybug infestation. The fungus grows on the sticky excretions (honeydew) of these sucking pests. Although the mold itself is harmless (though it may block photosynthesis), wipe it off to improve the plant's appearance, then deal with the pests. For aphids, you can attract native predators by planting pollen and nectar flowers, such as yarrow, tansy, candytuft, and goldenrod, or purchase and release aphid midges, lady beetles, lacewings, or parasitic wasps. You may also try spraying insecticidal soap.

Zones: USDA Hardiness Zones 9–10, AHS Heat Zones 12–3

Podocarpus macrophyllus (yew pine)

Plant Description: Podocarpus is an evergreen shrub or tree that grows up to 50 feet tall where summers are long, hot, and humid, but it remains more shrublike in cooler climates. Even in regions where it wants to shoot up tall, it can be kept to a smaller size and shape with pruning. The bright green, leathery leaves grow 2½ to 4 inches long. The plant takes well to espalier and topiary training and also lends itself to a clipped hedge, a screen, or even a container-grown specimen.

Preferred Growing Conditions: A heat- and drought-tolerant shrub, podocarpus does best in full sun or partial shade in average garden soil.

Maintenance Tip: Podocarpus is rarely bothered by pests or diseases.

Zones: USDA Hardiness Zones 7–10

Rhaphiolepis indica (Indian hawthorn)

Plant Description: A compact shrub that grows 4 to 5 feet tall and wide (pruning can keep it smaller, and named varieties have different growth potential), Indian hawthorn has pointed, leathery, dark green leaves that are 1½ to 3 inches long. In spring and early summer, the plant is laden with clusters of ½-inch-wide white or pink flowers, depending on the hybrid.

Preferred Growing Conditions: Indian hawthorn is a drought-tolerant shrub that will grow in full sun or light shade, though flowers will be less profuse and the form will be less compact in shady spots.

Maintenance Tips: Pinch branch tips annually after flowering to maintain a bushy, compact form. If you are aiming for an open structure, leave them be, except to thin out branches as necessary to emphasize the form.

Zones: USDA Hardiness Zones 8–10, AHS Heat Zones 9–3

Taxus spp. (yew)

Plant Description: Long-lived, slow-growing evergreen conifers that take heavy shearing and pruning, yews are an excellent shrub for hedges. The finely textured, dark green foliage makes the plants a superb background for perennial borders. Some yews grow tall and wide (*T. baccata* ultimately reaches a height of 30 to 70 feet); others, such as *T. x media* 'Densiformis', stay at 3 to 4 feet. *T. cuspidata* 'Nana' will take about 20 years to reach a 3-foot height and 6-foot spread. Depending on what you plant, yews are suitable as specimen trees, hedges, screens, and formal clipped topiary shapes, such as spheres and boxes. Choose one that has a growth habit that best suits the application you have in mind.

Preferred Growing Conditions: Yews grow well in both full sun and deep shade in either alkaline or acidic soil. They are picky about drainage, however, and will likely die of root rot if the soil remains waterlogged.

Maintenance Tips: For hedges, shear plants in summer and early autumn. Old plants that have overgrown their site can withstand severe renovation pruning.

Zones: USDA Hardiness Zones 4–7, AHS Heat Zones 7–1

Taxus x *media* 'Thayarae'

Trees

Depending on the genera and species, trees may be tall and stately, medium-sized or small-scale, deciduous or evergreen, flowering or not. The overall shape of the tree may be columnar, fastigate, round, oval, weeping, or conical. The canopy may be open, allowing light and rain to filter through to the ground, or dense, providing deep shade. When you select trees for your garden, bear in mind their ultimate, mature height and spread. A common mistake is to plant too large a tree in too small a space. Also consider leaf color and texture, the possibility of a colorful display in autumn, interesting bark in winter, and any potential for flowers and/or berries.

Acer griseum (paperbark maple)

Plant Description: A deciduous tree that grows slowly to about 25 feet at maturity, paperbark maple has a narrow, oval to rounded crown that makes a striking winter silhouette. Perhaps its most alluring feature is the orange-brown bark that peels off in curly strips. In summer, the leaves, which are divided into three lobes, are dark green on top and silvery underneath. In fall, the foliage turns brilliant red.

Preferred Growing Conditions: Paperbark maple grows best in rich, acidic soil in a sunny spot. Although it can withstand an occasional drought, it does better when given regular water.

Maintenance Tip: If you live in the right climate zone, paperbark maple is an excellent small landscape tree. A healthy tree should be able to survive any pests that come its way.

Zones: USDA Hardiness Zones 4–8

Acer palmatum (Japanese maple)

Plant Description: A slow-growing tree that ultimately reaches about 20 feet tall, Japanese maple deserves its huge popularity. Its ornamental qualities are evident year-round: In spring, the new growth is a fresh red; with the exception of the red-leafed hybrids, the finely toothed leaves evolve to a soft green for the summer months before turning scarlet, yellow, or orange for their autumn display. In winter, the bare, twisted branches make beautiful patterns in the landscape. Among the many excellent grafted cultivars are 'Bloodgood', which is a heat-tolerant cultivar with dark red-purple leaves; 'Bonfire', which has a beautifully twisted trunk and orange-pink spring and fall foliage; and 'Dissectum Atropurpureum', which has red-purple leaves that are more finely lobed than those of the species.

Preferred Growing Conditions: Unlike most maples, *A. palmatum* prefers a little shade, especially in parts of the country that have hot, dry winds.

Maintenance Tips: If you choose a variety, such as 'Butterfly' or 'Ever Red', that stays small, a Japanese maple makes an excellent container plant. Select a large container and fill it with a planting mix that drains quickly but still retains moisture. Water regularly so the plant never experiences the stress of wilting. During the summer months, when the tree is in leaf, feed it with a slow-release fertilizer every 4 to 6 weeks. Place the container in a partially shaded spot that is sheltered from wind.

Zones: USDA Hardiness Zones 4–8, AHS Heat Zones 10–3

Albizia julibrissin (silk tree or mimosa)

Plant Description: Left to its own devices, this deciduous tree will quickly reach 40 feet tall and wide, but you can head it back (prune back the central leader stem) to make a 10- to 20-foot-tall tree with a lovely spreading canopy like an umbrella. In summer, pink powder-puff flowers stand out on the ferny-leafed branches. With noninvasive roots and a wide canopy, it is a great tree to shade a patio. It's also a pretty tree to look down on, as the flowers grow on top of the crown. As is typical of fast-growing trees and shrubs, this one is short-lived and will begin to decline after about 20 years. In fall, the prolific seeds can be a nuisance.

Preferred Growing Conditions: Silk tree flowers best in full sun.

Maintenance Tips: *Albizia* is susceptible to webworms, which weave their silken nests between the branches. When the 1-inch-long brown caterpillars hatch, they go on a feeding frenzy and skeletonize the foliage. If you can reach them, remove the nests before the caterpillars have a chance to do any damage.

Zones: USDA Hardiness Zones 6–10

Amelanchier arborea (serviceberry)

Plant Description: A native of eastern North America, serviceberry is multistemmed and grows to about 25 feet tall with a 30-foot spread. The 1½- to 3-inch-long, ovate leaves are mid-green in summer and turn from orange to red in autumn. Fragrant white flowers borne on 2- to 3-inch racemes grace the tree in mid-spring.

Preferred Growing Conditions: In its native habitat, serviceberry grows on the forest fringe. Plant it in moist, acidic soil in sun or partial shade.

Maintenance Tip: In late winter or early spring, when the tree is still dormant, prune away any excess shoots growing toward the center of the tree, particularly those that are crossing other branches. That way, you'll maintain a permanent, healthy framework for the tree.

Zones: USDA Hardiness Zones 4–9, AHS Heat Zones 8–3

Cedrus atlantica (Atlas cedar)

Plant Description: Atlas cedar, which grows slowly, ultimately reaching 60 feet or more with a 30-foot spread, makes a magnificent specimen tree. The needlelike foliage is less than 1 inch long and generally a bluish green. The foliage of 'Aurea' has a yellow tint; 'Glauca' (blue Atlas cedar) is silvery blue. Another well-loved variety is 'Glauca Pendula', which has blue foliage and a weeping form. It is one of the few trees you can train to droop over a swimming pool, because it doesn't shed.

Preferred Growing Conditions: Plant in well-drained soil in full sun.

Maintenance Tips: Pinch back the branch tips of young trees to keep them from growing too long and heavy. Water the trees, especially young ones, during periods of drought.

Zones: USDA Hardiness Zones 6–9, AHS Heat Zones 7–2

Cercis canadensis (eastern redbud)

Plant Description: A North American native, eastern redbud is prized for its small, vibrant pink, pealike flowers that cover the bare stems in spring before the leaves appear. Often multistemmed, the tree grows quickly to 25 to 35 feet tall with a rounded canopy and horizontally tiered branches. The rich green, heart-shaped leaves are about 4 inches long. The foliage provides fall color after the first frost. 'Alba' blossoms with white flowers; 'Forest Pansy' has dark red-purple leaves.

Preferred Growing Conditions: Eastern redbud's natural habitat is the fringes of wooded areas, so it prefers full sun or partial shade. It does best in deep, fertile soil that is moist but well drained.

Maintenance Tip: When the tree is dormant, in late winter or early spring, prune out any internal

Chamaecyparis obtusa 'Crippsii'

branches that are crossing each other to promote a graceful, healthy framework for the tree.

Zones: USDA Hardiness Zones 6–9, AHS Heat Zones 12–9

Cercis occidentalis (California redbud)

Plant Description: A small, deciduous tree native to California, Arizona, and Utah, California redbud grows 10 to 18 feet tall and wide and usually has multiple trunks. In spring, the bare branches are covered with tiny, magenta, pealike flowers. The tree flowers best if it is exposed to winter temperatures in the area of 28°F. The flowers are followed by blue-green, kidney-shaped leaves that turn bright yellow or red in fall. Magenta seedpods turn brown as the season progresses and remain on the tree through winter. Because of its compact size and many-season interest, California redbud is an ideal patio tree.

Preferred Growing Conditions: California redbud enjoys full sun or partial shade. Although tolerant of most soils, it thrives in fertile conditions with good drainage.

Maintenance Tip: Prune as necessary when the tree is dormant to maintain an attractive, open framework.

Zones: USDA Hardiness Zones 7–10, AHS Heat Zones 12–9

Chamaecyparis obtusa (Hinoki false cypress)

Plant Description: There are scores of varieties of Hinoki false cypress, ranging from tall specimens that top out at 25 feet to dwarf cultivars, such as 'Nana', that reach a height of only 2 or 3 feet. Normally, the scalelike foliage is dark green on top of the flattened sprays and silvery underneath; however, there are cultivars with gold-tipped foliage ('Nana Lutea' is one), as well as fern-leafed forms. The slow-growing dwarf varieties are valuable for rock gardens and foundation plantings because they add bulk and texture without taking up too much space.

Preferred Growing Conditions: Hinoki false cypress enjoys well-drained, fertile soil that is slightly acidic. It is susceptible to root rot if drainage is poor. Grow it in full sun or partial shade.

Maintenance Tip: Over time, the foliage on the inner, older wood will die, either of natural causes or because of mites. In either case, aim a strong jet of water from a hose at the dead foliage. The force of the water will knock off the mites as well as the unattractive dead leaves.
Zones: USDA Hardiness Zones 4–8, AHS Heat Zones 8–3

Chionanthus retusus (Chinese fringe tree), and C. virginicus (white fringe tree)

Plant Description: The lacy clusters of fragrant white flowers that grace these small trees or large shrubs account for the common name, fringe tree. The genus name comprises the Greek words *chion* (snow) and *anthos* (flower). Chinese fringe tree tends to be the smaller of the two, maturing at a height of about 20 feet. It flowers in June and July, followed by blue-black fruit about ½ inch in diameter. In contrast, white fringe tree, which is native from Pennsylvania to Florida and Texas, reaches maturity at about 30 feet tall, though it is very slow growing. It can take 10 years for it to reach 12 feet. Fortunately, it blooms at a young age. Its flower clusters are twice as big as those borne by Chinese fringe tree and appear in May, also followed by blue-black fruit. The glossy, dark green leaves of both species turn deep yellow in fall.
Preferred Growing Conditions: Heat- and sun-loving fringe trees flower best in regions where summers are long and hot. Grow them in fertile, well-drained soil.
Maintenance Tips: These are low-maintenance trees that are rarely bothered by pests or diseases. Remove the lower branches of *C. virginicus* to encourage a more treelike form.
Zones: *C. retusus,* USDA Hardiness Zones 6–10; *C. virginicus,* USDA Hardiness Zones 5–9

Cladrastis lutea (yellowwood)

Plant Description: A deciduous, dome-shaped tree that grows quickly to 50 feet tall with a 40- to 50-foot spread, yellowwood is considered by many authorities to be one of the outstanding American flowering trees native to the

Cornus florida

Southeast. The leaves open in spring with a bright yellowish green color that matures to a light green. They are composed of 7 to 11 broadly ovate leaflets along a 12-inch stem. In fall, they change again to pure yellow. In late May and June, fragrant white flower panicles light up the tree, drooping from 15-inch pendants. A pink cultivar, 'Rosea', is also available. The winter silhouette is striking in the landscape because its smooth, pale gray bark catches the light for a luminescent effect. As a bonus, the roots support nitrogen-fixing bacteria, thus improving the surrounding soil. This is an underused tree that deserves more attention.
Preferred Growing Conditions: Grow yellowwood in full sun in loamy or sandy soil. It will adapt to both alkaline and acidic conditions. Drainage is particularly important, as it cannot tolerate wet feet. In the wild, it tends to grow on limestone cliffs and ridges. Once established, it can withstand periods of extreme drought.
Maintenance Tips: Prune only in summer (the tree is susceptible to bleeding). The wood is brittle and liable to snap in a strong wind, so it helps to clean out excessive wood from the tree's center and train a good branching structure to avoid bad crotches that are likely to split or crack. The tree

is almost completely disease- and insect-free.
Zones: USDA Hardiness Zones 3–8

Cornus florida (flowering dogwood)

Plant Description: A small, deciduous tree that grows slowly to 20 feet tall with a 25-foot spread, dogwood provide year-round interest with its attractive winter silhouette; brilliant pink or white late-spring floral display; and tidy summer foliage followed by oval, bright red berries. The actual dogwood flowers are the small green centers that are surrounded by the four bracts, each 1½ to 2 inches long, and are white or pink, depending on the variety or cultivar.
Preferred Growing Conditions: Growing naturally as an understory tree in the eastern U.S., flowering dogwood enjoys bright shade or full sun (partial shade is better in hotter areas) and moist, acidic soil enriched with organic matter.
Maintenance Tips: The fungal disease dogwood anthracnose has ravaged the dogwood population in the eastern United States. Symptoms include blighted and dying leaves and lower-limb dieback; ultimately the tree dies. To give the trees a fighting chance against the fungus, protect them from drought stress by mulching and irrigating. Avoid wetting the foliage when you water (a deep soaking at the roots is best), and keep the mulch material 3 to 4 inches away from the tree trunk. Improve vigor by feeding the tree with a balanced fertilizer. To keep possible infection from spreading, dispose of fallen leaves, rather than composting or recycling them, and prune away and destroy deadwood. If you are planting a new tree, select a site that receives at least half a day of sunshine and has good air circulation.
Zones: USDA Hardiness Zones 5–8, AHS Heat Zones 9–1

Cornus kousa (Kousa dogwood)

Plant Description: A slow-growing tree, Kousa dogwood reaches 20 to 30 feet in height with an equal spread under optimum conditions. Distinctive for its horizontal branching character, the tree has dark green summer foliage that changes to reddish purple or scarlet in fall. The foliage display lasts for 3 to 5 weeks, depending on weather conditions. Two to 3 weeks after *C. florida* flowers, Kousa dogwood is filled with inconspicuous true flowers highlighted with creamy white bracts that stand out from the foliage. Lasting for nearly 6 weeks, the bracts age to a soft pink. As the tree ages, the bark exfoliates to reveal a mottled mosaic of gray, tan, and brown.

Preferred Growing Conditions: Kousa dogwood flourishes in bright shade or full sun in moist, neutral to acidic sandy soil enriched with organic material. It is more drought tolerant than is *C. florida*.

Maintenance Tip: Kousa dogwood is a disease- and pest-resistant tree. Give it the growing conditions it requires, and it will reward you with excellent performance.

Zones: USDA Hardiness Zones 5–8, AHS Heat Zones 9–1

Lagerstroemia 'Yuma'

Franklinia alatamaha (Franklin tree)

Plant Description: A handsome, small specimen tree that reaches 10 to 30 feet in height with a 6- to 15-foot spread, Franklin tree was first discovered along the banks of the Altamaha River in Georgia by botanist John Bartram in 1770. He collected specimens and propagated the trees for his nursery business. Mysteriously, no wild specimens have been seen since 1790, so it is believed that all modern examples are descended from Bartram's original collection. The handsome foliage is a lustrous dark green in summer, changing to orange and red in fall. From late July into August, the tree produces fragrant, cupped white flowers featuring five petals around a center of yellow stamens. The flowers are typically about 3 inches in diameter. Although the tree is a native of Georgia, modern specimens tend to perform better in the North, perhaps because there they are not subject to a soilborne disease associated with cotton. Franklin tree does well as a lawn or patio tree.

Preferred Growing Conditions: Franklin tree grows best in well-drained, humus-rich, acidic to neutral soil in full sun. Add plenty of organic matter to the planting hole.

Maintenance Tip: The tree is tricky to transplant because of the sparse, fibrous root system, so either purchase container or balled-and-burlapped

trees or grow it from seed. A seed-sown tree will flower in 6 to 7 years.

Zones: USDA Hardiness Zones 5–8

Gordonia lasianthus (loblolly bay)

Plant Description: A medium-sized evergreen tree with an erect to slightly spreading habit, loblolly bay blossoms from July to September, sporting fragrant, single, white, camellia-like flowers 2 to 3 inches in diameter, each with five to seven large petals and a yellow stamen center. A fast grower, the tree will ultimately grow 36 to 60 feet tall, casting light shade because of its upright form and compact crown. The glossy, dark green foliage is narrowly elliptic and up to 7 inches long, with fine blunt teeth along the edges. In fall, the leaves turn a reddish color.

Preferred Growing Conditions: Grow loblolly bay in full sun or dappled shade in acidic soil that is either loamy or sandy. Found in the wild in swampy areas, the tree is tolerant of wet conditions, and appreciates regular watering.

Maintenance Tips: Prune in late winter or early spring as necessary to remove wayward branches.

Zones: USDA Hardiness Zones 8–10

Lagerstroemia spp. (crape myrtle)

Plant Description: A summer-flowering tree that enjoys hot weather, crape myrtle is ideal near a

swimming pool, where it will provide lively color during the time of year when you're most likely to be enjoying the poolside garden. It is an upright, multi-trunked tree (or large shrub) with peeling bark in shades of copper, brown, cream, and gray that looks marvelous in winter as well as summer. The dark green leaves grow about 3 inches long and are bronze when young. Flower colors include white, shades of pink, variations of purple and lavender, and red. Tree size varies with the hybrid. Large varieties, such as 'Centennial Spirit' (dark red flowers) and 'Muskogee' (lavender blooms), grow to 20 feet tall, and 'Natchez' (white flowers) reaches a stately 30 feet. 'Sioux' (bright pink blossoms) and 'Yuma' (lavender flowers) grow to 15 feet tall. Dwarf varieties that stay at 3 feet or shorter include 'Centennial' (bright purple flowers), 'Chickasaw' (pink blossoms), and 'Pixie White' (white flowers).

Preferred Growing Conditions: Crape myrtle does well in moderately fertile, well-drained soil in full sun.

Maintenance Tips: To increase the potential for a second flush of bloom, cut off the small round seedpods that form after the flowers have dropped. The practice (humorously referred to as crape murder) of cutting back young specimens to a few feet above the ground in

February or March ruins the natural shape of the tree and causes dense growth that impairs air circulation. It also increases risk of sooty mold and powdery mildew. You are better off allowing the tree to grow free, except for removing unwanted internal branches that crisscross each other.

Zones: USDA Hardiness Zones 7–9, AHS Heat Zones 10–2

Malus spp. (crab apple)

Plant Description: These are excellent small, deciduous ornamental trees that are covered in pink, red, or white flowers in spring and attractive little apples in late summer and into fall and winter. Plant crab apples away from the swimming pool, however, or you'll be skimming off spent flower petals in spring and removing fallen apples in autumn. The trees typically grow 15 to 25 feet tall, depending on the variety. The leaves, which are oval and pointed and in some cases fuzzy, range in color from deep green to almost purple, depending on the variety. The purple-leafed types hold their color best in full sun. Versatile landscape trees, crab apples are excellent in lawns, along fences, as a screen, in matched rows to create an avenue, espaliered against a fence or wall, or freestanding as a cordon.

Preferred Growing Conditions: Crab apples flourish in moist, well-drained soil in full sun. They are adaptable to a wide range of soil types.

Maintenance Tips: Prune the trees as necessary to keep an open, vaselike interior structure to encourage good air circulation and lots of light. To avoid common problems such as fire blight, cedar-apple rust, powdery mildew, and apple scab, opt for resistant cultivars, such as 'Donald Wyman' (red and pink buds open to single white flowers followed by bright red fruit); 'Indian Summer' (rose-red flowers and bright red fruit); 'Prairifire' (red buds, pinkish red flowers, and dark red-purple fruit); 'Red Jade' (red buds, white or pink flowers, and red fruit); and 'Sugar Tyme' (pale pink buds, fragrant white flowers, and persistent red fruit). Many of these varieties are available in weeping form. Check with your local Cooperative

Extension for the hybrids that are best suited to your area. Healthy, vigorous trees also are more resistant to pests and diseases.

Zones: USDA Hardiness Zones 4–8, AHS Zones 8–2

Pistacia chinensis (Chinese pistachio)

Plant Description: An excellent street, patio, or lawn tree, Chinese pistachio eventually reaches 60 feet tall and 50 feet wide, so give it plenty of room to grow. The bark develops shallow ridges that mature into gray scales. As the scales flake away, they expose a salmon-colored bark underneath. The 10-inch-long leaves, which comprise 10 to 16 paired leaflets, are a glossy dark green in summer, turning to scarlet, crimson, orange, and yellow in fall. It's the only deciduous tree that provides scarlet coloring in the desert in fall. Female trees produce bright red fruit that matures to dark blue.

Preferred Growing Conditions: Adaptable to most soil conditions, Chinese pistachio prefers full sun. It will tolerate excessive watering as well as drought (in deep soils).

Maintenance Tips: Stake young trees, and prune off lower branches as necessary to raise the canopy high enough to walk under. Chinese pistachio is almost completely insect- and disease-free.

Zones: USDA Hardiness Zones 6–9, AHS Heat Zones 12–4

Sophora japonica (Japanese pagoda tree)

Plant Description: This spreading, deciduous tree grows fairly quickly to 20 feet tall, then slows down, ultimately stretching to 40 feet or more with equal spread. Japanese pagoda tree is an excellent shade tree in a lawn or near a patio. The leaves are about 10 inches long, each with up to 17 lance-shaped dark green leaflets. From July to September, it produces 8 to 10 long clusters of pealike, yellowish white, ½-inch-long fragrant flowers. These mature into 2- to 3½-inch-long seedpods that dangle from the branches. The young wood is dark grayish green and smooth. As it ages, it becomes more

gnarled and rugged-looking. Because the tree sheds flower petals (which make an attractive carpet under the tree when they first fall), seedpods, and leaves, plant it away from the immediate vicinity of the swimming pool.

Preferred Growing Conditions: Although not overly fussy about soil and water, Japanese pagoda tree prefers loamy, well-drained soil. It grows well in full sun or partial shade, and flowers less reliably where summers are damp and cool. It is tolerant of pollution, making it an excellent city tree. Once established, it is heat and drought tolerant.

Maintenance Tip: Prune in fall to remove internal branches that cross each other and to create an attractive framework for the tree.

Zones: USDA Hardiness Zones 4–8

Syringa reticulata (Japanese tree lilac)

Plant Description: A member of the lilac family, Japanese tree lilac is a deciduous tree with glossy, reddish brown bark and lance-shaped, 6-inch-long dark green leaves with grayish green undersides. The mature height is 20 to 30 feet with a 15- to 25-foot spread. For 2 weeks from early to mid-June, it is bright with fragrant (similar to the scent of privet), showy white flowers borne on 6- to 12-inch-long panicles. Grow it as a large shrub or a small specimen tree or along a fence or building. For a more compact hybrid, look for 'Ivory Silk', which flowers when young and grows just 10 to 12 feet tall and 6 feet wide.

Preferred Growing Conditions: All lilacs grow best in loose, well-drained soil. Although adaptable to different pH conditions, Japanese tree lilac particularly likes slightly acidic soil. Plant it where it will receive full sun. It prefers regions with cool summers.

Maintenance Tips: Prune Japanese tree lilac after flowering to remove spent blossoms before the fruit forms. Look for plants grown on their own roots, rather than ones grafted onto privet rootstock.

Zones: USDA Hardiness Zones 3–7, AHS Heat Zones 8–3

USDA Hardiness Zone Map

Created by the United States Department of Agriculture (USDA), this map is a useful tool for selecting and cultivating plants. The map divides North America into 11 zones based on each region's average minimum winter temperature. Zone 1 is the coldest and Zone 11 the warmest. Locate your zone, and then use that information to select plants that are most likely to thrive in your climate.

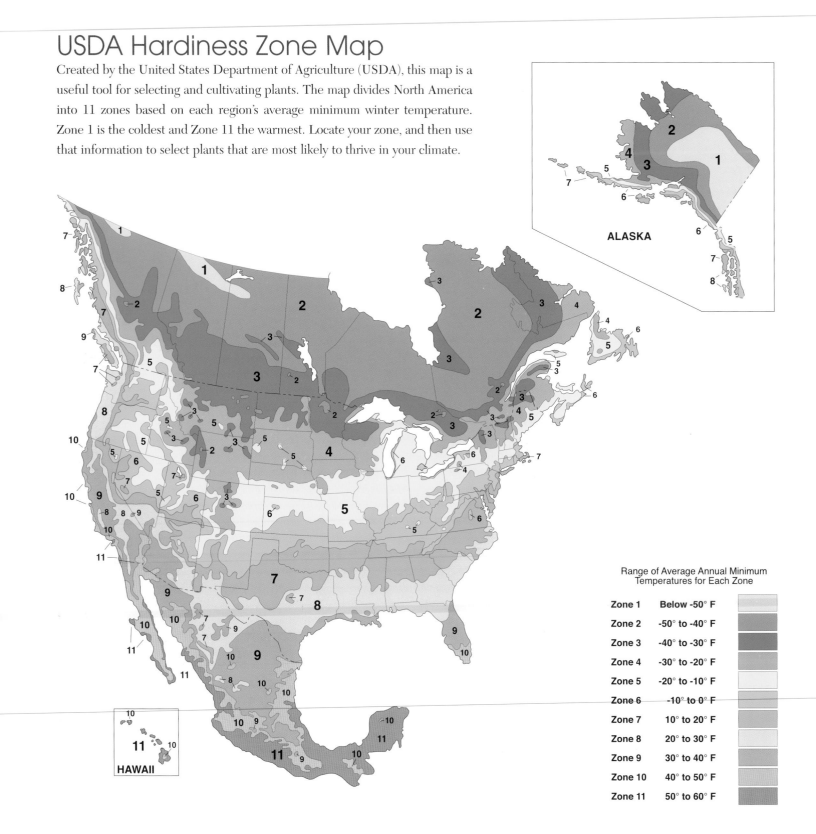

ALASKA

HAWAII

Range of Average Annual Minimum Temperatures for Each Zone

Zone 1	Below -50° F	
Zone 2	-50° to -40° F	
Zone 3	-40° to -30° F	
Zone 4	-30° to -20° F	
Zone 5	-20° to -10° F	
Zone 6	-10° to 0° F	
Zone 7	10° to 20° F	
Zone 8	20° to 30° F	
Zone 9	30° to 40° F	
Zone 10	40° to 50° F	
Zone 11	50° to 60° F	

AHS Plant Heat-Zone Map

Created by the American Horticultural Society (AHS), this map provides guidance for selecting plants that tolerate the upper temperature ranges where you live. It divides the United States into 12 zones, based on the average number of days each year a region experiences heat days (days when temperatures rise over 86°F/30°C). This is the point at which plants begin to suffer physiological damage from heat. Zone 1 has less than one heat day, while Zone 12 has more than 210 heat days. For more information, see the American Horticultural Society's website: www.AHS.org.

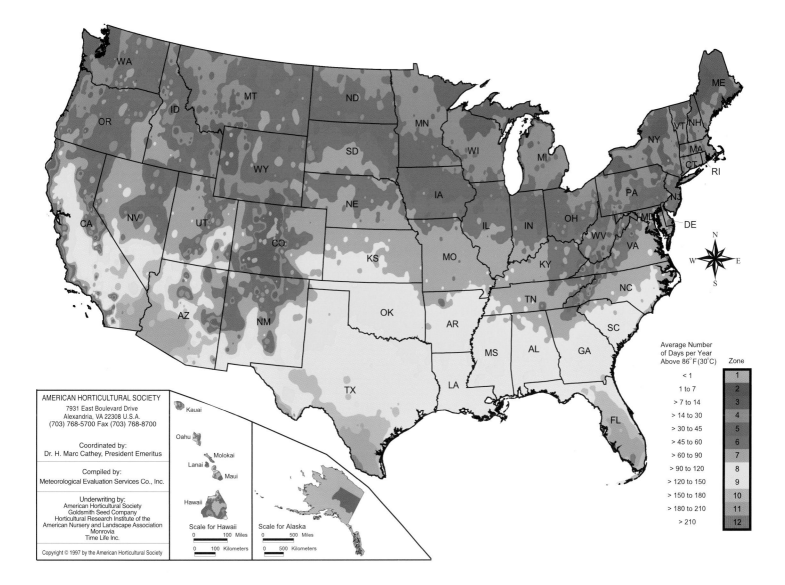

AMERICAN HORTICULTURAL SOCIETY

7931 East Boulevard Drive
Alexandria, VA 22308 U.S.A.
(703) 768-5700 Fax (703) 768-8700

Coordinated by:
Dr. H. Marc Cathey, President Emeritus

Compiled by:
Meteorological Evaluation Services Co., Inc.

Underwriting by:
American Horticultural Society
Goldsmith Seed Company
Horticultural Research Institute of the
American Nursery and Landscape Association
Monrovia
Time Life Inc.

Copyright © 1997 by the American Horticultural Society

Scale for Hawaii
0   100 Miles
0   100 Kilometers

Scale for Alaska
0   500 Miles
0   500 Kilometers

Average Number of Days per Year Above 86°F (30°C)	Zone
< 1	1
1 to 7	2
> 7 to 14	3
> 14 to 30	4
> 30 to 45	5
> 45 to 60	6
> 60 to 90	7
> 90 to 120	8
> 120 to 150	9
> 150 to 180	10
> 180 to 210	11
> 210	12

Additional Information

Brick Industry Association
11490 Commerce Park Drive
Reston, Virginia 20191-1525
Tel: (703) 620-0010; Fax: (703) 620-3928
www.brickinfo.org
For specifications on building a pier-and-panel wall without footings, ask for Technical Notes on Brick Construction 29A, Revised 2002.

Natural Swimming Ponds
Michael Littlewood
The Old Forge; The Pound
Shepton Beauchamp
Ilminster, Somerset TA19 0LD
England
Tel/Fax: 011 44 1460 241847
michael@ecodesign.freeserve.co.uk

Garden Lights
The Web site of Outdoor Illumination in Washington, D.C., includes hot links to major garden light manufacturers. Go to www.outdoorillumination.com.

Acknowledgments

One of the nicest things about being a garden writer and photographer is having the opportunity to meet fascinating people in the field. Working on this book was no exception. Colleagues and experts in the swimming pool world have all been extremely generous with their time and expertise. I would particularly like to thank architect Norm Applebaum; landscape architects Richard Arentz, Elizabeth Bartels, and Phillippe Lizarraga; landscape lighting expert Mark Oxley; pool designers Ron Gibbons, Skip Phillips, and Ian Spicer; Jon Dewey of Jud Tile, Ltd. in Vienna, Virginia; David Modine of the stone supplier Jack T. Irwin, Inc. in Rockville, Maryland; and my colleagues Debra Baldwin and Nan Sterman, who gave me many valuable introductions. *The Landscape Lighting Book* by Janet Lennox Moyer also was an invaluable and comprehensive resource.

In addition to the generosity of experts, many people opened their homes to me, sharing their gardening and pool ownership experiences and allowing me to take photographs. I'd like to offer special thanks to John and Laura Alioto; James and Rebecca Allen; Lyle and Helen Arnold; Elizabeth Bartels; Linda Bateman; Robert Bell; Kerry Blockley; Jane G. Briggs; Edward and Terry Carr; Marjorie Casey; Licia and Michael Conforti; Laurie Connable; Roger Cornell; Dewar and Alison Donnithorne-Tait; Mary Edgerton; Richard and Jodie Elliott; Joe and Susannah Haber; Jim and Jane Heekin; Richard and Jane Mears; Allen Mushinsky; John Nickum and Linda Lear; Carol and Dick Paul; John and Barbara Quarles; Tim and Tish Rickard; Barney and Pat Shine; Kathleen Tansey; Phil and Gayle Tauber; Gordon and Lisa Tudor and their three sons, Grant, Reid, and Cole; Jim and Jane Sleeva; Susi Torre-Bueno; Diane Uke; Tammy Valley; John and Mary Walsh; Margo Washburn; Phillip Watson; and Tim Webb.

Photography Credits

Photographs by Catriona Tudor Erler, except for the following:

Biotop Natural Pools: 86
© Gary Conaughton: 22
© Joseph De Sciose: 50, 150
© Roger Foley: 2, 6–7, 8–9, 10, 11, 12, 20, 28–29, 30, 40, 44–45, 52, 55, 56, 68–69, 72, 73, 74, 76, 85, 88–89, 110, 123, 130–131, 156, 157, 172–173

© Global Book Publishing Pty. Ltd.: 66
© Harry Haralambou: 32, 43, 79, 144, 147, 148, 154
© Robert Hebb/Apis Images: 67, 175, 176, 179, 180, 181, 182, 185, 186, 187, 188, 189, 191, 192, 193, 194
© Dency Kane: 19, 31, 91, 93, 155

© Janet Loughrey: 42, 49, 92
© Maggie Oster: 142–143
Giles Prett: 26
© Carl Saporitti: 121, 153

Garden Design Credits

Norm Applebaum, 90, 168
Richard Arentz, 28–29, 30, 74, 85, 88–89, 110, 123
Elizabeth Bartels, 17
Robert Bell, 138 (right)
Charlie Bowers, Garden Gate Landscaping, Inc., 21, 25 (left), 171
Yunghi Choi, 12
Ron Gibbons, Ron Gibbons Swimming Pools, Inc., 121, 153

Michael Holt, 114, 148
Eric Jensen, 16, 165
Raymond Jungles, 11, 40, 156
Arabella Lennox-Boyd, 135
Tom Mannion, 6–7, 56, 73, 162–63
Mission Pools, Escondido, CA, 169
Allen Mushinsky, 24, 77
Oehme, van Sweden & Associates: cover, 2, 10, 20, 44–45, 52, 55, 68–69, 72, 76, 172–73

Mark Oxley (lighting), 104–105, 106-107, 111, 112, 117, 118
Skip Phillips, Questar Pools and Spas, Inc., 113, 134
Peter Poirier, 22
Osamu Shimizu, 8–9, 130–31
John Snitzer, 82, 104-105, 106–107
Gary Stone, 53
Philip Watson, Washington Gardens, 71, 78

Index

Page numbers in *italics* indicate photos or illustrations.

bird-of-paradise, 70, 134

black bamboo, 83

black-eyed Susan, 78, *78*, 178

bloody cranesbill, 41

blue fescue, 41, 183

blue oat grass, 184

bog garden, 86–87, *86*

bollard lights, 122

Bonin Island juniper, 41

Boston ivy, 187

Bougainvillea spp., 49, 90, 152

box honeysuckle, 67

boxwood, 60, 65, 66, 70–71, 74

Brassica oleracea, 92

brick
  coping, 43
  paving, 36–37, *36, 37*
  walls, 52–53, *52*

Brick Industry Association, 53, 197

bridges, 153–155

broadleaf, 67

broad-leafed paperbark, 66

buckthorn, Indian, 85

bull-nosed coping, 42, *42*

burning bush, 48, 96, 189, *189*

Buxus microphylla var. *japonica*, 60

Buxus spp. *See* boxwood

C

cabanas, 145–146, *147*

cabbage, ornamental, 92

Calamagrostis x *acutiflora*, 183

Calendula officinalis, 41

calico flower, 152

California redbud, 192

calla lily, 84

Camellia spp., 67, 188

Campsis radicans, 152, 186, *186*

Canadian hemlock, 83

Canadian poplar, 66

canary bird vine, 152

Canary Island ivy, 85

candytuft, 41, 177

Canna spp., 82, 91

cape honeysuckle, 152

caraway thyme, 41

Carolina jessamine, 152

Carpinus betulus. See European
  hornbeam

cast-iron furniture, 158, 160, 161

catmint (catnip), *50, 73*, 92

cat's-claw vine, 152

cedars, 66, 192. *See also* Western red
  cedar

Cedrus atlantica, 192

Cedrus deodara, 66

Cephalotaxus fortunei, 66

Cerastium tomentosum, 180, *180*

Cercis canadensis, 192

Cercis occidentalis, 192

Cestrum nocturnum, 84

chain-link fence, 49

chairs, 156–160

Chamaecyparis lawsoniana, 66, *66*

Chamaecyparis obtusa, 192–193, *192*

Chamaecyparis spp., 188

Chamaemelum nobile, 41

chamomile, 41

Chilean potato vine, 152

Chinese fringe tree, 193

Chinese gooseberry vine, 152

Chinese holly, 65, 67

Chinese juniper, 66

Chinese pistachio, 195

Chinese plum yew, 66

Chinese (tropical) hibiscus, 69, 96,
  189

Chinese wisteria, 152, 187, *187*

Chionanthus retusus, 193

Chionanthus virginicus, 193

Choisya ternata, 84

Cistus spp., 41, 69, 188–189

Cistus x *purpureus*, 188

Cladrastis lutea, 193

Clematis armandii, 51

Clematis spp., 92, 152, 186

Cleome hasslerana, 84

climbing hydrangea, 152, 186

clock vine, 92, 152

Clytostoma callistegioides, 152

coleus, 82

Colocasia esculenta, 82

color
  in container gardening, 92
  in lighting design, 108, 111
  of pools, 24–25

common juniper, 66

common lilac, 96

common thyme, 96

compost, 101

concrete, 22–23, 39–40, *40*

coneflower, 78, 84, 175

conifers, 66

construction materials
  coping, 42–43
  paving, 31–40
  pools, 22–25

container gardening, 88–103
  choosing containers, 98
  overwintering, 93, 99
  routine care, 100–103
  topiary sculpture, 94–97, *94, 95*

container-grown plants, 62–64

Convallaria majalis, 84, 180

copings, 42–43

coralbells, 177

coral vine, 152, 186

cordyline, 92

Coreopsis spp., *50, 56*, 78, 175

Coreopsis verticillata, 92

Cornus alba, 85

Cornus alternifolia, 85

Cornus controversa, 85

Cornus florida, 193, *193*

Cornus kousa, 193–194

Corydalis lutea, 41

flagstone, *30, 31,* 33–36, 43
flax, New Zealand, 92
floodlights, 122, *122*
flowering dogwood, 193, *193*
flowering maple, 92
flowering quince, 58
foliage texture, 92
Forsythia spp., 58, 74
fountain bamboo, 83
fountain grass, 76, 78, 92, 184
fountains, *118,* 119, 138–141
four-o'clock, 84
Fragaria vesca, 85
fragrant plants, 41, 70–71, 84
Franklinia alatamaha, 194
Franklin tree, 194
Freesia alba, 84
Freesia lactea, 84
French lavender, 96
fringed lavender, 96
fringe trees, 193
fruit trees, 58, 59
Fuchsia spp., 96
furniture, 156–161
furniture covers, 161

G

Gardenia augusta, 84
garden lights. *See* lighting fixtures
garden phlox. See *Phlox paniculata*
garden sheds. *See* pool houses
gates, *48,* 54–55, *54, 55*
Gaultheria procumbens, 181
Gazania rigens, 181, *181*
gazebos, 146–149
Gelsemium sempervirens, 152
Geranium incanum, 41
Geranium sanguineum, 41
Geranium spp., 99, 176
geraniums. See *Geranium* spp.;
    Pelargonium spp.
giant bird-of-paradise, 134

giant dogwood, 85
giant feather grass, 185
giant fir, 66
giant hyssop, *112*
giant reed, 183
ginger, European wild, 179
ginger lily, 84
glass bridge, *153,* 155
glass mosaic tile, 38, *38*
glass walls, 53, *53*
Gleditsia triacanthos, 62, *71*
globe lights, 123
glossy abelia, 66, *66,* 188
golden bamboo, 83
golden dewdrop, 67
golden hops, 152
gooseberry vine, Chinese, 152
Gordonia lasianthus, 194
granite, 34–35, *35*
grasses, ornamental. *See* ornamental
    grasses
Griselinia littoralis, 67
ground covers, 179–183
Guinea gold vine, 152
Gypsophila paniculata, 176

H

Hakonechloa macra. See Japanese
    forest grass
halogen lights, 122–123
hand-painted tile, 15
hanging baskets, *92*
Hardenbergia comptoniana, 152
Hardiness Zone map, 174, *196*
harmony (in design), 72–74, 108–109
hawthorns, 61, 66, 170, 190
heather (heath), 41
Heat Zone map, 174, *197*
heavenly bamboo. See *Nandina
    domestica*
Hedera canariensis, 85
Hedera colchica, 85

Hedera helix, 85, 181
hedges, 60–67
    maintenance of, 65, *65*
    planting of, 62–64
    plant selection for, 60, 66–67, 83
Hedychium coronarium, 84
Helianthemum nummularium, 181
Helianthemum spp., 41
Helianthus annuus, 84
Helichrysum italicum, 96
Helichrysum petiolare, 96
Helictotrichon sempervirens, 184
heliotrope, 84
Heliotropium arborescens, 84
Hemerocallis spp. *See* daylily
hemlock, Canadian, 66
hen-and-chickens, 41
Hesperis matronalis, 84
Heuchera spp., 177
Hibbertia scandens, 152
Hibiscus rosa-sinensis, 69, 96, 189
Hibiscus spp., 67
Hibiscus syriacus, 96, 189
Hinoki false cypress, 192–193, *192*
Holcus mollis, 85
hollies, 60, 65, 66–67, 74, 85, 188
honey locust, 62, *71*
honeysuckle, 67, 84, 90, 92, 152
hop bush, 67
hops, golden, 152
hornbeam, 60, 66, 74
Hosta albomarginata, 85
Hosta fortunei, 85
Hosta plantaginea, 84
Hosta sieboldiana, 85
Hosta spp., 73, *111,* 177
hot tubs, 164, 167–168
houseleeks, 41
Howea palm tree, 170, *170*
Humulus lupulus, 152
Hydrangea macrophylla, 56, *57,* 85,
    190

Other Storey Titles You Will Enjoy

Deckscaping, by Barbara W. Ellis. When surrounded by shrubs and small trees, perennials and annuals, ornamental grasses and vines, a deck becomes an appealing link between home and yard. Using dozens of creative ideas and fail-proof techniques, Barbara Ellis shows readers how to create their own dream deck environment. 176 pages. Paperback with French flaps. ISBN 1-58017-408-6. Hardcover with jacket. ISBN 1-58017-459-0.

The Flower Gardener's Bible, by Lewis and Nancy Hill. This great, friendly, indispensable book is written with wit and authority by Lewis and Nancy Hill, who share their joy in growing flowers and more than 75 years of combined experience. Painstakingly thorough and stunningly photographed, this new primer covers every facet of growing perennials, annuals, bulbs, wildflowers, small trees, shrubs, and vines. 384 pages. Paperback. ISBN 1-58017-462-0. Hardcover with jacket. ISBN 1-58017-463-9.

Garden Stone, by Barbara Pleasant. Full-color photographs and clear instructions provide readers with visual inspiration and creative ways to use stone in the garden. 240 pages. Paperback. ISBN 1-58017-544-9. Hardcover with jacket. ISBN 1-58017-406-X.

Grasses, by Nancy Ondra. Whether on their own or as backdrops for colorful flowers, ornamental grasses provide color, movement, and texture to any garden setting. Learn how to use them for dramatic effect, care for them, and combine them with other plants. 144 pages. Paperback with French flaps. ISBN 1-58017-423-X.

Lawn and Garden Owner's Manual, by Lewis and Nancy Hill. This homeowner's ultimate landscape care and maintenance manual allows the reader to diagnose and cure lawn and garden problems, rejuvenate neglected landscaping, and maintain beautiful and healthy grounds throughout the year. 192 pages. Paperback. ISBN 1-58017-214-8.

The Practical Guide to Container Gardening, by Susan Berry and Steve Bradley. This inspiring and beautiful book is a comprehensive reference for choosing the best containers for specific plants, planning seasonal planting schemes, and using simple planting techniques and proper plant maintenance. 160 pages. Paperback. ISBN 1-58017-329-2.

Quick and Easy Topiary and Green Sculpture, by Jenny Hendy. In this fully illustrated handy guide, readers will find everything they need to know to create instant plant designs using a wide range of topiary frames and a full range of plants. 128 pages. Paperback. ISBN 0-88266-920-6.

Shady Retreats, by Barbara Ellis. Lifelong gardener and successful author Barbara Ellis provides detailed plans for 20 gardens with shade as the theme. Each design includes a plant list, ideas for great design, an easy-to-read blueprint, and a glorious oil painting of what the garden will look like. 192 pages. Paperback. ISBN 1-58017-472-8.

Simple Fountains, by Dorcas Adkins. Fountain designer and manufacturer Dorcas Adkins reveals her trade secrets for making 20 creative fountains {m} from a small, tabletop fountain to a full-sized waterfall. 160 pages. Hardcover with jacket. ISBN 1-58017-190-7.

What Color Is Your Swimming Pool?, by Alan E. Sanderfoot. This classic, time-tested resource for pool owners provides information on the latest swimming pool technology, spas and hot tubs, water treatment and filtration systems, pool accessories, and selecting and caring for equipment. 144 pages. Paperback. ISBN 1-58017-309-8.

These and other books from Storey Publishing are available wherever quality books are sold or by calling 1-800-441-5700.
Visit us at www.storey.com.